EVERYMAN'S DATABASE PRIMER
featuring dBASE III™

Robert A. Byers

ASHTON·TATE ■

Editor:	Monet Thomson
Technical Editor:	Robert Hoffman
Text Design:	Thomas Clark
Cover Design:	D.A. Gray
Illustrations:	Stephanie Behasa

Copyright © Ashton-Tate, 1984

Published by Ashton-Tate Publishing Group
10150 W. Jefferson Boulevard
Culver City, California 90230

ISBN0-912677-31-7

Acknowledgement

It's been tremendously satisfying over the last couple of years to witness the positive public response to both dBASE II and the *Primer*. The help and encouragement of George Tate and Wayne Ratliff and skillful editing by Virginia Bare made the *Primer* a reality. With the enthusiasm and support of all of the Ashton-Tate family the *Primer* became successful.

It is a real pleasure to participate in the continuing growth of dBASE with this *Primer* for dBASE III. My special thanks go to the Publications Staff at Ashton-Tate, and particularly to Monet Thomson and Robert Hoffman, for their help in changing this text from dBASE II to dBASE III while preserving its essential character.

Robert A. Byers

CONTENTS

CONTENTS

FEATURING dBASE III

SECTION ONE

Section One introduces "databases" and acquaints us with how they work. Databases are very common in our daily surroundings, and we rarely think twice about their part in our routine activities. A "database management system" is simply the way these familiar databases are contained in and manipulated by a computer.

We will take a close look at some common database examples and dissect the pieces in order to understand how a database system works to provide us with organized information. The process is simple: we will start right away, turn our computer on, and design our first computer databases.

1

DATABASE

3

"Database" is computer jargon for a familiar and essential item in our everyday lives. A database is a collection of information organized and presented to serve a specific purpose.

One of the more familiar database examples is the Telephone Directory. This common printed database contains the names, addresses, and telephone numbers of individuals, businesses, and government agencies. The addresses and telephone numbers have little value by themselves. They are useful only when they are related to a name.

The number of databases we are familiar with is astonishing. Some of the more common databases are a dictionary, a cookbook, a Sears-Roebuck Catalog, an encyclopedia, the card catalog at the library, your checkbook, and so on. Other familiar databases are the stock market report in the newspaper, an accounts receivable ledger, and a personnel file.

CHAPTER ONE

Why are these examples databases? Why isn't the newspaper, or a non-fiction book considered a database? After all, they too contain information. The reason is specific. In each of the examples given above, information is presented in a manner which makes it easy for you to locate some particular piece of information of interest. In the telephone directory example, telephone numbers and addresses are related to the name. The names are presented in alphabetical order so you can find them easily. Find the name and you find the phone number. The name is the *key* to using the phone book. The dictionary example is similar. There is a word and a definition. The words are listed alphabetically so that they can be found, and the definition is related to the word. The *key* to use of the dictionary is the word.

The common element in all of the examples is *organized information presented in a way that makes it easy to find* by the use of some *key*. In other words, information that can be presented as tables (rows and columns) can be a database. Some examples of column headings in tables that could be considered databases are shown in Figure 1-1.

4

```
Examples        Column Headings

PHONE BOOK:     NAME   ADDRESS           PHONE NUMBER

DICTIONARY:     WORD   DEFINITION

CATALOG:        ITEM   DESCRIPTION       SIZE    PART NO.    COST


STOCK REPORT: STOCK   SHARES TRADED     HIGH    LOW
```

**Figure 1.1 Examples of Column Headings From
Some Common Paper Databases**

5

By now you should have a general concept of database, and you might be asking, "O.K., but what's a *computer* database? What can I do with it that I can't do without it?" The computer database can't do anything you couldn't do yourself from a printed database. However, some things possible without the computer are simply not practical. As an example, we have all found a scrap of paper with a phone number on it—no name, just a number. If we want to find out who the number belongs to, the telephone book isn't much help. If, however, the telephone directory is in the form of a computer database, we can ask the computer to check the phone number and the name will promptly appear.

As another example, suppose you want the phone number of someone named Smith who lives on Santa Monica Boulevard in Los Angeles. You can ask the computer's L.A. phone book file (maybe named "LAPHONE") for the names, addresses, and phone numbers of all the Smiths on Santa Monica Boulevard. It may not give you a single name and number, but it will surely narrow it down.

The computer is no panacea. It can't do anything you can't. But (and it's a big but) it can *help* you do the things you want to do quickly and easily. It is a tool to help you accomplish things that are simply not practical without it.

Using a personal phone book as an example, a simple database might look something like the one shown in Figure 1-2.

NAME	ADDRESS	PHONE NUMBER
Byers, Robert A Sr	9999 Glencrest, Standale	555-9242
Byers, Robert A Jr	48 N. Catalina, Pasadena	555-9540
Cassidy, Butch	4800 Rimrock Ct., Sunland	878-1121
Evans, Sydney H.	398 S. Calif. Blvd., Encino	998-1234
Goose, Sil E.	21809 Cottage Ln., Montecito	675-1212
Hedman, Gene	139 Luxury Dr., Bev. Hills	987-6543
Maori, Stanislas	2800 Oak St. #344, Red. Bch.	324-8529
Robertson, James	5892 Glencrest, Standale	997-2741

Figure 1-2. A Sample Database

Of course, a real database can contain many, many more items of information. In fact, the above database is much better kept in a small notebook than in a computer. You can carry it around with you, make notes in it, and it's a lot cheaper. The value of a computer is in the need to process a lot of information—so much information that you can't efficiently do so without the computer. The purpose of this book is to teach you about databases and how to use them. Therefore, we are going to use very small databases for examples. Exactly the same principles would apply if this personal phone book were from the white pages for

Los Angeles County. There is absolutely no difference other than there are a lot more entries in the white pages.

To better acquaint you with computer databases:

- how to plan them
- how to make them
- how to use them
- how to change them

we are going to build a computer database from a simple telephone book example. We will use the microcomputer database system *dBASE III*. *dBASE III* is representative of the better database management systems currently available for microcomputers. A database management system is a system that can be installed on a computer, takes care of all of the details involved with a database, and lets you use, manipulate, and change the database contents.

If you own or have access to a microcomputer with *dBASE III*, you can follow the instructions in this book and work along using your computer. If you do not have either a microcomputer or *dBASE III* you will still be able to follow along without difficulty. A description of what you do, and what the computer does, will be provided at each step. What you type in will be in uppercase.

FROM PERSONAL PHONE BOOK TO COMPUTER DATABASE: THE QUESTION OF TERMINOLOGY

L et's look again at the data from our personal phone book.

The Record

      Byers, Robert A Sr   9999 Glencrest, Standale   555-9242

The entry as shown above is called a Record. Pieces of information that make up a record are seen horizontally— displayed in rows across the page on screen. Our phone book has eight rows—eight records—eight sets of name + address + phone number.

The Field

If we were to draw lines between the names and addresses and the addresses and phone numbers in our telephone book, we would isolate columns of similar information. We separate three groups of vertically arranged data—a column of names, a column of addresses, and a column of phone numbers. In computer terminology, these columns are called FIELDS.

Fieldnames

The column titles—name, address, and phone number—are called FIELDNAMES. Conceptually, you can create a computer database with paper and pencil. Obviously, both a paper database and a computer database exist to be used. An appropriate question is then: What do you actually *do* with your phone book?

8

You write in new acquaintances, perhaps change names, addresses, or phone numbers of people who move, get a new phone, marry, or divorce. Maybe you cross some people out (or erase them, if you've had enough foresight to keep your records in pencil). When you want to use the information stored there, you are likely trying to make a call, going to a party at a particular address, mailing a letter, or so on. Thus your phone book, if you keep it up-to-date, reflects a process of change and, at any given time, will supply you with the information you're looking for. The same is true of your computer databases. You can very easily add, take out, or change the information in a computer database. Likewise, you can easily view information from your database as well.

In your everyday activites, you are always adding and subtracting from information at hand, changing it, selecting what you want to see, and ignoring what you don't want to see. This activity is basic to our thinking process. But, we are talking about putting all this information we're so accustomed to having strewn all around us into a computer database.

There will be something holding this information, and you need to become comfortable with the fact that it's in there. You need to know that you can retrieve the information when you need it. After you become comfortable, you'll be amazed at how much a computer database can actually do for your information needs.

Using your computer will become as easy as using your phone book. Like anything you do in life, it takes some thought, some planning, and some "how-to" knowledge. You need to know how to create, how to use, and how to change your store of information. In the learning process, it will not be necessary for you to re-invent the wheel. You are only learning a new function—a new set of mechanics for a new machine—designed to support your efforts to perceive and process all kinds of information already familiar to you.

This book will introduce you to computer databases. Together we will build and use some simple ones. So that you can easily relate the principles and common examples to actual practice, we will use *dBASE III*, a commercial microcomputer database management system, for our examples.

9

SOME SIMPLE ANALOGIES

Let's look at another simple example to illustrate the concept behind a database management system. Say you need a part for your car. You go to an auto parts store and tell the clerk which part you want, and he looks up the part in a catalog.

- The first book gives him an identifying number for the part.
- He then looks up this part number in another book. This book tells him where the part is located within the store.
- After he locates the part, he again uses the number to find the cost of the part from a price list.

CHAPTER ONE

In this analogy, the actual automotive parts correspond to the data items in a database. The clerk, catalogs, lists, storage bins, and so on correspond to the database management system. To use this "automotive parts management system" you tell the clerk what you want, in a language that he understands (English), using terminology related to cars. "I need a carburetor for a 76 Belchfire 8." The clerk takes care of all of the business of locating the parts, keeping the books current, updating his knowledge of the books, and so forth. All you need to do is have a reasonable idea of what you want. The clerk, his books, and catalogs take care of the rest.

The same is true for a computer database management system (DBMS). As soon as a DBMS is installed on a computer, the computer becomes an expert at all of the details involved in storing, cataloging, and retrieving data. All you need to do is have a reasonable idea of what you want and know a little computer terminology. This book provides you with the computer terminology you need. The computer and the database management system take care of the rest.

Incidentally, don't be intimidated by the need to install the database management system on the computer. It's nothing as complicated as the ready-to-assemble children's toys. It's simple.

Another analogy to database management system is a large library. In many large libraries, particularly university research libraries, you are not ordinarily allowed access to the shelves where the books are stored. To acquire a book, you must consult the card catalog, copy information from the index card on a slip of paper, and hand the paper to a librarian. Unseen by you, a "gnome" will scuttle through dark passageways to retrieve the book and deliver it to the librarian, who in turn delivers it to you.

When you return the book, much of this process is reversed. The librarian gives the book to a gnome who scuttles back to place the book in its original location. Again, the card catalog, the librarian, the gnomes, and the storage facilities correspond to the computer database management system. The book corresponds to the data item. All that is required of you is a little knowledge of how to use this system; the system does all the work.

OUR FIRST COMPUTER DATABASE

We have talked at length about our personal phone book, which makes a good basis for our first computer database. We will use it as an example and, as we proceed, you'll see that the process isn't much different from putting the information on a sheet of paper with an ordinary typewriter.

Say we were going to type this information on a piece of paper. The typist might do the following:

- Enter column headings such as Name, Address, and Phone Number.
- Figure out how many spaces to use for each column to keep everything neat and orderly.
- Type in a page heading or title for the page.

In a computer database, these activities are not optional.

- You must assign FIELDNAMES for each column (FIELD).
- You must figure out the size of each column. This is called the FIELD WIDTH.
- And, you must give the database a title. The database title is called a FILENAME.

We are almost ready to start our computerized version of a personal phone book. But before proceeding, you should know that computers have limitations.

If you were to take a pencil and paper and make a list of your friends' names, addresses, and telephone numbers, you could give the list a title such as "phone book," "telephone list," etc. Before you can get a

CHAPTER ONE

computer to accept a list, you *must* give it a title. This title will be the name of the database.

Generally, a database is called a FILE and the title is called a FILENAME. Filenames have certain peculiarities.

- They cannot have more than eight letters and numbers.
- They cannot contain any unused or blank spaces.
- They must start with a letter.

In addition, the filename is normally preceded by an additional symbol. This identifies for the computer which disk drive is to be used for the data file. (A disk drive stores information. Computer storage devices, such as disk drives, will be more fully explained in Chapter Four.)

There is often more than one such disk drive attached to the computer. The disk identifier informs the computer which device is to be used. In this text the disk drives are identified by a letter followed by a colon, such as "A:".

Some possible titles (filenames) for our computerized telephone book (database) are shown in Figure 1-3. Please bear in mind that you can give the database any name you choose so long as you use eight letters or fewer.

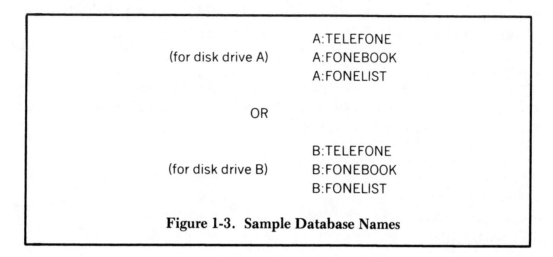

Figure 1-3. Sample Database Names

The filenames in the above example are called mnemonics. A mnemonic is a device to aid the memory, and it is a good idea to choose filenames that you can easily remember. The following five words are examples of eligible mnemonic filenames.

ACCTSPAY   ACCTSREC   PAYROLL   PERSONNL   QTRLYTAX

Fieldname

Column headings (FIELDNAMES) must be assigned to each of the columns (FIELDS) in the database. Fieldnames have limitations similar to those for filenames.

- They cannot have more than ten letters and numbers.
- They cannot contain spaces.
- They must begin with a letter.

Our simple phone list has three column headings (fieldnames): name, address, and phone number. The first two (name, address) are usable as fieldnames, but "phone number" is not. It has more than ten letters and contains a space which is not a letter or a number. So, we have to name this column with a mnemonic something like FONENUMBER or PHONE or NUMBER to conform to the ten character rule.

Fieldtype

Since the computer deals differently with different kinds of fields, it will need to know which of the available fields is appropriate to our needs. Fields can be one of five kinds:

CHARACTER
DATE
MEMO
LOGICAL
NUMERIC

In our example, all the fields are CHARACTER FIELDS and may contain letters, numbers, spaces and other standard typewriter symbols. Numeric, date, memo, and logical fields will be explained fully in later examples.

Fieldwidth

It is also necessary to tell the computer how many characters, (letters, numbers, spaces and other symbols) will be needed for each field. You will enter a number equal to the total "slots" necessary to hold the characters, spaces, and other symbols.

The computer does some things on its own. Each time a record is entered the computer automatically gives it a number. It calls the first row, which is the first record, RECORD 1, the second RECORD 2 and so forth. You could, indeed, work with databases for a long time and do some very involved work without ever using a record number. They are, however, convenient for some things, and we will discuss their usefulness later in this book.

We have covered, then, some basic, pertinent terminology. Make sure you are comfortable with the concepts because we are next going to construct a simple database. Remember:

- Rows are records, automatically numbered by the computer.
- Columns are fields: they need titles called fieldnames (ten characters maximum, no spaces, start with a letter).
- You must tell the computer where (which disk drive) to put the data (Example: A:FONEBOOK will put it on "A" drive).
- Tell the computer the form and arrangement of information to be entered. You know about filename and fieldnames. Finish the task by (1) allocating the number of spaces necessary to accommodate information for each field, and (2) telling the computer what kind of information is to be stored in the field—the fieldtype.

OUR FIRST EXERCISE

In this first exercise we will really start from scratch. When the computer is first turned on, the video screen will display something similar to Screen 1-1.

15

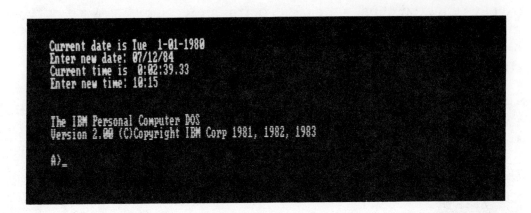

```
Current date is Tue  1-01-1980
Enter new date: 07/12/84
Current time is  0:02:39.33
Enter new time: 10:15


The IBM Personal Computer DOS
Version 2.00 (C)Copyright IBM Corp 1981, 1982, 1983

A)_
```

Screen 1 - 1

The Operating System

PC-DOS (MS-DOS) is a widely used operating system for microcomputers. An operating system helps you to operate the computer. Database management systems such as *dBASE III* use the operating system to perform routine tasks. Although the operating system sometimes imposes specific ways of doing things on the database system, you will not need to learn the details of the operating system to use a database management system.

The A> is a prompt. It is the operating system's way of telling you "I'm ready, tell me what to do." The symbol to the right of the > is called the cursor. The cursor is a light marker which appears on the screen to show you where you are. It is the computer's equivalent of a pencil point. Letters you type on the screen by pressing keys on the keyboard will appear where the cursor is. As each letter is typed, the cursor moves to the right.

16

Getting Your Computer To Use dBASE

Getting the computer ready to use your database management system is called loading the database. To begin, simply type in the letters DBASE. The video display will now look like Screen 1-2.

```
Current date is Tue  1-01-1980
Enter new date: 07/12/84
Current time is  0:02:39.33
Enter new time: 10:15


The IBM Personal Computer DOS
Version 2.00 (C)Copyright IBM Corp 1981, 1982, 1983

A)dbase_
```

Screen 1 - 2

17

Press the <RETURN> key (the name is borrowed from the carriage return on an electric typewriter). For most computer operations it indicates to the computer "O.K., that's it, I'm through entering this item—now do it." On the IBM and most compatible computers the key looks like ⬅ .

The computer will respond as shown in Screen 1-3.

18

```
dBASE III  version 1.00  8 June 1984 IBM/MSDOS ***

COPYRIGHT (c) ASHTON-TATE 1984
AS AN UNPUBLISHED LICENSED PROPRIETARY WORK.
ALL RIGHTS RESERVED.

Use of this software and the other materials contained in the software package
(the "Materials") has been provided under a Software License Agreement (please
read in full). In summary, Ashton-Tate grants you a paid-up, non-transferrable,
personal license to use the Materials only on a single or subsequent (but not
additional) computer terminal for fifty years from the time the sealed diskette
has been opened. You receive the right to use the Materials, but you do not
become the owner of them. You may not alter, decompile, or reverse-assemble the
software, and YOU MAY NOT COPY the Materials. The Materials are protected by
copyright, trade secrets, and trademark law, the violation of which can result
in civil damages and criminal prosecution.

dBASE, dBASE III and ASHTON-TATE are trademarks of Ashton-Tate.



Type a command (or HELP) and press the return key (←┘).
.
```

Screen 1 - 3

The period in the lower left hand corner of the screen under the asterisks is important. In *dBASE* it is called a dot prompt. The dot prompt is the computer's way of telling you "I'm ready, tell me to do something." The things that you will tell it to do are called commands.

The top line on the screen tells you exactly what you have installed. *dBASE III* is the name of the database management system, "Version 1.0" tells you what "edition" of *dBASE III* you are using, and the date that follows is the release date of version 1.0. A version number is like a model identifier, and normally each new version will have all of the features of earlier versions, plus new and/or improved features.

To get out of *dBASE*, you simply type the word QUIT after a dot prompt:

```
. QUIT
```

The computer will respond with.

```
***END RUN dBASE III
A>
```

You are now back to your computer's operating system.

We are ready to start the process of CREATING the database B:FONEBOOK. The dialog between the user and the computer is shown in Screens 1-4 and 1-5. The computer responses (PROMPTS) and the corresponding keyboard entries are shown as they might appear on a video terminal. The computer prompts are in lower case. The keyboard entries are in upper case. Note that what we have done so far remains on the screen as we proceed.

19

```
. CREATE
Enter the name of the new file: _
```

Screen 1 - 4a

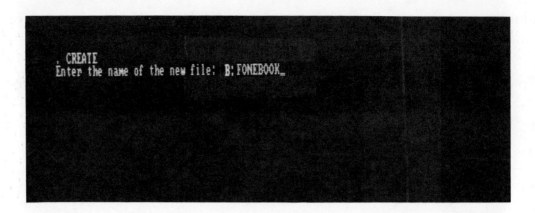

. CREATE
Enter the name of the new file: B:FONEBOOK_

Screen 1 - 4 b

Now we will enter the information which defines the form and arrangement of the database.

Just after the dot prompt, type in the word CREATE. Then press the <RETURN> key. CREATE is the dBASE command that starts the process of building the database. <RETURN> tells the computer to accept the command that you have just typed in (CREATE). Remember, the computer will do nothing until you press <RETURN>.

After you have entered CREATE (and pressed the <RETURN> key), the computer will respond with the prompt "Enter the name of the new file:." The proper keyboard entry is: (1) disk drive identifier, (2) colon, and (3) the eight-letter (and number) filename. In our example, the keyboard entry is B:FONEBOOK.

The next screen (Screen 1-5) lets you define the fields to be contained in the database. For each new field you are prompted to enter the fieldname and the fieldtype. If the fieldtype is either character or numeric, you will also need to enter the width (size of the field). dBASE will not let you make an illegal entry.

20

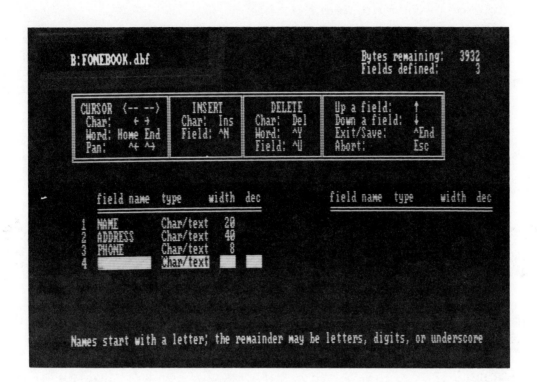

Screen 1 - 5

Remember, the fieldname may have up to ten characters. It must begin with a letter and cannot have embedded blank spaces. dBASE will discard any characters to the right of an embedded blank. If the fieldname is less than ten characters long, press the <RETURN> key to advance to the type column.

The fieldtype is selected by typing in the first character of the desired fieldtype (character, date, memo, logical, or numeric). dBASE will automatically enter the rest of the characters in the filetype and advance the cursor to the next item.

The field width is only entered for character and numeric fields.

The first field in our example is NAME. NAME is a character field that is twenty spaces wide. When the field definition for NAME is complete, the system is ready to accept the definition for the next field. This process will continue until you have either entered 128 fields (the maximum for *dBASE III*), or you signal that you want to terminate the process. Don't worry if you need more than 128 fields—it is possible, and you will learn later how to accommodate more than 128 fields.

You signal dBASE that you want to stop this field definition process by pressing the <RETURN> key instead of entering a new fieldname. In this example, the <RETURN> key was pressed when the computer asked for the fieldname for field four. That is because we are only using three fields (NAME, ADDRESS, PHONE) in this database.

22

ENTERING DATA

The computer will now ask you if you want to input (enter) data. You should respond with a Y for yes or an N for no. You won't need to press the <RETURN> key; the computer will respond directly to the Y or N in this case. A yes response will cause the computer to clear the video screen and begin prompting you to enter the names, addresses, and phone numbers (data). Enter Y and the video screen will appear as shown in Screen 1-6.

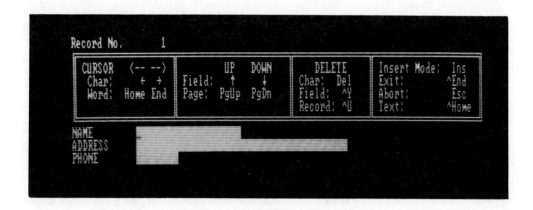

Screen 1 - 6

This kind of display is a full-screen prompt. It prompts you to provide all information needed for the entire screen (as opposed to a dot prompt which asks for just one line of input). The computer displays the fieldnames and a space in which you are expected to enter the information belonging to the field (column).

As you enter the data for the name field, for example, the cursor will move to the right until the field is full. At this point, a bell will ring and the cursor will jump to the left-most position of the next field. If, as is most likely, the name entered does not completely fill the space allocated to the name field, you must press the <RETURN> key when the name has been completely entered. When you press the <RETURN> key the cursor will move to the next field (in this case the address field).

When you have entered all of the data for a record, as shown in Screen 1-7, the computer will automatically clear the screen and begin prompting you to enter data for the following record. This process is continued until you have entered all of the data.

23

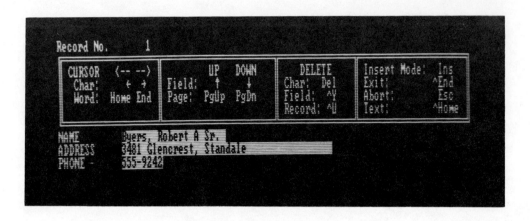

Screen 1 - 7

24

Earlier we had identified fields as *vertical* columns. Now the data for the vertical columns is entered as consecutive rows on the screen. This is done for convenience in entering the data. The computer places each field entry into a vertical column in the database. When you have entered the data for the eight records of our example, the screen will look like Screen 6 except the Record Number will read 9, awaiting the ninth record. But we don't have a ninth this time.

If you press the <RETURN> key now, with the cursor positioned as shown, the computer will exit from CREATE, and will respond with a DOT PROMPT, indicating that it is ready to accept further commands.

USING THE DATABASE

We now have a database. It has eight records and three fields: NAME, ADDRESS, PHONE. Its FILENAME (title) is FONEBOOK, and it is on the B drive. To use the database we type USE B:FONEBOOK (and a <RETURN>) after a dot prompt.

```
.  USE  B : FONEBOOK
```

The computer responds with another dot prompt on the next line. Via "B:FONEBOOK" you tell the computer you want to work specifically with the database located on B: drive, whose filename is FONEBOOK. USE is the dBASE command, roughly analogous to saying to your assistant, "Chatsworth, please get me the phone book." The transactions will look like this:

```
. USE  B:FONEBOOK
. □
```

When the computer responds with the dot prompt on the line just below USE B:FONEBOOK, the database FONEBOOK is ready for use. Let's "use" it first to look at the structure as we recently set it up. The structure of the database is really determined by the definition of the fields (columns). To review the structure, type DISPLAY STRUCTURE following a dot prompt. The computer will respond with the display shown in Screen 1-8.

25

```
. DISPLAY STRUCTURE
Structure for database : B:FONEBOOK.dbf
Number of data records :        0
Date of last update    : 01/01/80
Field  Field name  Type       Width    Dec
    1  NAME        Character     20
    2  ADDRESS     Character     40
    3  PHONE       Character      8
** Total **                     69
: =
```

Screen 1 - 8

You should notice that the computer has added .dbf to the filename of the database. Note also that the TOTAL is one more than the visible total of the number of characters used.

.dbf is a filetype and the filetype tells the computer how to deal with a specific file. The date of the last update represents the computer system date when the last change was made to the database. The item total at the bottom indicates the number of characters (plus one) in a record. This is the record size indicator, and its significance will be discussed later.

Now that we have USEd B:FONEBOOK and viewed the structure, let's move on to the major application for databases: the storage and retrieval of information. Say we want to retrieve some of the information we have stored so we can look at it. One way to look at the information is to type DISPLAY ALL after a dot prompt. DISPLAY ALL is the dBASE command that displays the contents of the database. The result of this command appears in Screen 1-9.

```
. DISPLAY ALL
Record#  NAME                  ADDRESS                            PHONE
      1  Byers, Robert A Sr.   3481 Glencrest, Standale           555-3242
      2  Byers, Robert A Jr.   48 N. Catalina, Pasadena           555-3548
      3  Cassidy, Butch        4800 Rimrock Ct, Sunland           878-1121
      4  Evans, Sydney H.      398 S. Calif. Blvd., Encino        998-1234
      5  Goose, Sil E.         21809 Cottage Ln, Montecito        675-1212
      6  Hedman, Gene          139 Luxury Dr. Beverly Hills       987-6543
      7  Maori, Stanislas      2800 Oak St. #344, Redondo Beach   324-8529
      8  Robertson, James      5892 Glencrest, Standale           997-2741
. =
```

Screen 1 - 9

The left-hand column displays the automatically assigned RECORD NUMBER we discussed previously. If you do not want the record number displayed, type DISPLAY ALL OFF instead of DISPLAY ALL. The computer will generate the same display, except the record numbers will not be shown.

Earlier in this chapter we gave some examples of the kinds of tasks the computer can easily perform. One of these examples had to do with a phone number on a scrap of paper. The dBASE command DISPLAY will give us the owner of that phone number (if it is in the database). To accomplish this, we must tell the computer what we want it to do in a way that it will understand. The computer may be fast, but it's not particularly bright.

So, we use the DISPLAY command to give us the owner of the telephone number on the scrap of paper we found. The transaction looks like this:

27

```
. DISPLAY FOR PHONE = '998-1234'
Record#  NAME                 ADDRESS                              PHONE
       4  Evans, Sydney H.     398 S. Calif. Blvd., Encino          998-1234

. =
```

28

This is very straightforward. The word PHONE is the fieldname of the field (column) containing the phone numbers. What you are really telling the computer with the short instruction above is to look through the entire database and display each record containing the characters 998-1234 in the phone column.

The apostrophes are called DELIMITERS. They are there to identify to the computer the beginning and the end of what is called a CHARACTER STRING. What is contained between the apostrophes is specifically, to the letter and the space, what you are looking for.

Phone numbers are character strings because we identified the phone number field (PHONE) as a character field when we created the database. Numbers can be either numbers or characters. You must tell the computer which they are by using the delimiters. As an example, 555 is a number to the computer, while '555' is a character string. Numbers should normally be entered as characters unless they are to be used in arithmetic.

As another example, let's find everyone who lives in Standale. This transaction is as follows:

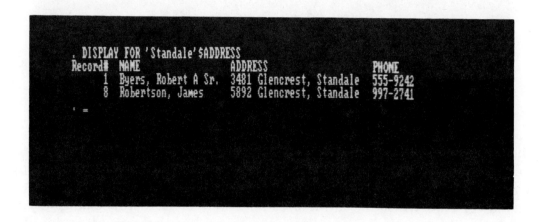

. DISPLAY FOR 'Standale'$ADDRESS
Record# NAME   ADDRESS   PHONE
      1 Byers, Robert A Sr. 3481 Glencrest, Standale 555-9242
      8 Robertson, James   5892 Glencrest, Standale 997-2741

. =

Screen 1 - 10

Just as before, the character string is enclosed in apostrophes. This example, however, looks a little more exotic. The dollar sign is a sort of shorthand for "contained in." What we tell the machine to do is look through the entire database and display each record that contains the characters "Standale" in the address column. If there is a Standale Avenue somewhere in that field of the database, that record is reported along with the two Standale town addresses reported. Again, what it's looking for is a *sequence of characters*. To further illustrate the character sequence concept we tell the computer to:

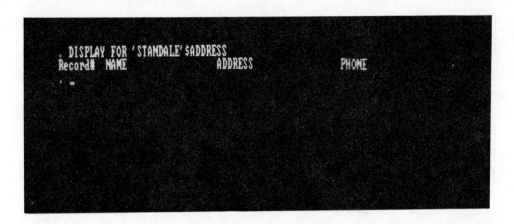

Screen 1 - 11

30

The computer responds with a dot prompt. This means there are no records with the character string STANDALE in the address field. The two character strings Standale and STANDALE are different. The first uses lower case while the latter uses all upper case. In this example you and I would know they mean the same thing, but the computer doesn't. The computer's interpretation is very literal.

As another example of the computer's literal interpretation, let's tell the computer to display all the records containing the CHARACTER STRING 'Robert'. The computer's response is shown in Screen 1-12.

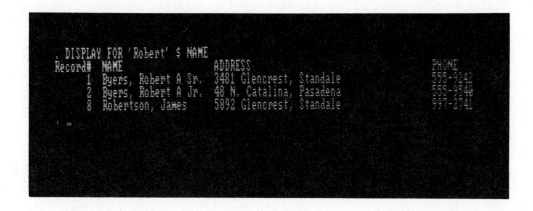

```
. DISPLAY FOR 'Robert' $ NAME
Record#  NAME                ADDRESS                        PHONE
    1  Byers, Robert A Sr.  3481 Glencrest, Standale       555-1242
    2  Byers, Robert A Jr.  48 N. Catalina, Pasadena       555-3540
    8  Robertson, James     5892 Glencrest, Standale       997-2741
. =
```

Screen 1 - 12

This is a graphic example of a character string search where the computer gave more information than we thought we asked it for. The point to make here is that *it did exactly what it was told.* In this case, we wanted a display of everyone whose first name was Robert. This would have been obtained by using ', Robert' instead of 'Robert' in the instructions. This is because 'Robert' as a first name always follows a comma.

To remove a little more of the mystique (if it even had any) from computer database operations, let's take a look at what process happens when we say DISPLAY FOR 'Standale'$ADDRESS.

● The computer goes to the beginning of the database (Record 1) and looks through the ADDRESS field of Record 1 to see if the character string 'Standale' is there.
● If it is there, the computer will display all of Record 1 on the video terminal.
● If it is not there, the computer will not display any part of Record 1.
● When Record 1 has been examined and either displayed on the terminal or not, the computer will proceed to examine Record 2 in exactly the same manner.

31

FEATURING dBASE III

● This record by record examination of the ADDRESS field continues until every record has been examined.

Let's recap what we've done so far. We've learned a little of the terminology, we've learned that databases can be likened to things we use everyday, and that databases and computers can't do anything you can't do without them—if you have lots and lots of time.

Up to this point, a paper and pencil would have been much faster, cheaper, and you wouldn't have needed to learn any computer terminology. Bear in mind, however, that this list could easily be eighty, 800, or 8,000 names long. Examples in this book never have more than fifteen records (in the interest of conserving paper and your interest). In order to appreciate what this particular computer technology can do for you, you should think of these examples as small sections of databases containing hundreds or thousands of records.

This entire process is very much like creating a table with paper and pencil.

● You must plan your layout, decide what information is to go in which columns, and determine the physical size of each column.
● Next you enter all of the information.
● It is only after this is all accomplished that you can actually use the table for its intended purpose. In this chapter we only used the database one way—we viewed it, that is, DISPLAYed it.

The process of creating a table on paper is analagous to designing a computer database. The database must be planned and data must be entered. Then, and only then, can you use it to perform calculations. The nice part is that you can accomplish all of this knowing nothing about the internal workings of the computer. All you have to do is to follow the rules. It's a little like learning to drive an automobile with an automatic, as opposed to a manual, transmission.

The language you use to talk to the computer is a *very* limited English. Nearly all commercially available databases have "English" vocabularies of less than a hundred words. Furthermore, unlike grammatical English, there are no special cases. Each English word in the computer's vocabulary has a very specific meaning with no room for interpretation. The meaning will be *one* of the common English meanings for the word.

Finally, you have nothing to worry about. While you are learning, you can't break the computer, and if you aren't quite sure about something, just try a few different commands and see if they work. Probably the hardest thing to learn is that there is really nothing difficult about working with the computer: it is an easy thing to master. You use only a limited vocabulary, and no difficult physical coordination (such as using an automobile clutch) is required.

33

SIMPLE DATABASE USES: HOW THEY WORK

Now that you're familiar with what a database is, we are ready to discuss some simple database uses and how they work. We have already discussed one simple use: DISPLAY. With it, we looked at the structure and contents of a very simple database. In this chapter, we will learn to change the database by both adding and deleting information, to produce standard reports, and to index and sort database contents. In this chapter we will also CREATE a more complex database than B:FONEBOOK of Chapter One.

35

So, thus far we have discussed two simple ways to USE the database.

- As a way to look at its structure.
- As a means to view all or selective parts of the database contents.

The next process that will concern us is *change*. It is very important to know how easily we can accommodate necessary changes.

CHAPTER TWO

Continuing with the personal telephone directory example, we would expect to easily erase names, addresses, and phone numbers and enter new ones in their places. This is exactly the case. This capability is necessary for several reasons. Mistakes are made while entering data—the wrong address and phone number are entered for a name, words are misspelled, numbers are left out, and so forth. People move and telephone numbers and addresses change; others get married and their names change. Some people disappear from our lives altogether—others enter. If the world were truly static and nothing changed, the value of a data storage system would be significantly lower. The world, however, is in a constant state of flux. It is changing at a fast pace, and this makes the value of databases considerable.

CHANGE

There are generally three kinds of change the computer can accommodate:

- One is to add or delete entire records.
- Another is to change the contents of a record.
- The last is to change the structure of the database by adding or erasing entire fields (columns).

DELETING RECORDS

Deleting a record is a two-step process, which provides a safeguard against accidental erasure. In dBASE, two separate commands are used: DELETE and PACK. To illustrate the procedure we will erase the record for Sydney Evans (Record 4). The transaction with the computer is illustrated by Screen 2-1.

```
. DELETE FOR NAME = 'Evans, Sydney H'
      1 record deleted

. DISPLAY FOR DELETED()
Record# NAME                ADDRESS                              PHONE
     4 *Evans, Sydney H.    398 S. Calif. Blvd., Encino          998-1234
.
. PACK
      7 records copied
.
. =
```

Screen 2 - 1

We tell the computer "delete the record that contains Sydney Evans." The DELETE command places a mark (*) in front of the record or records we want to remove and the computer then tells us how many records were marked for deletion. At this point, the record is still in the database. If it had found another Sydney Evans, the response would have been "2 Records deleted," a clue to us that something unexpected had occurred.

The DISPLAY FOR DELETED( ) command tells the computer to display the records marked for removal. The computer displays a single record, the one marked for elimination. Notice that the * symbol appears between the record number and the record. The ( ) after the word DELETED indicates that the word DELETED is a special dBASE function.

The command PACK actually removes the record. This eliminates all the records marked by the DELETE command and renumbers all remaining record numbers.

If we now display the entire database, we see that the record for Sydney Evans is gone. There are now only seven records, and the record that was

37

CHAPTER TWO

formerly number five is now four, and so forth. The revised database is shown in Screen 2-2.

Screen 2 - 2

38

ADDING RECORDS (APPEND)

Adding a record to the database is a simple, one-step process. In *dBASE*, the command to add a record is APPEND. Entering data for APPEND is exactly the same as entering data for CREATE. When the computer is told to APPEND, the computer will clear the screen and generate the display shown in Screen 2-3.

EVERYMAN'S DATABASE PRIMER

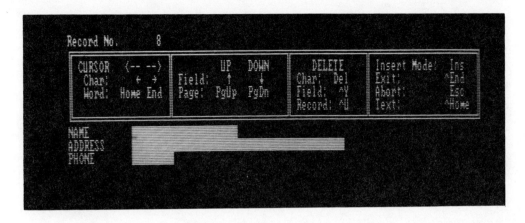

Screen 2 - 3

To add the record, fill in the blanks as in the CREATE process. It's just like filling in a form with a typewriter. You may add as many records as you desire. To exit from APPEND, press <Ctrl-End> or the <RETURN> key when the cursor is in the first position of the first field of the new record.

The new entry is shown in Screen 2-4. In this example we did not know the address for T. E. Deum, so a <RETURN> was entered to advance the cursor to the PHONE field.

39

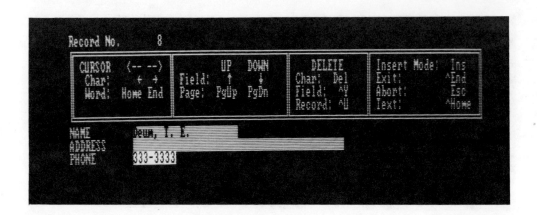

Screen 2 - 4

40

As in the CREATE example, the computer automatically advances to the next record (Record 9) and prompts you to enter the data. Pressing the <RETURN> key will stop the APPEND process and have the computer respond with a dot prompt.

EDIT & REPLACE

Now, suppose we acquire an address for T. E. Deum and his phone number changes. Two of the principal commands used to edit (change) the fields within a record are EDIT and REPLACE.

The EDIT command is similar to the APPEND command except that it does not add a record. Unlike the APPEND command, however, it requires a knowledge of the record number. It is one of the few *dBASE* commands requiring a knowledge of record numbers. But, a record may be EDITed without knowing the record number by using the CHANGE command. Use of the EDIT command is described below. To invoke the EDIT function, after a dot prompt type EDIT followed by the desired record number.

. EDIT 8

EDIT is similar to APPEND, except that instead of displaying empty FIELDS as in APPEND, the contents of the desired record are displayed. As in APPEND, the cursor will appear in the first position of the first field. In this example, we will add the address and change the phone number.

To change the address, we must move the cursor to the ADDRESS field. Record 8 is now displayed on our screen, with the cursor positioned in the NAME field.

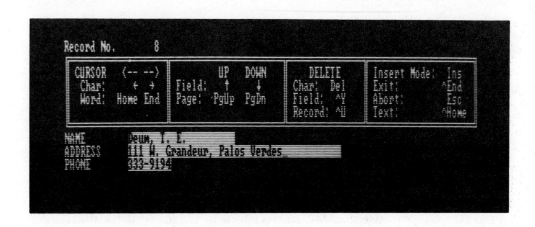

Screen 2 - 5

To move the cursor to the ADDRESS field, press the down arrow. This moves the cursor to the first character position of the ADDRESS field. Enter the address as shown in Screen 2-5. Entering a <RETURN> will position the cursor to the beginning of the PHONE field. To change the phone number, just type the new number directly over the old one.

When the "4" was entered in the phone number above, the computer automatically exited from the EDIT command. It did this because we had entered the last character in the last field of the last record of the database. If this had not been the last field of the last record, we would have had to purposefully exit from EDIT. This is done with <Ctrl-End>. Hold down the <Ctrl> key and press the <End> key. The key combination writes the new information to the disk and exits from EDIT. The act of "exiting" says you are finished with your changes and what is done should be "written" to the disk for permanent storage.

The other change command, REPLACE, allows selective change of one or more records. With REPLACE, you change the content of one or more fields by telling the computer the fieldnames, the new contents, and the criteria for making a change.

As an example, suppose the last entry, T. E. Deum, has moved his residence. He has a new address and a new telephone number. To change the telephone number and address with the REPLACE command, the transaction looks like this:

```
. REPLACE  PHONE  WITH  '222-6661', ADDRESS WITH ;
'200 Splendid Ave, Escondido' FOR NAME='Deum, T. E.'
1 Record replaced
```

The semicolon at the end of the line tells dBASE not to execute the command yet—you just needed more room to finish writing it on the next line. You can actually write command lines up to 254 characters long.

Even though the two fields were changed (replaced), the computer's response of "1 Record replaced" refers to the number of records changed by the command. The command changed both the telephone number and the address to reflect the new information.

Both EDIT and REPLACE have extensive uses for modifying the contents of the database. EDIT is what is called a full-screen operation. The database record, in a sense, *is on the screen* and can be changed by typing new information right over the old. REPLACE automatically replaces old data with new data according to criteria established by you. The change is

SIMPLE DATABASE USES: HOW THEY WORK

made in the computer but is not actually seen on the screen. If visual confirmation is desired, you must use a separate display command.

The personal telephone book exercise covers familiar territory we can all relate to. It is, however, very limited, and does not offer enough material to demonstrate the full range of computer database capabilities.

It is time to begin our second database project. Our new project will demonstrate more facets of computer database capability. The concept behind this database is familiar to us all, and it is based on the needs of a retail store inventory. We will conduct an annual inventory similar to what might be undertaken by the proprietor of a very small liquor store.

What items might be of interest to the liquor store owner? Likely items include

Type of liquor
Brand name
Size
Amount of stock on hand
Retail prices

43

These items then become the columns (fields) needed in our new database. Our next three steps are all part of one process which defines the database form and arrangement. First, we assign fieldnames. Second, we assign a category to each field (character, numeric, logical, date, memo). Third, we decide upon the size (width) of each field.

• In this example, the fieldname for the column containing the type of liquor is LIQUOR. It is a character field ten spaces wide.
• The column for the brandnames has the fieldname BRAND. This is a character field and is twenty spaces wide.
• That for container size is SIZE, it is a character field, and is seven spaces wide.

FEATURING dBASE III

● The amount of stock is QUANTITY, a number field, and is three digits wide. This allows up to 999 containers of each size of each brand in the inventory of this small store.

● The last two fields, called COST and PRICE, are also number fields. These two fields will contain decimal values, however, and are entered in a slightly different manner. For both, we will allow three digits to the left of the decimal place and two digits to the right. This yields a maximum of 999.99. The field width for each of these two fields is six (five digits plus the decimal point).

As to choosing a name for our example, we have exactly the same problem in choosing a filename (title) for this database as we did in the example of the personal telephone directory. Liquor Store Inventory is too large and contains blank spaces. We will instead use INVENTRY as the filename. It is descriptive and has eight letters.

CREATE A DATABASE

The process we have just been through is shown in Screens 2-6A and B. The database (file) INVENTRY will be placed on the B disk drive.

44

Screen 2 - 6

When prompted to define field 7, press the <RETURN> key to signal dBASE that you have finished defining the database structure. dBASE will ask you

```
Input data records now? (Y/N)
```

With your Y (yes) response, the computer begins prompting you to enter the data for the first record. The video display is shown in Screen 2-7.

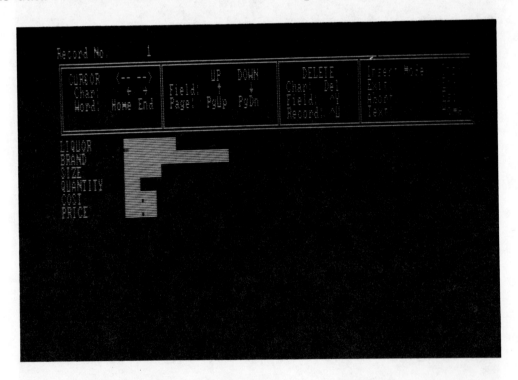

Screen 2 - 7

We will now enter the data into the database INVENTRY. Screen 2-8 shows a representative record.

SIMPLE DATABASE USES: HOW THEY WORK

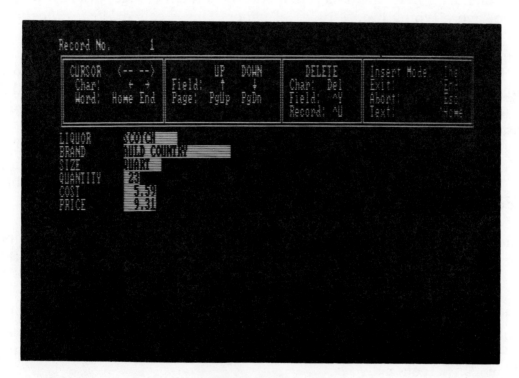

Screen 2 - 8

This process will continue, filling in record by record, until all of the data for the fifteen records has been entered (see Screen 2-9). A <RETURN> at the beginning of Record 16 gets us out of the data entry mode.

FEATURING dBASE III

NOTES ON ENTERING DATA

Data entry begins at the left hand edge for each field. If the field is a character field, the data remains at the left hand edge, just as it would if you were typing it on a piece of paper. This is called *left justification*.

For number fields, the data is entered beginning at the left hand edge just as for character fields. However, when you press the <RETURN> key (telling the computer that you have finished entering the field), the computer will move the numbers into a column. This is called *right justification*. The computer will right justify number fields.

If you attempt to enter a letter into a numeric field, *dBASE* will not allow it. The letter will not be accepted and the terminal will sound an audible alarm.

The data entry process can go on until the inventory is completed (or there is enough data for our example). Our sample database B:INVENTRY has six FIELDS and fifteen RECORDS.

When we exit from the data entry mode we are "using" our database. To look at the contents of the database B:INVENTRY we enter the command LIST. The complete contents of our sample database B:INVENTRY are shown in Screen 2-9.

48

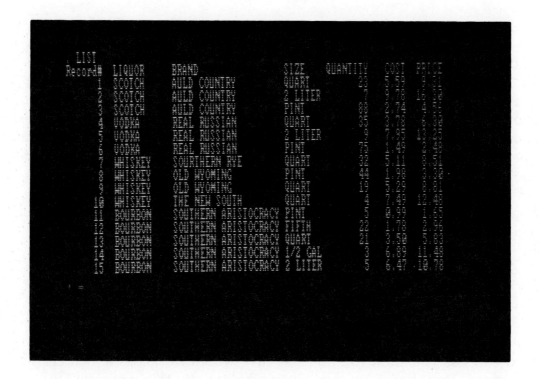

Screen 2 - 9

One of the objectives of an inventory is to determine the amount of tied-up capital. When we finish an inventory with the conventional pencil and paper, we can compute the inventory value by multiplying each quantity by the corresponding cost and adding the results. If the inventory is done with a microcomputer and a database management system we can get the same result almost immediately. The system gives us power and speed. From this example we can begin to see the power of the database.

CHAPTER TWO

The dBASE command requesting the value of the inventory looks like this:

```
. SUM COST*QUANTITY
    15 records summed
COST*QUANTITY
    1305.49
```

We have asked for the sum (total) of cost times quantity. The asterisk symbol "*" requests multiplication of the computer, and the result of this operation (1305.49) is shown below the command. The computer applies the above command to the entire database.

Suppose you only wanted to know how much capital is invested in Scotch. The transaction is shown below.

```
. SUM COST*QUANTITY FOR LIQUOR='SCOTCH'
    3 records summed
COST*QUANTITY
    438.15
```

Now suppose you want to know the investment in quarts of Scotch. The command and the result are shown below. In this example, we see another important requirement: AND must be preceded and followed by a period so it looks like ".AND."

```
. SUM COST*QUANTITY FOR LIQUOR='SCOTCH'.AND.SIZE='QUART'
    1 record summed
COST*QUANTITY
    128.57
```

Simple computations such as these mark only the surface of the information readily available via database transactions. You can actually obtain entire reports, organized to use and display your information according to your specific needs, with just two commands.

STANDARD REPORTS

*d*BASE III, like most database management systems, has a built-in "report generation" feature called REPORT. This feature prepares formal reports, such as the one shown in Figure 2-1, from a Report Form. The Report Form itself is created directly from the keyboard with the help of CREATE REPORT. The report form can be used over and over again to produce as many copies of a report as desired and is saved on disk for future use.

Type CREATE REPORT after a dot prompt as shown in Screen 2-10.

51

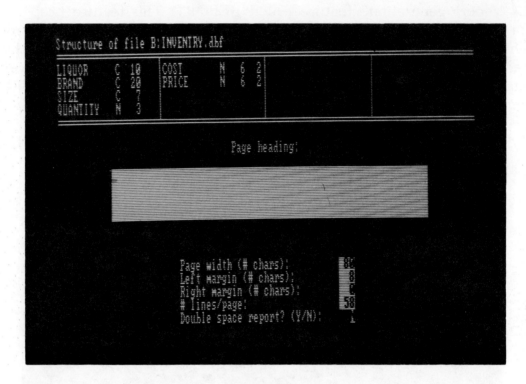

Screen 2 - 10

dBASE will respond by asking a series of questions appearing as a sequence of screen forms. You type in the answers just as you would when filling out any form.

The first question (prompt) is a request for a REPORT FORM NAME. This is another kind of filename, similar to the filename for the database. Filenames for report forms follow the same rules as filenames for databases. They must begin with a letter and can contain both letters and numbers. They may be up to eight characters long and may not contain embedded blank spaces. Since we are using the database B:INVENTRY, we will name the report B:INVENTRY also.

You may wonder how the computer can tell the difference between B:INVENTRY (the database) and B:INVENTRY (the report form). In *dBASE*, as in most database management systems (DBMS), there are different types of files. The DBMS has its own labeling system to keep them separately identified. *dBASE* adds .dbf (for database file) to the names of databases such as B:FONEBOOK, and it adds .frm (for report form) to the filename. This is done automatically and allows us to assign the file the same name as the database file.

After you enter the report filename, the computer prompts you for the information it needs to prepare a report. The top of the screen is used to display helpful information in the form of either a help menu or a listing of the fields in the database. To switch between these displays press the function key <F1>.

The first page of the report form (Screen 2-11) provides an area to enter an optional report title.

53

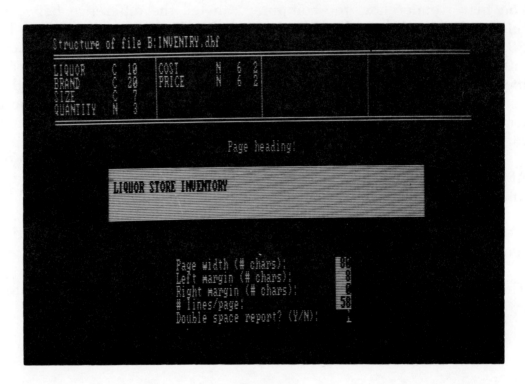

Screen 2 - 11

It also asks five questions to help in formatting your report. These are the page width, left and right margins, number of lines per page, and whether or not the report is to be double spaced. Standard (default) values are already entered for you. To advance to the next page press the <PgDn> key.

The second page (Screen 2-12) lets you subtotal and sub-subtotal. In our report we want subtotals for each kind of liquor, so we enter LIQUOR in the large box titled "Group/subtotal on:".

The next question is "Summary report only? (Y/N)." A summary report contains only the kind of liquor and the subtotals. Entering an N to this prompt indicates that you want a full report.

The question "Eject after each group/subtotal? (Y/N)" is really asking you if you want each subtotal category to begin on a fresh page (for printed reports). Answering Y (yes) to this question would print our sample report on four separate pages.

55

56

```
Structure of file B:INVENTRY.dbf

LIQUOR    C 10  COST     N 6 2
BRAND     C 20  PRICE    N 6 2
SIZE      C 7
QUANTITY  N 3

Group/subtotal on:           LIQUOR




Summary report only? (Y/N): N    Eject after each group/subtotal? (Y/N): N

Group/subtotal heading:


Subgroup/sub-subtotal on:



Subgroup/subsubtotal heading:
```

Screen 2 - 12

The block provided for Group/subtotal heading is optional. Look at Figure 2-1. Notice that the content of the liquor field (subtotal category) is printed just above the group of entries for each category. If we had entered a heading, it would have been displayed *in front* of the category but on the *same line.*

Sub-subtotalling provides an additional level of calculation within each category when appropriate. We are not using this level of subtotalling in our sample report, so it is left blank.

To advance to the next page (Screen 2-13) press the <PgDn> key. This form lets you define each of the columns to be displayed by the report. The large block labeled Field Content defines the display. The small blocks for Number of Decimal Places and Totals can be changed only when the item to be displayed in a column is numeric. The large block labeled Field Header lets you define a column title, and the small block, Width, just beneath it displays the standard size for the column. You may make the column width either wider or narrower than the content. If the column width is narrower than its content, the content will be printed on two or more lines.

Our first column will contain the content of the field BRAND, and the column title will be BRAND. The field is twenty characters, which we will use for the column size. This column definition appears in Screen 2-13.

57

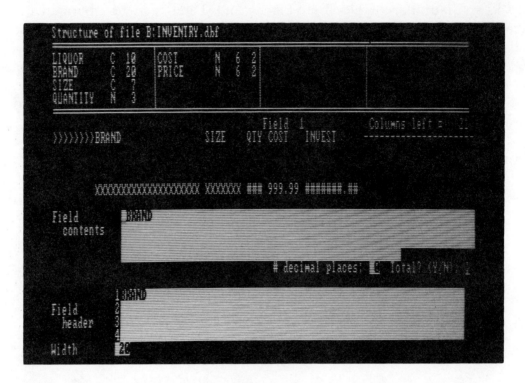

Screen 2 - 13

Our report will use five columns, and these are defined below:

Field Content	Field Header	Width	# of Decimals	Totals
BRAND	BRAND	20		
SIZE	SIZE	7		
QUANTITY	QTY	3	0	Y
COST	COST	6	2	N
COST * QUANTITY	INVEST	7	2	Y

Note the last item. The content of a column can be either a FIELDNAME or an expression such as COST * QUANTITY. When the content is described by a fieldname, the report will contain the contents of the FIELD. But, when the content is described by an expression, the report will contain the result of the expression.

At any point in the process, you can back up to a previous page by use of the <PgUp> key. Alternatively to return to where you were, use the <PgDn> key. To save the report form, press either the <RETURN> key when prompted to define a new column, or press <Ctrl-End>. To abort the report, press <Esc>.

Finally, the report form can be changed at any time by the MODIFY REPORT command. MODIFY REPORT is used exactly like CREATE REPORT.

By completing this initial work, any time you enter the command REPORT FORM with the filename B:INVENTRY at the dot prompt, the computer gives the report shown in Figure 2-1. The command . REPORT FORM TO PRINT produces a printed copy.

59

```
PAGE NO. 00001
09/15/81
                    LIQUOR STORE INVENTORY

        BRAND            SIZE      QTY      COST     INVEST

*   SCOTCH
AULD COUNTRY             QUART      23       5.59     128.57
AULD COUNTRY             1/2 LIT     7       9.78      68.46
AULD COUNTRY             PINT       88       2.74     241.12

**  SUBTOTAL **                    118                438.15

*   VODKA
REAL RUSSIAN             QUART      35       3.78     132.30
REAL RUSSIAN             1/2 LIT     9       7.95      71.55
REAL RUSSIAN             PINT       75       1.49     111.75

**  SUBTOTAL **                    119                315.60

*   WHISKEY
SOUTHERN RYE            QUART       32       5.11     163.52
OLD WYOMING             PINT        44       1.98      87.12
OLD WYOMING             QUART       19       5.29     100.51
THE NEW SOUTH           QUART        4       7.49      29.96

**  SUBTOTAL **                     99                381.11

*   BOURBON
SOUTHERN ARISTOCRACY    PINT         5       0.99       4.95
SOUTHERN ARISTOCRACY    FIFTH       22       1.78      39.16
SOUTHERN ARISTOCRACY    QUART       21       3.50      73.50
SOUTHERN ARISTOCRACY    1/2 GAL      3       6.89      20.67
SOUTHERN ARISTOCRACY    1/2 LIT      5       6.47      32.35

**  SUBTOTAL **                     56                170.63

**  TOTAL **                       392               1305.49
```

Figure 2-1. Computer Report On Liquor Store Inventory

So what have we done? What might we have done? If we had actually conducted an inventory of a small liquor store, most likely we would have used paper and pencil and adding machine. Now we can do the same thing with a computer database management system, and the results will be available within minutes of inventory completion. In addition, we significantly reduce the opportunity for error by eliminating the adding machine. And, all of this is possible without knowing anything about computer programming or database management systems. All we have to do is follow the same steps we have been through in the last few pages. If you think about it, this example is remarkable: all of this from two commands—CREATE and REPORT.

To give us a different feel for what is in our inventory, we might want to re-organize our listing of inventory items. For instance, our stocking scheme may key on the sizes of different kinds and brands of liquor. Within the database, we have the ability to INDEX or SORT. Indexing and sorting are similar in concept but entirely different in application.

INDEXING OR SORTING

If we SORT a database, we physically rearrange it. A non-computer example of this is to sort a deck of cards. We can arrange the cards in many different ways, but only in one way at a time. Suppose we arrange the cards in suits, and then in value within the suits. If this is the case, and we want the Jack of Diamonds, we know where to look. If we take the cards and rearrange them (SORT) by value, we have an entirely different sequence of cards, but we will still know where to find the Jack of Diamonds.

A very clever way to accomplish the same result is to INDEX the cards. This leaves the physical arrangement of the database in its original order. INDEX creates a separate list that describes the location of the item we want. To illustrate this, let's look at the deck of cards. On a sheet of paper, make a list of each card in the order shown in Figure 2-2.

SUIT	CARD	POSITION
Spades	Ace	
	King	
	Queen	
	.	
	.	
	.	
	Two	
Hearts	Ace	
	.	
	Two	
Diamonds	.	
Clubs	.	

Figure 2-2

You now have an ordered list of the fifty-two cards in the deck. Now, take the cards and shuffle them well.

Take the first card from the top of the deck. Locate the card in the list and write the number "1" under "POSITION" across from the card description (Spades. . . .Ace. . . . .1). Place the card on the table and repeat this operation until you have entered all of the cards in the deck.

The list is now an INDEX. Any card can be located by finding it in the list and counting card by card from the bottom of the deck. For example, if the Jack of Diamonds has the number ten written after it on the list, it is the tenth card from the bottom of the deck. The card location numbers on the list are called POINTERS.

We can also make a list that describes another possible card arrangement: the cards arranged by face value and suit within value. Such an arrangement is shown in Figure 2-3.

CARD	SUIT	POSITION
Ace	Spades	
	Hearts	
	Clubs	
	Diamonds	
King	Spades	
	Hearts	
	.	
	.	
	.	
	Etc.	
Etc.		

Figure 2-3. Another Card List

If we go through our deck again and list card positions, we will end up with two lists which describe the same physical arrangement of the card deck. As long as we do not change the order of the cards, we can find them quickly using either index.

A library offers another common example of INDEXES and POINTERS. If you go to the library knowing you want a particular book, you can find it in one of two ways: either wander around starting with the first shelf and continuing a shelf at a time until you find the book, or use the card catalog which tells you which shelf the book is on. The card catalog is a multiple index. There are index cards to locate books based on title, author, and subject. Each card contains pointers to tell you where to find the book.

63

CHAPTER TWO

Depending on the type of database you have, you can maintain one or more indexes on the records. With the kind of database we are using, we can use the database B:INVENTRY and make an index on the size of the liquor bottle, for example. When we do this, we must have an INDEX FILE where the desired order of records is stored. In this example, call the index file B:SIZINDEX. We first USE our inventory file B:INVENTRY and then index on the size. Size, of course, doesn't really mean anything to the computer. The index groups the records by an "alphabetical" ordering of the contents of the size field. This groups all like sizes together because they start with the same letter and are spelled the same.

This operation and the result are shown in Screen 2-14.

```
. USE B:INVENTRY
. INDEX ON SIZE TO B:INVENTRY
     15 records indexed
. LIST
Record#  LIQUOR   BRAND                 SIZE     QUANTITY   COST   PRICE
     14  BOURBON  SOUTHERN ARISTOCRACY  1/2 GAL         3   6.89   11.48
      2  SCOTCH   AULD COUNTRY          2 LITER         7   9.78   16.30
      5  VODKA    REAL RUSSIAN          2 LITER         9   7.95   13.25
     15  BOURBON  SOUTHERN ARISTOCRACY  2 LITER         5   6.47   10.78
     12  BOURBON  SOUTHERN ARISTOCRACY  FIFTH          22   1.78    2.96
      3  SCOTCH   AULD COUNTRY          PINT           88   2.74    4.56
      6  VODKA    REAL RUSSIAN          PINT           75   1.49    2.48
      8  WHISKEY  OLD WYOMING           PINT           44   1.98    3.30
     11  BOURBON  SOUTHERN ARISTOCRACY  PINT            5   0.99    1.65
      1  SCOTCH   AULD COUNTRY          QUART          23   5.59    9.31
      4  VODKA    REAL RUSSIAN          QUART          35   3.78    6.30
      7  WHISKEY  SOUTHERN RYE          QUART          32   5.11    8.51
      9  WHISKEY  OLD WYOMING           QUART          19   5.29    8.01
     10  WHISKEY  THE NEW SOUTH         QUART           4   7.49   12.48
     13  BOURBON  SOUTHERN ARISTOCRACY  QUART          21   3.50    5.83
```

Screen 2 - 14

64

SIMPLE DATABASE USES: HOW THEY WORK

By making use of INDEX and an INDEX FILE, we leave the physical database in the order of its original data entry. The record number column reflects where each entry is in the database. What has happened here is very similar to the example of the card deck and the lists. That is, the display is controlled by the INDEX file B:SIZINDEX instead of the order in which the data was entered. Thus, one of the really nice features of INDEX is that you don't have to be concerned about the order in which records are entered, and the computer can quickly arrange them into nearly any sequence or grouping you desire.

In these first two chapters, we have discussed some basic concepts and workings of microcomputer database management systems. This basic orientation and beginning "hands-on" experience is the foundation for bigger and better things. These systems use the speed of the computer to perform tasks that, in the past, we performed manually with the aid of "paper databases."

• The database management system provides a mechanism for storing data in the computer, for retrieving, manipulating, and changing that data, and for preparing reports based upon that data.

• The modern microcomputer database systems do not require that the user either have or acquire a technical background.

• For the most part, computers have been successfully adapted to the needs of the user, rather than forcing the user to adapt to the computer. These systems will eventually become the basis for everyday computer use.

CHAPTER THREE

HELP AND ASSISTANCE

Most current database management systems now offer their users elaborate help systems of one kind or another. *dBASE III* is no exception. Two kinds of direct assistance are provided. The first, called the dBASE Assistant, provides a series of menus that allow you to use dBASE before you learn its command language. The second, HELP, provides information about how to use dBASE and the dBASE command language.

To get the most out of modern database management systems, you should learn the command language. System designers are beginning to understand that many users need to have immediate use of at least the basic parts of the database system. The real power features that are available through the commands can then be learned at a more leisurely pace.

CHAPTER THREE

THE DBASE ASSISTANT

The dBASE Assistant uses menus to provide you access to the basic database management capabilities. Among the available options are the ability to:

- Create and use databases
- Prepare and produce reports and labels
- Make changes to existing databases
- Obtain information
- Sort and index
- Copy, delete, and rename files

The dBASE Assistant is invoked by the command ASSIST. The function key <F2> will also bring up the dBASE Assistant. Later in this chapter we'll describe a way to have the Assistant brought up automatically whenever *dBASE III* is entered.

. ASSIST

will clear the screen and present the display shown as Screen 1. This first screen describes the functions of keys that are used with ASSIST.

Screen 3 - 1

Press <RETURN> to advance you to the Assistant's Main Menu (Screen 2).

```
                          dBASE III Assistant
 Set Up      Modify      Position     Retrieve    Organize     Uncounter
 Use or Create a database and Create Reports or Label Forms.

 ┌────────────────────────────────────────────────────────────────────┐
 │                         SET UP ENVIRONMENT                           │
 │                                                                      │
 │  The  SET UP menu allows you to establish the active database file, either │
 │  by  creating a new one or selecting an existing one.  It also  lets  you  │
 │  create  label and report layouts.   Other menu options are inactive until │
 │  an active database is available.                                    │
 │                                                                      │
 │  Use      Set Drive      Create      Create Label      Create Report │
 │                                                                      │
 └────────────────────────────────────────────────────────────────────┘

 No database is in use. Press ↓ to select SET UP to define a USE file.

 Drive B:    Previous Menu: ↑  Left: ←  Right: →  Next: ↓ (or ENTER)    Help: F1
```

Screen 3 - 2

This main menu is a "Menu of Menus." The menu selections are the six items on the second line, beginning with Set Up. The last line on the screen tells you what your options are. Press the right or left arrow keys. Each time a left or right arrow key is pressed a different menu option will be highlighted. In Screen 2, the option Set Up is highlighted. If a database has not yet been selected you cannot move to any option other than Set Up. If you press the Up Arrow you will return to Screen 1.

The center of Screen 2 describes the Set Up menu and lists the options on the line beginning with USE. Press either the down arrow or the <RETURN> key to select the highlighted option. This will bring up the Set Up menu (Screen 3).

Screen 3 - 3

The Set Up menu allows you to select one of the menu options listed on the second line of the screen.

USE (a database file)
SET DRIVE
CREATE (a database file)
CREATE LABEL
CREATE REPORT

Each time the left or right arrow is pressed, a different menu option will be highlighted. Four seconds after an option is highlighted a description of the option is displayed in the center screen area. A highlighted command line is displayed near the bottom of the screen. The dBASE command associated with the menu option is displayed in this command line. By observing this line you will gradually become familiar with the dBASE command language.

The CREATE option is identical to the command CREATE in that it is used to create a new database file. CREATE has already been discussed in this book. We'll assume that we have a number of database files available to us on the B disk drive.

Press the down arrow or <RETURN> key when the USE option is highlighted. The display shown will be similar to that of Screen 4. The available disk drives (A, B, C, etc.) for your computer will be displayed. Each time the left or right arrow key is pressed, a different disk drive will be highlighted.

72

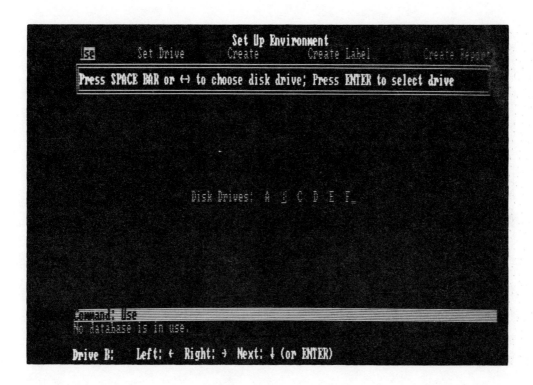

Screen 3 - 4

To select a drive, press the arrow key until the desired drive is highlighted—then press <RETURN>.

This will bring up the database selection screen (Screen 5). All of the database files on the selected disk drive are displayed in the center area of the screen. Use the arrow keys to highlight the desired database file. When the desired file is highlighted press the <RETURN> key to select it.

74

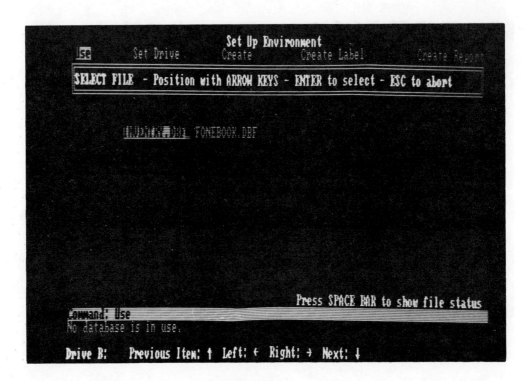

Screen 3 - 5

All menu options may be viewed at any time by pressing the function key <F1>. This changes the description at center screen to that shown in Screen 6.

```
                    dBASE III Assistant
SET UP      Modify      Position      Retrieve      Organize
Use or Create a database and Create Reports or Label Forms.


              ASSIST COMMAND NAVIGATION GUIDE

►Set up    ↔    Modify ↔ Position ↔ Retrieve ↔ Organize ↔ Utilities
  ↑ ↓            ↑ ↓      ↑ ↓        ↑ ↓        ↑ ↓        ↑ ↓
Use            Append   Find       Display    Index      Set Drive
Set Drive      Browse   Locate     Sum        Sort       Copy File
Create         Edit     Continue   Average    Copy       Dir
Create Label   Delete   Skip       Count      Pack       Rename
Create Report  Recall   Go         Label                 Erase
               Replace  Modify     Report                Modify Stru
               Position Retrieve   Position



File in use: B:INVENTRY.dbf Current record #:    1    Size (records):    15

Drive B:    Previous Menu: ↑  Left: ←  Right: →  Next: ↓ (or ENTER)    Help: F1
```

Screen 3 - 6

Once a database file has been placed in USE, return to the Main Menu
with the up arrow. You may now change the highlighted option by using
the left and right arrow keys. The display produced when each of the
options is highlighted is shown as Screens 7 through 11.

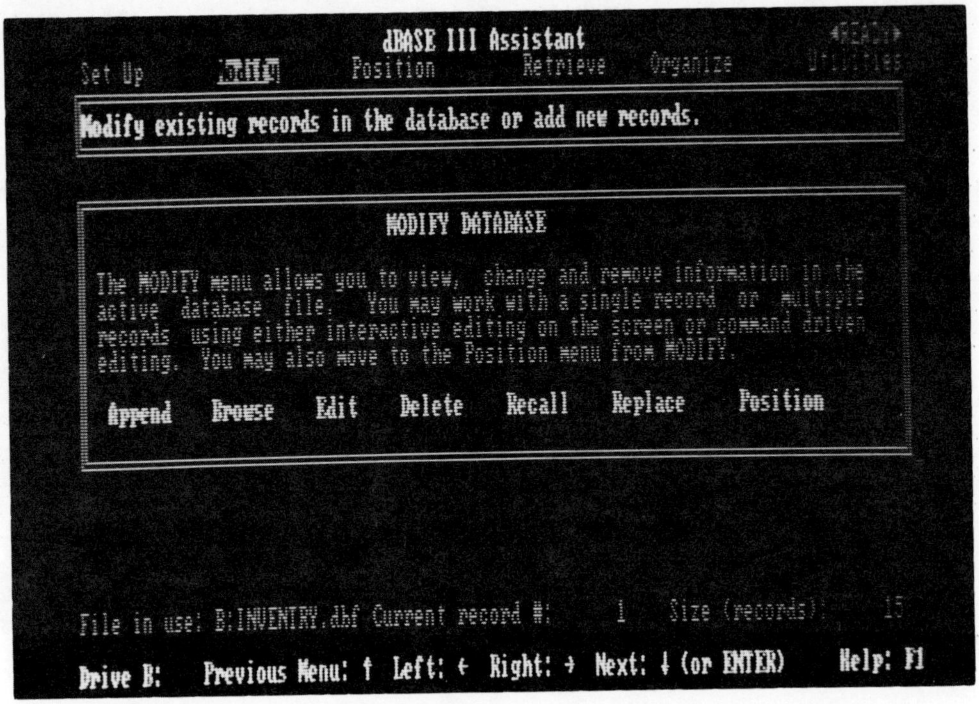
dBASE III Assistant
Set Up Modify Position Retrieve Organize
Modify existing records in the database or add new records.
MODIFY DATABASE
The MODIFY menu allows you to view, change and remove information in the active database file. You may work with a single record or multiple records using either interactive editing on the screen or command driven editing. You may also move to the Position menu from MODIFY.
Append Browse Edit Delete Recall Replace Position
File in use: B:INVENTRY.dbf Current record #: 1 Size (records): 15
Drive B: Previous Menu: ↑ Left: ← Right: → Next: ↓ (or ENTER) Help: F1

Screen 3 - 7

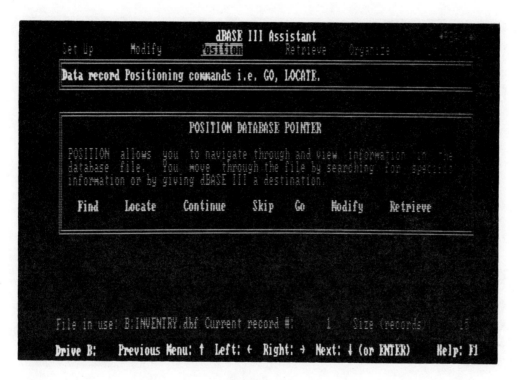

Screen 3 - 8

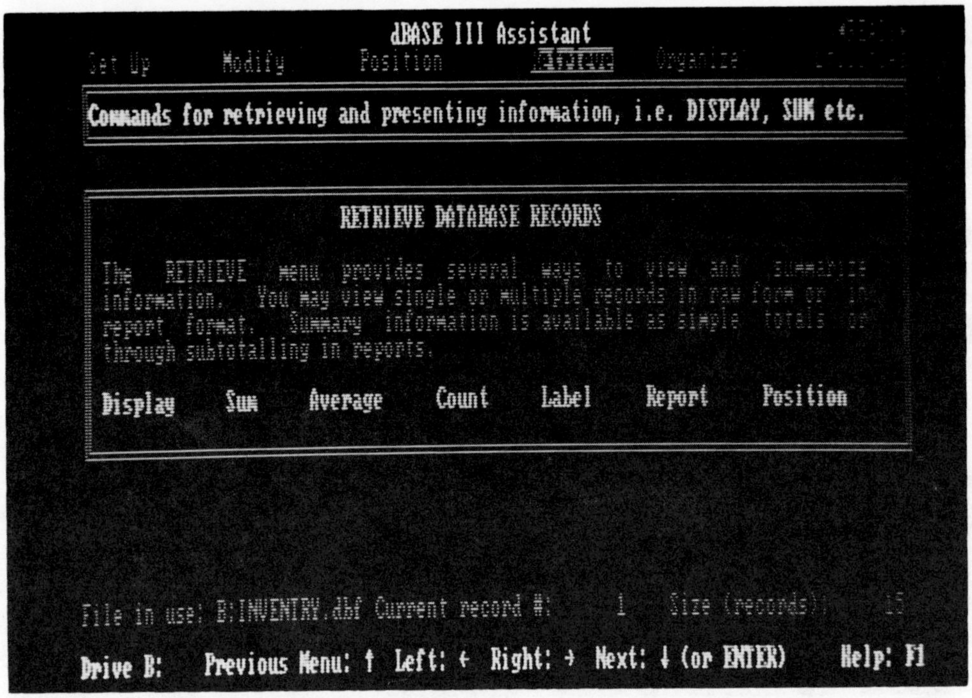
dBASE III Assistant
Set Up
Modify
Position
Retrieve
Organize
Commands for retrieving and presenting information, i.e. DISPLAY, SUM etc.
RETRIEVE DATABASE RECORDS
The RETRIEVE menu provides several ways to view and summarize information. You may view single or multiple records in raw form or in report format. Summary information is available as simple totals or through subtotalling in reports.
Display
Sum
Average
Count
Label
Report
Position
File in use: B:INVENTRY.dbf Current record #: 1 Size (records):
Drive B:
Previous Menu: ↑ Left: ← Right: → Next: ↓ (or ENTER)
Help: F1

Screen 3 - 9

```
                           dBASE III Assistant
 Set Up      Modify      Position      Retrieve      Organize      Database

┌──────────────────────────────────────────────────────────────────────────┐
│ Do operations on the database as a whole.                                  │
└──────────────────────────────────────────────────────────────────────────┘

┌──────────────────────────────────────────────────────────────────────────┐
│                                                                            │
│                          ORGANIZE DATABASE                                 │
│                                                                            │
│  The ORGANIZE menu is used to create indexes for fast key searches, sort a │
│  database file by field contents, copy a database file and remove          │
│  information marked for deletion.                                          │
│                                                                            │
│  Index            Sort               Copy              Pack                │
│                                                                            │
└──────────────────────────────────────────────────────────────────────────┘

 File in use: B:INVENTRY.dbf Current record #:      1    Size (records):     15
 Drive B:    Previous Menu: ↑  Left: ←  Right: →  Next: ↓ (or ENTER)    Help: F1
```

Screen 3 - 10

79

CHAPTER THREE

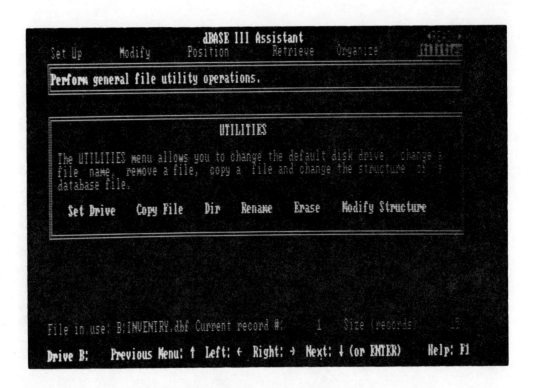

Screen 3 - 11

To illustrate using the Assistant to retrieve data from the database INVENTRY, use the Set Up option to select INVENTRY as the active database file. Press the up arrow to return to the Main Menu. Then press the right arrow until the RETRIEVE option is highlighted. Press <RETURN>. This will produce the display of Screen 12. Note that the highlighted command line shows DISPLAY as the command. The complete dBASE command will be built up on this line.

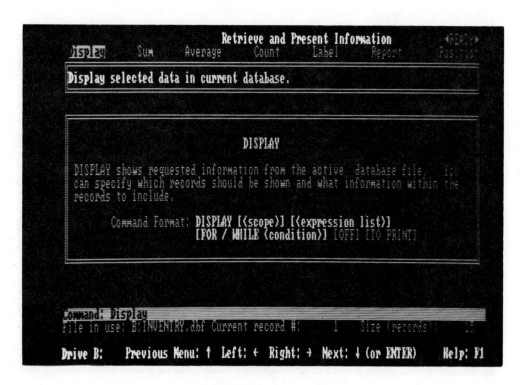

Screen 3 - 12

Press the <RETURN> key when the option DISPLAY is highlighted. This brings us to the screen display shown as Screen 13.

Screen 3 - 13

This screen allows us to specify the part of the database that we want to work with. Use the up and down arrows to highlight your selection. To make the selection, press the right arrow when the desired option is highlighted. For our example we want to work with all of the records. To do this we would use the down arrow to highlight the ALL option. Then press <RETURN>.

This brings us to Screen 14. Note that the command line now says Display ALL.

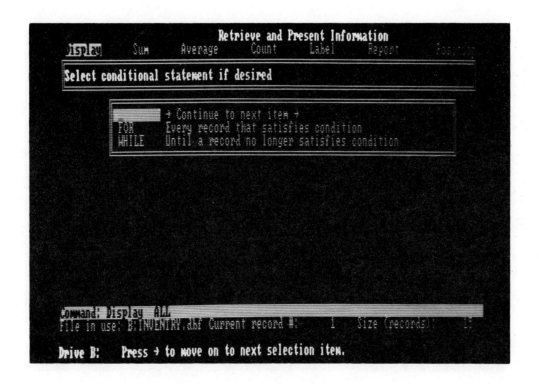

Screen 3 - 14

This screen allows us to indicate that we want to specify records that meet a particular criteria. We want to display those records where the contents of the LIQUOR field are WHISKEY. Use the down arrow key to highlight the FOR option. Then press <RETURN> to obtain Screen 15.

Screen 15 provides a list of fields. To select specific records from the database, we need to identity a field and the desired content of the field (e.g. LIQUOR = 'WHISKEY'). Screen 15 allows us to identify the field to be used in our comparison.

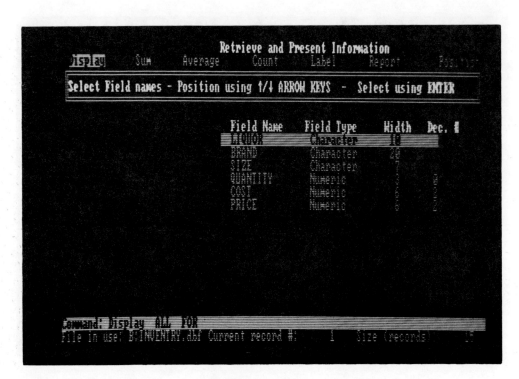

Screen 3 - 15

A field is selected by using the up or down arrow keys to highlight the desired fieldname, and then pressing the <RETURN> key. In our example, we press the <RETURN> key when LIQUOR is highlighted. This brings us to Screen 16. Note that the command line of Screen 16 indicates DISPLAY ALL FOR LIQUOR.

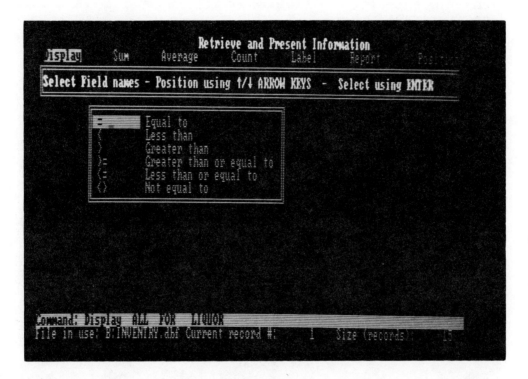

Screen 3 - 16

Screen 16 allows us to define the manner in which the specified content of the LIQUOR field will relate to the actual content. Again, the selection is made by highlighting our choice (in this case the = sign) and pressing <RETURN>.

Now we are asked (in Screen 17) to enter the content of the field. When the screen comes up, a single quote will already be displayed in the data area. dBASE knows that the field is a character string and that our entry must be enclosed by quotes (delimiters). We enter the word WHISKEY and press <RETURN>. Do NOT enter the closing quote mark. A closing quote mark will be entered by dBASE. If you enter one, there will be two quotes. Should this occur, the command will be displayed on the center of the screen. Use the arrow key to position the cursor to the extra closing quote and press the <Del> key.

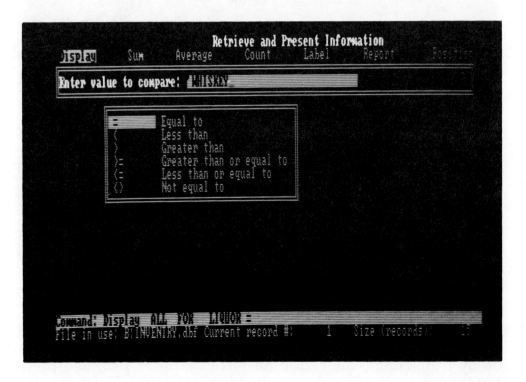

Screen 3 - 17

At this point the command line at the bottom of the screen will display the complete command DISPLAY ALL FOR LIQUOR = 'WHISKEY'. You are provided with an opportunity to add more conditions to the command, such as .AND. BRAND = 'OLD WYOMING'. This is shown in Screen 18. Press the right arrow key to avoid making a selection.

Screen 3 - 18

Screen 19 provides the opportunity to define which fields are to be displayed. To select a field, use the down arrow to highlight a field, then press <RETURN>. This process is repeated until all of the desired fields have been selected. Selected fields will have a triangular mark in front of the fieldname.

88

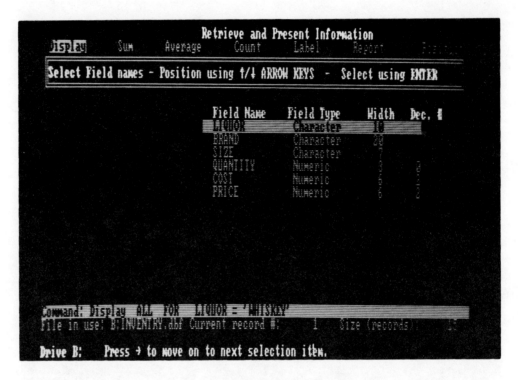

Screen 3 - 19

To terminate selection, press the right arrow key. If the right arrow key is pressed without first selecting one or more fields, all fields will be displayed. This provides the display shown in Screen 20.

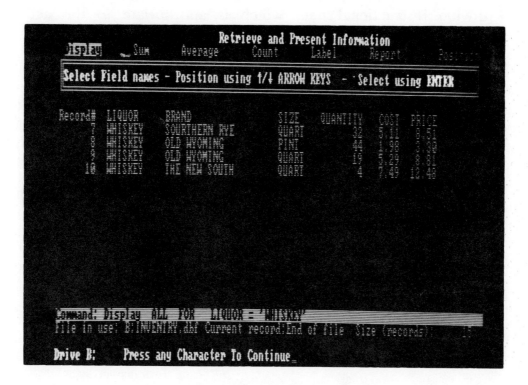

Screen 3 - 20

The use of any of the other menu options is similar to the above. You are walked through the process one step at a time. Selections are made by using the arrow keys to highlight an item and pressing the <RETURN> key when the desired item is highlighted. Instructions as to arrow key functions are displayed on the bottom line of the screen at each step.

When finished with the dBASE Assistant, press the <Esc> key one or more times until a dot prompt is obtained.

CHAPTER THREE

HELP

HELP is provided in a variety of ways. The function key <F1> will provide instructional help which is appropriate to the activity underway.

Press <F1> or type HELP after a dot prompt. This produces the display shown as Screen 21. The screen is oriented to someone who is a relative newcomer to *dBASE III*. Specific categories of help are displayed on the first page of a menu system. This is the main help menu. To select a category, use the arrow keys to highlight the desired menu option, then press <RETURN>.

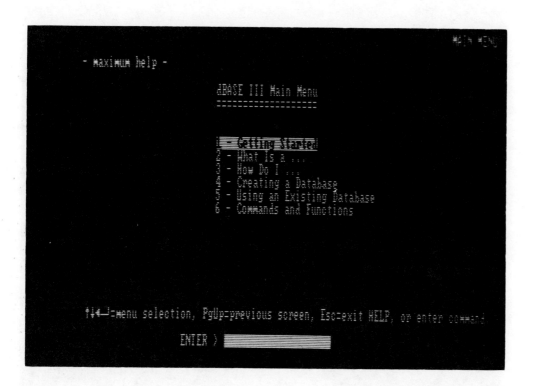

Screen 3 - 21

To illustrate, let's select the HELP option "How do I . . ." This gets us the display shown as Screen 22. If we select the first option we get a description of the QUIT command. To terminate the HELP system, press <Esc>.

92

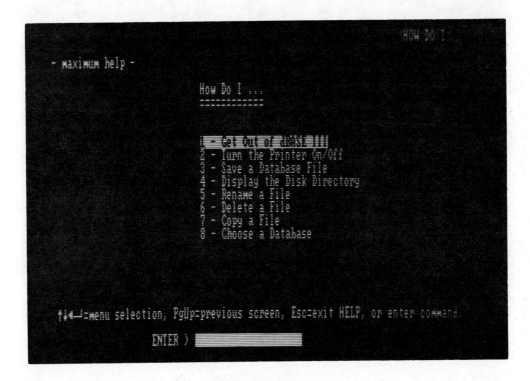

- maximum help -

```
                                    How Do I ...
                                    ============

                        1 - Get Out of HERE !!!
                        2 - Turn the Printer On/Off
                        3 - Save a Database File
                        4 - Display the Disk Directory
                        5 - Rename a File
                        6 - Delete a File
                        7 - Copy a File
                        8 - Choose a Database



    ↑↓←┘=menu selection, PgUp=previous screen, Esc=exit HELP, or enter command.

            ENTER ) ▨▨▨▨▨▨▨▨▨▨▨▨▨▨▨
```

Screen 3 - 22

If dBASE cannot execute a command as entered, the command will be echoed back as shown in Screen 23 and you will be asked if you want help. A "yes" response will produce a display describing the syntax and use of the command.

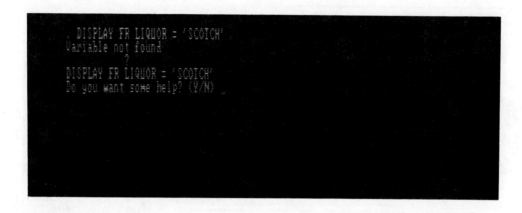

Screen 3 - 23

93

If you want help with the detailed syntax of a specific command, type HELP followed by the command name after a dot prompt.

. HELP CREATE

While in any of the full screen commands such as CREATE, EDIT, and so on, a help menu of key functions will be displayed on or removed from the screen by pressing the function key <F1>.

Most of the newer database management systems will provide a variation of at least the HELP system of *dBASE III*. Software designers have begun to recognize that they must provide a product that can be profitably used without a significant investment of learning time on the part of the user. It is probably safe to say that any software product that does *not* provide on-line assistance to the user will *not* be successful in today's marketplace.

CHAPTER FOUR

WHAT ABOUT HARDWARE SYSTEMS?

In the first two chapters, we did a survey of the field. We learned that a microcomputer and a database management system (DBMS) are easy to use and to understand. Our brief sample of how database management systems work and what they can do for us will be expanded in the following chapters. In the chapters to come we will go over this same material in much more detail. And, of course, we will also introduce new material.

In this chapter we will introduce microcomputer hardware systems. In order to use a database system you must have a computer (although, as we said earlier, you will be able to understand and follow the material without having a computer). In case you are unfamiliar with computers, this brief discussion will include the basic elements of computer systems and then indicate what you will need to be able to use a database system. As you will see in this chapter, as well as later chapters, your database needs have a significant effect on the computer hardware you select.

A typical microcomputer system is diagrammed in Figure 4-1.

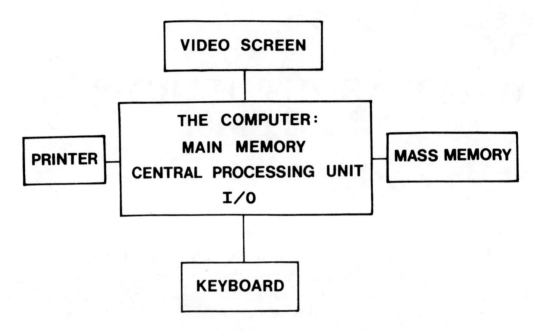

Figure 4-1. A Typical Microcomputer

The diagram above describes any computer system: it could be a microcomputer or a very large computer. The computer itself consists of what is inside the box labeled computer: the central processing unit, the main memory, and the I/O (input/output). The other four boxes—video screen, mass memory, printer, and keyboard—are called peripherals.

THE COMPUTER

The computer, as shown above, consists of the central processing unit, main memory, and I/O (input/output). The central processing unit is usually referred to as the CPU. It is the device that actually does the "computing." For it to function, however, it must have main memory. Main memory is used directly by the CPU.

Advertisements for microcomputers usually say something like

BUY A 256K Cucumber IV

The 256K refers to the amount of main memory in something called bytes. A byte is the amount of memory needed to store a typewriter character such as "m" or "$." K (for Kilo) stands for 1,000. In a computer system K actually stands for 1,024. Thus, a 256K computer system actually has 262,144 bytes of memory.

Main memory is relatively expensive when compared to mass memory. When you purchase a computer, you will want to select the amount of main memory with some care. The database system you select will require a minimum amount of main memory, and *you will need to acquire at least that amount of main memory for your computer system.*

I/O stands for input/output. By this means you connect the computer to the outside world. In this case the outside world consists of the peripherals. You might reasonably assume the I/O is a standard feature like tires on a car. This is not always true—computer I/O often costs extra. For microcomputers however, cost is a *relative* consideration.

THE PERIPHERALS

For most database uses, all but one of the peripherals shown in Figure 4-1 are required. That is, mass memory, video screen, and keyboard are mandatory. For some uses, the printer is also a must; other times the printer can be optional.

KEYBOARDS, MONITORS, TERMINALS

The keyboard is similar to a typewriter keyboard, and it is used to communicate with the computer. The computer, in turn, communicates with you by means of the video screen. The keyboard and video screen may be separate devices. When they are separate, video is supplied by a television-like device called a monitor. The keyboard and video screen are often incorporated into a single device called a computer terminal, a video terminal, or sometimes just CRT.

Whether you have a terminal or keyboard and monitor usually depends upon the brand of microcomputer system you own. There is no practical difference between a video terminal and a keyboard with separate monitor, and in this book we refer to it as terminal for convenience sake. Typical video screens can display twenty-four lines of eighty characters at a time, while some display less and others more. The keyboard and video screen are extremely important from a subjective point of view: these devices are your means of interaction with the computer. You "talk" to the computer via the keyboard; the computer "talks" to you via the video screen.

MASS MEMORY

Mass memory stores your information for future use. Mass memory is significantly less expensive than main memory, and it is also significantly slower (more than a thousand times). When power is turned off, main memory is erased while mass memory is not. Finally, mass memory must be deliberately changed.

Mass memory is used to store the information you want to save, much the same as an audio tape is used to save "memories" of sounds. Mass storage systems are designed so the computer can easily find the information it wants. There are two kinds of mass storage commonly used by microcomputers: tape and disk.

98

Tape systems usually employ cassettes similar to those used for audio storage. These systems are slow and, except for particular applications, are not suitable for use with database systems other than for "backing up" data.

Disk systems, often referred to as direct access storage devices (DASD), are like "magnetic phonographs." The information is magnetically stored on a rotating disk (hence the name) on tracks like a record. A device which is similar in concept to a tone arm (except that it has a magnetic head like those used on tape recorders) is used to "read" and "write" on the disk. The information is on magnetic tracks that, unlike a phonograph record, are invisible to the eye.

A disk drive is the mechanism which turns the disk and transfers information to and from the disk. The computer knows the location of each piece of information on each disk drive. It knows this by reading the disk directory for each disk. The disk directory is similar in concept to the label on a long playing record—it tells you which musical piece is located on each band on that record.

The disk drive must be controlled by a disk controller which connects to the I/O of the computer. As instructed by the CPU, the disk controller directs the magnetic disk. The disk controller provides a path for information flowing between the CPU and the disk. It also keeps the CPU informed about conditions on the disk.

For microcomputers there are two kinds of disk systems commonly used: "floppy disk systems" and " hard disk systems."

FLOPPY DISK SYSTEMS

Floppy disks are often called floppies or diskettes. They were developed by IBM in about 1970 for use on the IBM 370 computer system, and they are the most common mass storage medium for microcomputer systems. The cost of a floppy disk is about the same as the cost of a tape cassette, while the cost of the floppy disk drive is usually much greater than the cost of a cassette recorder.

Most microcomputer systems for personal, business, or professional applications are equipped with from one to four disk drives, and to run a database management systems, you will have at least one floppy disk drive. The floppy disk is a convenient way of introducing new software to the microcomputer and for transporting data or software to other microcomputers.

The floppy disk is made from an oxide-coated mylar film and resembles a 45 rpm phonograph record. The disk is packaged into a square plastic or paper envelope with holes or openings whereby the read/write head accesses to the disk. Another hole in the disk envelope is for index mark sensing. When the floppy disk is inserted into the disk drive, the envelope remains stationary while the mylar disk turns within it. Care must be taken to keep the mylar film clean: the mylar film must *not* be touched. Touching the film or exposing it to grease or dirt can cause severe damage to your data.

100

Since there are no universal standards for floppy disk systems, you can have problems in interchanging floppy disks between systems. The disk drives *must be compatible*. And then, of course, there is the matter of size. Floppy disks come in five and a quarter inch (called mini-floppies) and eight inch versions. Each can be single-sided (data can be on only one side of the disk) or double-sided. The density of stored information is either single-density or double-density (twice as much as single-density). There are also quad density systems.

The nominal amount of information that can be stored on each of these floppy disk types is shown in Table 4-1. These values provide a general guide to the storage capacity of "generic" diskettes. These values can vary considerably from system to system and manufacturer to manufacturer. In one sense this is unfortunate because this variation comes at the expense of interchangeability.

	5¼ inch	8 inch
single sided, single density	70K	240K
single sided, double density	160K	480K
double sided, double density	360K	960K

Table 4-1. Floppy Disk Storage Capacity In Bytes

Most eight inch single-density disks are recorded in IBM 3740 format. This format is used by the disk drive to record the data. It was originally used by IBM for the "3740 Key to Disk Data Entry System."

Each 3740 disk contains seventy-seven tracks and is divided into twenty-six sectors. A sector is a pie-shaped wedge as illustrated by the diagram in Figure 4-2. The outermost track is track 0 and the innermost track is track 76. The number of bytes stored within a sector on a track is usually independent of the track position. This means that if 100 bytes were stored in each sector of track 0 then 100 bytes will be stored in each sector of track 76. This particular arrangement allows the disk data transfer rate to be independent of track—the outer tracks move faster (inches per second) than the inner tracks.

Double-density eight inch disks are usually recorded in IBM 34 format. Recording in a compatible format is not enough to guarantee that disks can be exchanged between microcomputers, but it's a start. As a result, a good percentage of eight inch disks can be exchanged between different microcomputer systems.

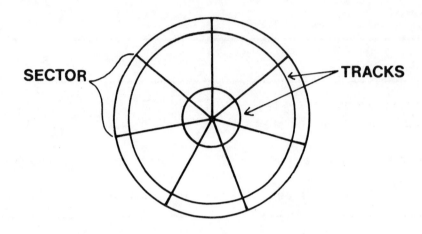

Figure 4-2. Schematic Diagram of a Disk

102

Unfortunately, the exchangeability situation is not as good for the five inch mini-floppy disks. For the smaller disks, there is, as yet, no single dominant recording format, although that used on the IBM PC is a good bet to become the five inch standard. As a rule, the odds are against exchanging five inch disks between different microcomputer systems. It's a good idea to test compatibility between systems before making big plans to exchange information via floppy disks.

HARD DISK SYSTEMS

Even though floppy disks are used pervasively in microcomputers, hard disks are certainly available and applicable. Hard disk simply describes a microcomputer disk system that does not use floppies. The physical difference is that the hard disk is a rigid disk made from a machined-metal plate. There are hard disks that are not removable and these are called Winchester disks.

Hard disks offer substantially higher performance than do floppy disks; they are also considerably more expensive. The storage capacity of hard disk systems starts at over a million bytes, although five to forty million bytes and more are common.

Other performance characteristics of disk systems that you may see in advertisements are track-to-track speed, average access speed, and data transfer rate. These are measures of the performance of the particular disk system. Track-to-track signifies the time required by the disk drive to move the head from one track to an adjacent track. Advertised values for this capability are usually a few milliseconds (1/1000 of a second). Average access speed is the average time required to reposition the head. Specifically, it is the time required to move the head from track 1 to the last track divided by two. It is normally several milliseconds for hard disk systems and is almost never advertised for floppy disk drives (100 to 500 milliseconds). It is a performance specification that can be very misleading in advertising and should ordinarily be ignored by you. Data transfer rate is another specification that vendors like and that you should ignore. Data transfer rates are normally specified in hundreds of thousands to millions of bytes per second.

103

Of far more interest to you is whether the disk drive device is compatible with your computer—that is, what has to be done to connect the device and make it work properly with your computer. For your information, connecting the device and making it work properly is called integration.

For the purposes of this book, mass memory is of particular importance. Databases are stored on disks of one type or another, and *no* database management approach will be satisfactory if you don't have adequate disk storage. Currently available microcomputers can hold only a relatively small database in main memory, and very large databases usually require a hard disk. Databases of moderate size may be contained on floppy disks of one type or another. Even large databases that are contained on hard disks may be backed up on floppy disks (backing up means to make a duplicate copy of the data). This extra copy protects against disk failures and provides an economical means of transferring the database from one microcomputer to another.

FEATURING dBASE III

THE PRINTER

A printer is always useful even when not absolutely mandatory. The two most common types of printers are the dot matrix and the daisy wheel.

- The daisy wheel printer produces a fully formed character like a typewriter does, and it is usually used where letter-quality is desired.
- The dot matrix printer uses a number of small dots to form the character.

Dot matrix printers are less expensive and of lower print quality than daisy wheel printers, but they are usually significantly faster. Typical print speeds for daisy wheel printers are 20 to 35 characters per second. Print speeds for dot matrix printers are often in excess of 100 characters per second. Also, dot matrix print does not always reproduce well on copying machines.

104

THE OPERATING SYSTEM

When most computers are turned on, the main memory is blank: the machine has no purpose and cannot process information. You need an *operating system* to let the computer peform its functions. Most microcomputer systems that are suitable for use with a database management system use a disk operating system (DOS). When the computer is turned on, the operating system is loaded into main memory from a disk. This may be done automatically, or you may have to press a key or keys on the computer. Loading the operating system is called *booting*. Don't fret—you will not need to know much about the operating system, now or ever, to use a database system.

The discussion in this book assumes that the operating system used is PC-DOS (or MS-DOS). A different operating system *may* have different rules for addressing disk drives and/or naming files.

A FEW LAST WORDS ON THE QUESTION OF HARDWARE

To get properly started you will need to have an adequate set of computer hardware. The most critical hardware item for a microcomputer database system is the disk drive system. If you own a computer and desire to use it for a database application you will want to carefully evaluate your disk capability. Remember that you need sufficient storage space to store the entire database on a single disk. (In Chapter Five, we discuss how to determine the size of your database in bytes.) In addition, the CPU can only use the data contained on the disk drives that are connected to it. That data is said to be *online*. If you have floppy disk drives, only the floppy disks that are actually inserted into the disk drives are *online*.

If you have not yet selected a computer, the best advice I can give you and your bankbook is this: select the database system, determine your storage requirements, and select a computer that, (1) is compatible with your database software system, and (2) supports your storage requirements and offers a reasonable way of adding additional mass storage if necessary.

SECTION TWO

In Section Two we will develop a more comprehensive understanding of database planning and use. We begin with a discussion of the importance of simplicity and good planning and proceed to build, modify, maintain and finally work with the databases.

CHAPTER FIVE

PLANNING YOUR DATABASE

Planning is often considered a nuisance, particularly by the beginner. This is not limited to the database beginner. But if you do not plan well, you may be unhappy with the result and, of course, you might have to begin all over again.

Take once again the example of constructing a paper database with a typewriter. If the typist does not plan the layout of the columns properly the database will, most likely, "fall off" the right margin of the paper, and it will have to be done over.

The same is true of our computer database. It is not going to fall off the paper, but if not properly planned, you may have to go back and start over. In fact, one good approach to planning your database is to take a shot at it expecting to have to redo it once or twice (this process is called *iterative enhancement*). One of the benefits of working with a computer database (as opposed to paper) is that you can make major changes to the database without having to re-enter the data. The computer can recover most, if not all, of the data stored in the database before the change was made.

CHAPTER FIVE

The first step in planning your database is to know what you want to accomplish with it. The next step is to make a list of the items (data) that must be included. Avoid concern over perfection. Nearly any shortcoming or omission can be easily repaired or overcome.

As a first example, let's look again at the liquor store database created in Chapter Two. This *inventory* database is intended to tell us the stock on hand and how much it is worth. When we created this database, we simply stated the column headings to establish the record structure. But to *plan* this database, we will make a list of the items to be included:

> Brand of liquor
> Size of container
> Kind of liquor
> Retail price
> Wholesale price
> Quantity on hand

This list describes what was included in the liquor store inventory from Chapter Two. Since we first set this up, we have thought of at least one additional item that should be included:

> Location of the item

This oversight is simple to correct. We will review the necessary process step by step, and you will see how easy it is to change the database. This should truly set your mind at ease.

You already have a database, B:INVENTRY, and it has a lot of data in it. What do you do? First, you need to add a field and you don't want to lose the data that you have already entered. You can solve this one from your keyboard in minutes without losing any data at all.

MODIFY THE STRUCTURE

dBASE III allows you to change the structure of the database with the command MODIFY STRUCTURE. But when we edit the structure in this way, all of the data is destroyed. Therefore, a copy of the data is automatically made to prevent this loss of data. After the structure is modified, data from the backup file is automatically copied to the new database structure. There must be enough space on the disk to contain both the database and the backup copy. We proceed to change the database with the commands shown in Screen 5-1.

Screen 5 - 1

This will bring up Screen 5-2.

111

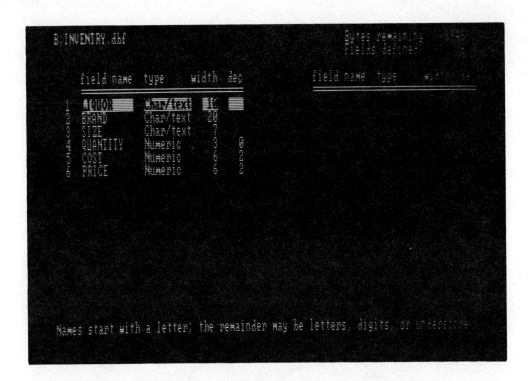

B:INVENTRY.dbf   Bytes remaining
                                                    Fields defined

    field name   type   width dec   field name   type   width

1   LIQUOR   Char/text   10
2   BRAND   Char/text   20
3   SIZE   Char/text   7
4   QUANTITY   Numeric   3   0
5   COST   Numeric   6   2
6   PRICE   Numeric   6   2

Names start with a letter; the remainder may be letters, digits, or underscore.

Screen 5 - 2

In this example we will insert a new field between QUANTITY and COST. To accomplish this we press the down arrow key four times. This positions the cursor at the beginning of the fieldname COST. Then,

● Press the <Ctrl> key and the <N> at the same time. This inserts a blank at field 5.
● Enter the new field definition. The display will look like Screen 5-3 below.

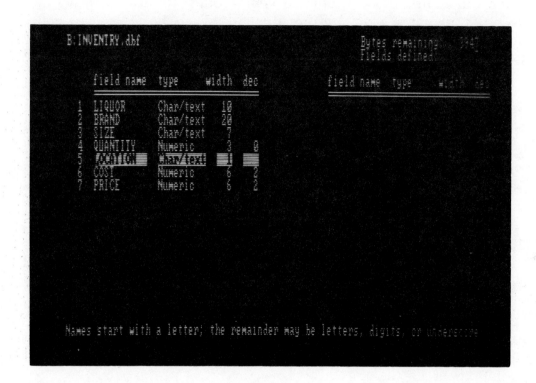

B:INVENTRY.dbf   Bytes remaining: 3947
                                                  Fields defined:

    field name   type   width dec   field name   type   width dec

  1 LIQUOR   Char/text   10
  2 BRAND   Char/text   20
  3 SIZE   Char/text   7
  4 QUANTITY   Numeric   3   0
  5 LOCATION   Char/text   1
  6 COST   Numeric   6   2
  7 PRICE   Numeric   6   2

  Names start with a letter; the remainder may be letters, digits, or underscore

Screen 5 - 3

Press <Ctrl-End>. The database B:NEWFILE now has the new field that you wanted to add. The existing data from the backup file B:INVENTRY.BAK will be added automatically. (You can use <Ctrl-U> to delete a field.)

At this point you have both the new and old versions of your database. Check the new database to make sure that everything is okay before deleting your old version.

CHAPTER FIVE

```
. LIST
```

When the computer's response to your request to "list" appears on the screen, you will see an additional blank space between the columns QUANTITY and COST. This blank space will hold the contents of the new field location. If everything looks all right, delete the old file B:INVENTRY. Simply:

```
. ERASE B:INVENTRY.BAK
File has been deleted
```

This completes Solution #2: The process of modifying the structure of your database.

You see, it's a piece of cake. Nothing to it. You can put in (CREATE) whatever you want in the beginning and then the process of iterative enhancement will let you refine your approach as you get deeper into the task.

Let's now move back a bit—back to the concept of planning before you get into CREATEing and USEing your database. You are ready to know more and need additional information about working characteristics and limitations of the database.

If you were to set up a database on paper using a typewriter you would need to do two things—assign column headings for each of the columns, and figure out how many spaces to use for each column. You must do both of these for a computer database. Determining the kind of information in each column is also part of planning your computer database.

There are five kinds of fields used in computer databases. These are:

Character Fields
Numeric Fields
Logical Fields
Date Fields
Memo Fields

Character fields are the most common kind of field. A character field may contain anything that can be input by a keyboard. This includes letters (both upper and lower case), numbers, and special symbols such as ?, &, <, and so on, as well as "space." Normally a character field can be used for any purpose. In fact, we can make every field in the database a character field. Some typical examples of character fields are NAME, ADDRESS, and PHONE from the telephone directory example in Chapter One.

The size (width) of a character field is the number of "typewriter" spaces that would be required to contain the longest entry for that field. Each letter, number, special symbol, and space counts as one character. Each character takes one byte of memory. Each time we relate the field width to space on a typewritten page, we can use that as an analogy to the space in the computer's memory. To summarize: field width is always represented in bytes, and the number of bytes is the same as the number of spaces required to put the field on a typewritten page.

115

Numeric fields can contain only numbers. They are normally used only when the numbers they contain are to be used for arithmetic calculations. They can contain either whole numbers (called integers) or decimal numbers. In addition to the digits, they can contain one decimal point (period) and a minus sign (-). A negative number such as -281.65 occupies seven spaces (bytes) and has two decimal places. In most database systems the positive (+) sign is understood and does not need to be entered. The minus sign and the decimal point each occupy a space and must be counted when determining the field width.

Numeric fields are right justified by the computer, and character fields are normally left justified by the computer. Examples of number columns that are right and left justified are shown in Figure 5-1.

LEFT JUSTIFIED	RIGHT JUSTIFIED
1	1
10	10
100	100

Figure 5-1. Justification

116

Logical fields are used when there are only two possibilities for the data. For example, bills are either paid or they are not. Students either attended a class or they did not. You are either reading this or you are not. Logical fields always take one byte (space). Data can be either true or false.

Date fields, as you must have guessed, are used to store dates. Date fields are always eight bytes long. Dates are entered and displayed as MM/DD/YY. These date fields will only accept proper dates.

Memo Fields are used to store large blocks of text. These fields are variable in length. Each memo field takes a minimum of ten bytes. As data is entered, *dBASE III* assigns additional space in increments of 512 bytes. The maximum size of a memo field is 4,096 bytes. Memo fields are stored in a special auxiliary file that has the same name as the database file. This auxilliary file is distinguished by the three-letter filetype .dbt.

Close on the heels of determining what type of field you want is assigning that field a fieldname. From Chapter One we know that the fieldname must contain ten or fewer characters. Fieldnames should be selected so that they are adequately descriptive, but as short as possible for convenience. For example, suppose you were to have fields that contained the inventory quantity for every month of the year. If you like to type, you might have fieldnames like JANUARY, FEBRUARY, etc. Otherwise, JAN and FEB should do just fine.

The other "decision option" is relevant only to numeric fields: does it contain decimal numbers, and if so, how many places minimum will you allow? That decision is pretty straightforward and we will see it made as we work again through the plan process—this time CREATEing the structure on our screen.

We are going to work through the plan—a database plan—for the inventory database created in Chapter Two. This is currently B:INVENTRY, amended to add the item's location. We will use the same fieldnames, fieldtypes, and widths that we used in the example. The new field containing the item's location will be a character field called LOCATION. For the purpose of this example, we will arbitrarily assign a width of ten to this field.

A plan for the database B:INVENTRY looks something like that shown in Figure 5-2. Notice that it resembles a database itself. If you have several databases, it is often wise to have a database which contains the database plans. We can call this database of plans a DATA DICTIONARY.

This database has seven fields and requires sixty-two bytes of memory for each record. Before you say, "Big deal, why should I go through this whole process for something that I can do in my head?" you should consider that your database could well require several dozen fields with hundreds of bytes for each record. If this should occur, then you must compare your plan with the resources available to you. Each database system, as well as your computer, has limitations that must be taken into account if your information is truly large. Computer limitations primarily concern the capacity of the disk drive(s). Consequently, they can normally be resolved

CHAPTER FIVE

FIELD DESCRIPTION	FIELDNAME	TYPE	WIDTH	DECIMALS
Kind of Liquor	LIQUOR	C	10	
Brand of Liquor	BRAND	C	20	
Size of Container	SIZE	C	7	
Retail Price	PRICE	N	6	2
Wholesale Price	COST	N	6	2
Quantity on Hand	QUANTITY	N	3	
Location of the Item	LOCATION	C	10	
TOTAL NUMBER OF BYTES			62	
EXPECTED NUMBER OF RECORDS			1000	

Figure 5-2. Sample Database Plan for B: INVENTRY

by either adding additional disk drives or purchasing disk drives with greater capacity.

The limitations imposed by the database system are more interesting. Database system limitations could easily lead you off on a quest for some new and wonderful database management system that will be a panacea for all your problems. The alternative to this potentially costly approach is to use your head.

The resource limitations imposed by the database system are typically as follows:

Number of Fields
Field Width
Number of Bytes in a Record
Number of Records in a File (database)

In *dBASE III*, 128 fields are allowed. Each field is limited to 254 bytes and each record to 4,000 bytes. The number of records is limited to one billion. The maximum size for each *dBASE III* database file is two billion bytes. That's pretty big. It's so big that you are unlikely to encounter the limits.

To give you an idea of just how big this is, consider the following. Using a standard typewriter paper (8 1/2 by 11), standard one-inch margins, and pica type, the database requires more than 569,000 pages. A microcomputer with a Winchester Disk can read the database at about 16,000 characters a second. This means that it takes the computer over thirty-four hours just to read the database. When you encounter databases that are this large you are likely to encounter limitations in either the computer hardware or the operating system.

119

One of the most common problems in database planning is that a plan requires more fields than are offered by the database system. The solution to this is easy. Simply split the plan into two or more databases. When this happens, each database becomes a file within a larger database, and perhaps you should refer to each of the databases as a file. All of the files taken together become the database.

When you split your plan into two or more files you must find a way to link the databases together. One way to do this is to have one or more common fields in each database file. As an example, let's look at a database for an elementary school. Our hypothetical database plan might have 130 fields and look like Figure 5-3.

FIELD	FIELD DESCRIPTION	FIELDNAME	TYPE	WIDTH	DECIMALS
1	Student's Name	NAME	C	30	
2	Room Assignment	ROOM	C	3	
3	Grade	GRADE	C	1	
4	Teacher's Name	TEACHER	C	15	
5	Retained last year Y/N	RETAINED	L	1	
—	—	—	—	—	
—	—	—	—	—	
127	Home Address	ADDRESS	C	30	
128	Home Telephone Number	PHONE	C	8	
129	Emergency Notification	ENAME	C	30	
130	Emergency Telephone	EMERGENCY	C	8	

TOTAL NUMBER OF BYTES   341

EXPECTED NUMBER OF RECORDS   600

Figure 5-3. Elementary School Database Plan

This is a good example of a moderately large database. It requires mass storage of a little over 200,000 bytes (characters). It's been estimated that more than 90% of all databases have less than 100,000 bytes. All of which illustrates an important and often overlooked point:

> *You should understand your application before you buy your hardware and software.*

For the application illustrated in Figure 5-3, the minimum hardware configuration should include two disk drives where at least one of the drives is capable of storing 500,000 bytes. You can get by with less, but you may be constrained within the range of your plans. For example, if you should want to add a field to a database, you will need 400,000 bytes to store the two databases at the point where you have appended all of the records from one database to the other.

The only database software limitation (for *dBASE III*) in this example involves the number of necessary fields: there are more fields than one database file can support (128). The solution is to break the database into two or more files. When databases are broken and occupy two or more files, we must link the files together. This is done using a "common element"—some piece of data that appears consistently across the whole database, like the student's name. Think about old-fashioned paper files. It is quite likely that each student's file (for paper files) is on more than one piece of paper. In a paper file, the student's name would commonly appear on each piece of paper. In our database, each file has a NAME field which contains the student's name. The total number of fields is now 131 and the total number of characters is 371. There are 131 fields because we have added NAME again in field 129 to identify the information in fields 129-130. This installs the necessary common element after 128—130 is split off from the first database.

The only problem arises when there are two students in the school with the same name, not an unlikely occurrence. We minimize this problem by making three fields—NAME, ROOM and GRADE—common to both files. The plan now requires 133 fields with 375 bytes per record. Using *dBASE III* our plan can be implemented with two files which form the complete database.

Another possible solution is to assign each student an identification number. This has some merit. It requires fewer bytes than the recommended solution and requires only two additional fields instead of three. On the negative side, it might require additional effort on someone's part to insure that the identification number is unique for each student.

121

CHAPTER FIVE

Let's take a look at the fields ROOM, GRADE, and TEACHER. In an elementary school, Mr. Jones would normally be assigned to room 201 and grade six. If this is the case, it is reasonable and efficient to establish a third database file which contains information regarding the teachers. Since it is likely that the school would have a file on personnel information, this allows the elimination of a field from the student file. In this particular case, that saves approximately 9,000 bytes of memory (600 records times 15 bytes)—plus the bother of typing the 600 names in the first place and changing it all when a teacher is replaced.

This school database now has three related files. This demonstrates, by the way, the definition of a *relational* database system. Files may be related to each other and needless duplication minimized. As a matter of fact, the technical term for a database file is *relation*. It is usually wise to group information that is used together into a single relation. It is simpler to work with one database than with two or more.

In our example, the three database files (relations) are linked as shown in Figure 5-4. This Figure illustrates the way in which the files can be tied together.

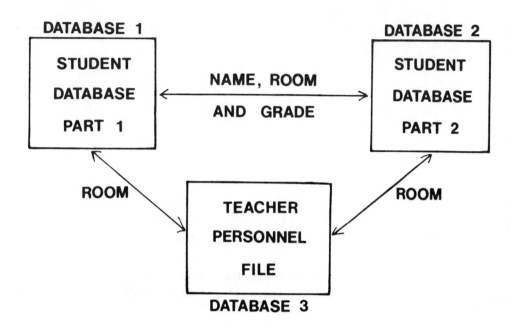

Figure 5-4

One other item to consider in planning is described by Figure 5-5.

Figure 5-5. Two Possible Sets of Fields

124

This figure demonstrates that an item can cover a lot of ground. In one case, we have three fields, in the second, eleven. Your application will likely be somewhere in the middle. However, to decide whether to combine data items into a single field or not requires an understanding of how the data will be used. One rule of thumb is that if the items are rarely (if ever) used separately, then they may be combined. Grouping items such as last name, first name, and middle initial into a single name field often allows for more efficient use of space. And it's certainly simpler to do.

The list in Figure 5-5 covers exactly the same information that we covered in the original telephone directory example. There is, however, information here that was left out of the original: the area code and zip code. These two items could be covered in the address and phone fields of the original example. In the second example of fields, you would most likely add a field for the zip code. Whether or not you add a field for area code or include it as a part of the phone number will depend on how you intend to use the information.

As your database gets larger, it takes more time for the computer to search through it. You may want to carefully consider the size of each field—and even if you should have the field at all.

Remember: although we used the number of spaces on a typewritten page to illustrate the number of bytes used in a field, a typewritten page also contains blank spaces used to separate the columns. *Do not do this in a database*. Unused bytes are not needed to separate the fields. If the field contains a student's age, and the maximum possible age is nine, use only one byte for that field. Separating the fields when they are displayed, either on the terminal or on a printer, is an issue covered in a later chapter.

As we mentioned at the beginning, planning is often considered a nuisance. The urge to get started is sometimes overwhelming. But, as you gain experience, you will also gain an appreciation of the immense value of thorough planning. Planning also forces you to think the problem through before you act. If it seems like a nuisance, remember that no planning will likely result in the larger nuisance of having to do the work over again. Think of planning in terms of iterative enhancement (improvement through repeated attempts).

● Begin with a workable "skeleton" of the plan.
● Build on this workable framework until you have the system ready to put on the computer.

The most serious trap you can get caught in is to seek perfection. This can cost you time, money, and energy.

Remember, you may be unfamiliar with computer database management systems, but the concept, construction, and use of computer databases is not difficult. There are a lot of parallel examples from the pencil and paper world that you are familiar with. Relax and make the necessary connections from your pool of experience. A computer database is an easy step to take into your future. Not to say that it's trivial—just easy.

BUILDING YOUR DATABASE

127

When you have finished the planning process, you are ready to begin construction of your database. First, you create the structure (framework) for the database, which we discussed in depth in Chapter Five. The construction phase is then completed by entering all of the data—a record at a time—into this structure. The most serious problem you are likely to encounter during this data entry period is to keep from being bored to death.

Prior to the development of microcomputers and database management systems, the process of creating a file wasn't easy. It was a lengthy and expensive process involving costly hardware and the use of professional programmers. Though you could have learned to program yourself, until recently there wasn't any way to avoid the use of expensive hardware. Today, with one of the available database management systems and inexpensive microcomputer hardware you can easily do everything yourself. And, unless you are a very slow typist, it can be done quickly.

CHAPTER SIX

SOME REVIEW FROM CHAPTER ONE

The process of data entry was illustrated in Chapter One by the construction of two sample databases, B:FONEBOOK and B:INVENTRY. In these examples, we learned that the mechanical process of creating the database structure is in two parts. *First*, select a filename (title) for the database. *Second*, define each of the fields (columns) in the database. The rules for selecting a filename are determined by the computer's operating system.

A filename may have eight or fewer letters and numbers. It must begin with a letter. It may not contain blank spaces. Some examples of valid filenames are:

    CHAPTER1
    SCHOOL
    FONEBOOK

Examples of *invalid* filenames are:

CHAPTER 1	Too long and contains a blank space
GOBBLEDEGOOK	Too long
8CHAPT	Starts with a number

The purpose of the filename is to identify to the computer which file you want to work with. If the computer has more than one disk drive, you usually must add a disk drive identifier in front of the filename. MS-DOS disk drives are identified by a letter followed by a colon (e.g. A:). The valid filenames from above could be identified as:

A:CHAPTER1	File is on the A drive
C:SCHOOL	File is on the C drive
B:FONEBOOK	File is on the B drive

BUILDING YOUR DATABASE

The disk drive identifier is not a permanent part of the filename. It varies according to which disk drive the disk is inserted in. For example, if we remove the disk containing the file CHAPTER1 from drive A and insert it into drive B, the file will then be identified as B:CHAPTER1.

You may have more than one database file with the same name as long as the files are not on the same disk. The system will not permit you to have two database files with the same name on a disk.

A database is a particular kind of FILE, a ".dbf file." There are other kinds of files the computer may work with. In Chapter One, we worked briefly with another kind of file called a FORM file (".frm" file), which we used to prepare the liquor store inventory example report. A database file and a form file may be on the same disk, and have the same filename. When a database file is created, *dBASE III* automatically appends ".dbf" to the filename. When a report is created ".frm" is automatically added to the filename. ".dbf" and ".frm" are examples of filetypes. The filename is determined by you, the user. In *dBASE III*, the filetype is determined by the system. The filetype is important to the system, which uses the information in the performance of its tasks.

129

Once you have selected a filename for your database, you are ready to define the database structure. The information that the computer needs is:

- How many FIELDS (columns) there are.
- The name of each column.
- The width of each column, that is, the number of characters or digits.
- The kind of information in each column (numbers, characters, dates, memos, or logical).

The database management system will prompt (ask) you for each item it needs as it needs it. An example of the dialogue that created the database B:INVENTRY is shown as Screens 6-1 and 6-2:

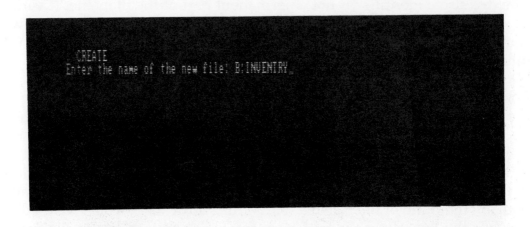

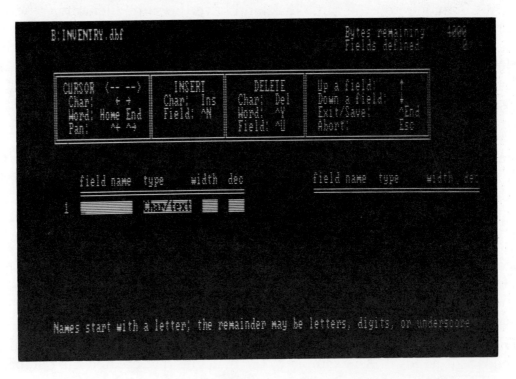

Screen 6 - 1

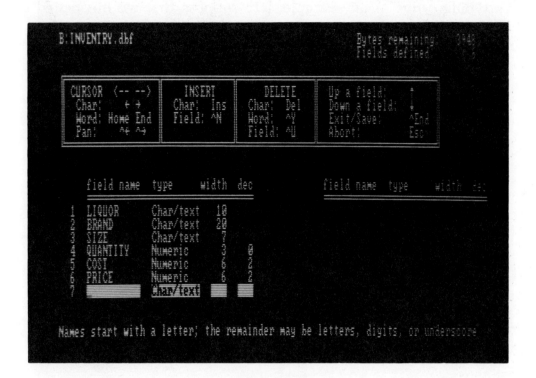

Screen 6 - 2

131

We have created a database with the filename INVENTRY which is located on disk drive B. A rough analogy to what we have done to this point is to take a new manila folder, write "INVENTORY" on the tab, type column headings on a blank paper, draw lines on the page separating the columns, place the paper in the manila folder, and then place the manila folder in a file cabinet.

SAME PROCESS: SOME NEW VARIABLES

As you enter the information shown in Screen 6-2, it is possible to make a typing error. As an example, let's suppose that we misspelled the entry SIZE in field three. We can correct this by using the arrow keys to back up to the error and type in the correct value. If you notice an error after you have moved to another field, use the up arrow to back up to it. To begin entering data into your new database, you must first open the file. In *dBASE III*, this is accomplished with the USE command. In our example this would be:

```
. USE B:INVENTRY
```

The data entry process is initiated by the command APPEND.

```
. APPEND
```

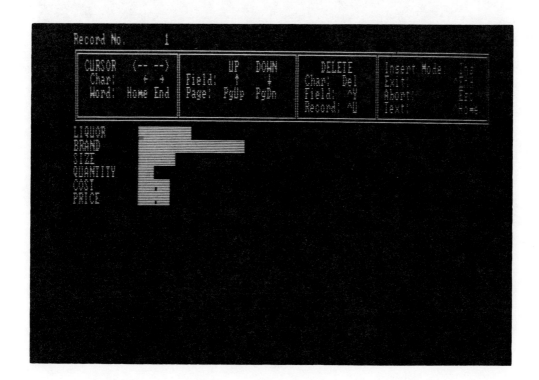

Screen 6 - 3

The computer will prompt you to enter the data for the first record as shown in Screen 6-3. Actually, the APPEND command adds records to the end of a database. So, if there were already forty-nine records in the database, the response to the APPEND command would be identical to Screen 6-3, except that the record number would be fifty.

When you have entered all of the data for a record, as shown in Screen 6-4, the computer will automatically clear the screen and begin prompting you to enter data for the next record.

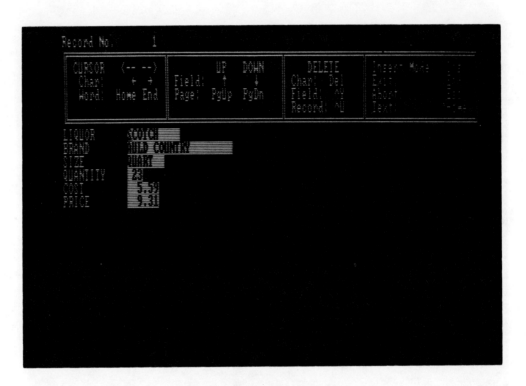

Screen 6 - 4

ON ENTERING DATA

The value of a database depends in large part upon its quality. It is of little solace to tell the tax auditor, "I know there are some errors, but it was really fast!" Because data entry is often dull and repetitious work, it is tempting, if not common practice, to turn this part of the process over to the lowest paid help available. This is a *bad* idea.

In many cases, there will be an enormous amount of data to enter into the new database. Most real liquor stores, for example, have far more than fifteen items in stock. Data entry will be, far and away, the most time consuming part of most database usage. Entry is done at human speed; retrieval is done at computer speed.

Data entry is the part of the process most prone to error. Though entering several records may be accomplished without error, error-free input for hundreds and, perhaps, thousands of records is not likely.

ERRORS WHILE ENTERING DATA

When you are adding a large number of new records to a database, such as during the initial construction, something may happen to cause you to lose track of where you are. Or, as you are busily working, it may dawn on you that you made an error during data entry on the last record. To correct an error or find your place, simply "back up" to the previous record. This is accomplished by pressing the <Pg Up> key. Each time you press <Pg Up>, you will move back one record in the database. To return to APPENDing, press the <Pg Dn> key to move forward (toward the end) of the database.

135

Errors in a record can be easily corrected by moving the cursor back to the error and typing in the correct information. On many terminals there are four keys with arrow symbols on them. These keys should allow you to move the cursor while entering data into the database. The "up" and "down" arrows should move the cursor a field backward and forward in the record. The "right" and "left" arrows should move the cursor one character space to the right and to the left.

Let's go through some sample corrections. Suppose that you have typed in TESSTT and you wanted TEST. The final T can be removed by placing the cursor on the last T and striking the space bar. The surplus S can be removed by placing the cursor on the second S and pressing the <Del> Key. <Del> eliminates the character that the cursor is on.

Of course, you could have just typed over the word TEST and used the space bar to clean up the extra two characters at the end. Regular keyboard characters can be printed on the screen wherever the cursor is located. It doesn't matter whether or not there were characters there already. The last character entered "wins."

The other side of removing characters is adding characters. Suppose that you typed TET when you wanted TEST. You want to insert the letter S between the E and the T. This can be accomplished by using the <Ins> key. Place the cursor on the last T. To insert the letter S, press the <Ins> key, type S, and then press <Ins> again.

<Ins> "toggles" the insert mode on and off. When the insert mode is on, the word "insert" is displayed on the top right of the screen.

There is another element in data entry besides error correction which may concern you. Perhaps you have available only part of the information necessary to complete a record, but you still want to enter what you have. Enter the information you have and then press <Pg Dn>. This will advance you to the next record without having to step through each of the remaining fields.

To this point, the process of constructing a database has been purely mechanical. You create a file structure according to simple rules and then you enter data. Data entry continues until all the data have been entered. At this point the database is ready to be used to fulfill some purpose—such as providing you with the information needed to help manage a business.

If the data entry job is small, the mechanical approach described above is probably the best way to get the job done. It is straightforward and simple.

If there is a lot of data to enter, it might be a good idea to find ways that the computer system can actually help with the entry process.

COMPUTER DATA ENTRY ASSISTANCE

There are some built-in data entry aids as well as some simple procedures that you can write which enable the computer to assist with or perform some of your data entry tasks for you. In the remaining pages of this chapter, we will discuss three such processes:

(1)   CUSTOM SCREEN FORMS
(2)   SET CARRY ON/OFF
(3)   MENU SYSTEMS

SET CARRY ON/OFF is a "built-in" aid, initiated by a simple command. CUSTOM SCREEN FORMS and MENU SYSTEMS are developed by simple procedures which you will learn to write to suit your needs. A "procedure" is an easy way of getting the computer to perform special things for you. The details of "teaching" the computer a procedure will be discussed in Section Four, which begins with Chapter Thirteen. The use of procedure-generated end products—custom prompts and menu systems—is included here because of their great added value to the data entry process.

137

Custom Forms
CUSTOM SCREEN FORMS illustrate the kind of assistance the computer can provide. In our liquor store example, the fieldnames are reasonably descriptive of the field contents. This is often, but not always, the case. When it is not the case, it's nice to be able to include more information. For example, we could make the prompt read something like:

```
ENTER THE KIND OF LIQUOR (SCOTCH, WHISKEY, ETC.):
```

This gives much more information than simply displaying the word LIQUOR. In general, this sort of help from the computer is very desirable, particularly if the filenames are not descriptive or if you have a lot of data and want someone else to help you enter it.

CHAPTER SIX

As we mentioned before, custom prompts such as this one can be provided with relative ease via format files.

Format files, like databases, have filenames. The same filename rules that apply to other files apply to format files. You must also identify which disk drive the format file is stored on.

To show you how a CUSTOM FORM might work, we will assume that a format file to provide descriptive prompts has been written. We will call our sample format file B:ENTRY. To have the computer use this format file, following a dot prompt, you enter:

```
. SET FORMAT TO B:ENTRY
```

SET FORMAT TO B:ENTRY produces Screen 6-5. From this point on, the custom form B:ENTRY will be used whenever the EDIT or APPEND commands are used.

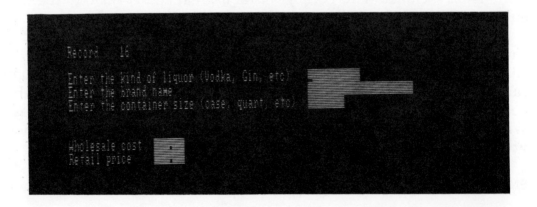

Screen 6 - 5

Incidentally, writing procedures for database management systems is not at all hard. In fact, it can be fun as well as rewarding.

Set Carry On/Off

We'll take a short break from what you can teach the computer to do and talk about another capability it has on its own. In many databases, there is often a lot of redundant data to be entered. In a school for example, there are far more children than there are rooms and teachers, so many teacher names and room numbers are repeated. In our liquor store example, there are several brand names for each kind of liquor. The stock on the shelves is grouped by kind of liquor—Vodka, Bourbon, etc.—for the convenience of the customer. The various sizes for a given brand are usually grouped within the brand.

In many cases, the data may be grouped in such a way as to reduce the amount of data that must be typed in. When redundancy is grouped, as in these two examples, the computer can reduce the amount of typing required by "carrying" the data forward from record to record. In *dBASE III*, this capability is "turned on" by the command SET CARRY ON. It is turned off by SET CARRY OFF.

139

Let's consider how data entry would progress for our example if CARRY were SET ON. First, with APPEND, we get an initial screen display and enter the data for Record 1.

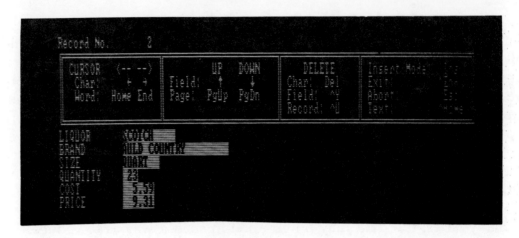

Screen 6 - 6

140

Normally, then, the display for Record 2 would appear blank. With CARRY ON, the display is exactly like Screen 6-6 with the record number advanced to 2. All we need do is change those fields which are different from Record 1. When we advance, the Record 3 display will be exactly as Record 2 at the time of the advance. This particular assistance can accomplish two things: it can reduce the amount of typing, and it can reduce the number of errors due to typing.

A Menu System
Now back to another technique you can teach the computer to do. With this technique, a procedure is written that provides the data entry person with a set of multiple choices to select from. This technique is called a MENU SYSTEM. It minimizes the possibility of typing error. Unfortunately, it increases the possibility of absolute error. It is profitably used where the data to be input has little in common from record to record and, consequently, the idea of carry forward is of no value.

Let's suppose that we have written a procedure to do a liquor store inventory using the MENU technique. In our hypothetical example, the terminal might provide the display shown in Screen 6-7.

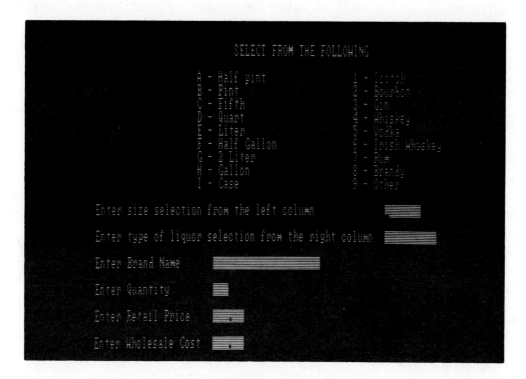

Screen 6 - 7

This particular example uses some of the helpful aspects of our earlier discussion of custom prompts, as well as the menu selection idea. The information "gallon of gin" is entered as H3.

In this example, the entire data entry and menu process is accomplished with one screen display. If the data to be entered is more extensive, we might require more than one screen display. For example, if there are thirty or forty choices for each of the liquor and size selections we might want to use one screen display for each of the two selection columns. This would lead directly to three successive screen displays for this menu example.

Menu procedures, as well as other elaborate prompt systems, can be profitably used when you need a lot of data entered and don't want to have to explain either the nature of the data or anything about the database system. There are cases where everything that needs to be entered can be menu selected.

Conditional Replacement

In addition to these three rather straightforward data entry aids, there is another, somewhat sneakier, method available for entering certain kinds of conditional information.

The example appropriate to this CONDITIONAL REPLACEMENT method comes from a student database built for an elementary school. The database contains the NAME, ROOM, GRADE, and TEACHER for each student. When the database is "built" only the NAME, ROOM, and GRADE need to be entered. When this is completed for each child, the TEACHER information can be added with an operation like the *dBASE III* command REPLACE.

```
. REPLACE TEACHER WITH 'Mr. Johnson' FOR ROOM='101'
. REPLACE TEACHER WITH 'Mrs. Adams' FOR ROOM='201'
```

The best thing about the process of building a database is that usually it is a one-time operation. This process—entering the data—is sometimes called *loading* database. The build process is critical to all future use of the database. If the information is not complete or if it is entered with errors, the ultimate results will be incomplete and erroneous. And you will be unhappy. If the data has been correctly entered, however, you can begin to make profitable use of it—which is what this is all about.

To summarize, the options you have when "building" the original database range from the simple and straightforward APPEND to increasingly elaborate procedures for more descriptive prompts. The aids that can be used to minimize your effort are:

- Use of custom screen forms
- Carrying data forward from record to record
- Menu selection
- Conditional replacement

These aids reduce the amount of typing required. The larger and more complicated your database, the more likely the procedure idea is to be of value to you.

143

MODIFYING AND MAINTAINING YOUR DATABASE

Once the database has been built, it will inevitably be changed. All kinds of changes necessitate record changes. In addition to internal record change in fields like QUANTITY and PRICE, some records must be added and some deleted. Evolving government regulations may require that new fields be added to the database. This major everyday activity—changing the database—is called *updating*.

Updating a database is certain to consume a lot of time since it is a manual operation. Routine reports and other output products are usually accomplished automatically at computer speeds and require relatively little time.

The frequency with which the database is updated will depend, in large part, on your needs. Ordinarily, there are updating tasks which must be done daily. Others are suitable for weekly or monthly update. Still others are done only as specifically needed.

Our Little Liquor Store, for example, might update an inventory database as each new shipment is received. Employee hours, depending upon the situation, might be updated either daily or weekly. The magnitude of the updating tasks will, of course, depend upon the particular application.

Change normally falls into one or more of three categories:

(1) Changing the database structure
(2) Adding and deleting records
(3) Changing the content of records

CHANGING THE STRUCTURE OF A DATABASE

Generally, the structure of a database is not often changed. Any structural change is normally in response to a change in the business environment—such as a new government regulation. Because of possible data loss consequences, great care should be taken whenever the structure is altered.

Whenever the structure of the database is changed (in *dBASE III* this is called MODIFYing) the contents of the database will be damaged. To protect against this, a copy of the database is automatically made before the database structure is changed. Once this copy is made, the structure can safely be modified. After the structure has been modified, the data from the backup copy is automatically appended back to the database.

An example of this process in the *dBASE III* system is shown in Screen 7-1.

146

Screen 7 - 1

Changes that may be made to the structure include:

- Adding fields
- Deleting fields
- Changing the name of a field
- Changing the size of a field
- Changing the fieldtype

If a fieldname or a fieldtype is to be changed, no other changes should be made to the database with the same MODIFY STRUCTURE. If other changes are to be made, there is no way for the system to know whether you meant to add a new field and delete an existing one, or simply wanted to change a fieldname. For example, if we attempted to add a new field and rename an existing field in the same session with one use of MODIFY STRUCTURE, the computer would add two new fields (the new field and the renamed field) and discard all data in the field that was renamed. If this had been done in two steps, with renaming the field one step and creating the new field another step, no data would have been lost.

The computer will display the database structure on the terminal as shown in Screen 7-2.

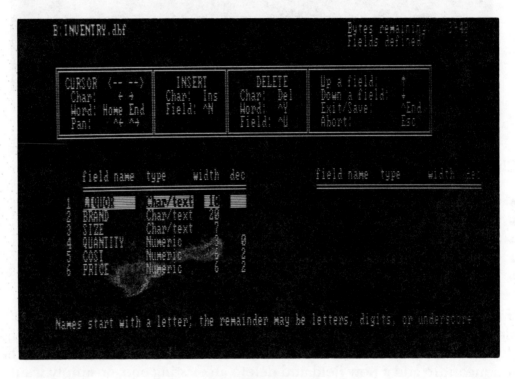

Screen 7 - 2

In this mode you are able to move the cursor about on the screen in order to effect the desired changes. The cursor may be moved using the arrow keys. A field can be deleted by positioning the cursor on the fieldname and pressing <Ctrl-U>. A field can be added by positioning the cursor to the desired location of the new field and pressing <Ctrl-N>. This will move all of the following fields down one position and display a blank field at the cursor. Enter the fieldname, fieldtype, and width to complete adding the field. Existing fields can be modified by positioning the cursor to the field to be modified and typing the new information in over the old information. Typing <Ctrl-End> tells the computer that you have completed modifying the structure. Press <Esc> to abort the change.

KEY	EFFECT
←	Moves cursor 1 character left
→	Moves cursor 1 character right
↑	Moves cursor 1 field back
↓	Moves cursor 1 field forward
^U	Deletes field
^N	Inserts blank field space at cursor location
^End	Save new file structure
Esc	Abort the change operation

Figure 7-1. Control Key Functions for MODIFY STRUCTURE

149

At this point you have a copy of the old database and a new database which has no records. The data from the old database that belongs in the new one is loaded (*reloaded*) into the new database automatically.

The contents of all fields that are common to both the new and the old databases are added to the new. New fields will be blank. A field which has been made smaller will truncate the data when it is added to the new database. Character fields will lose their rightmost characters. In number fields, an overflow (all asterisks) will be displayed in the new numeric field.

It is reasonable to expect that the structure of a database will not be changed often. When changing the structure is undertaken, it is wise to make an extra copy—just in case something goes wrong. This is one case where the penalty for error is extreme.

CHANGING RECORD CONTENTS

There are several ways that you can change the contents of data fields. When you are making specific changes to individual records—such as entering the number of hours an employee worked on Monday—these changes are best made one at a time with one of the full screen operations:

* EDIT
* CHANGE
* BROWSE

150

Let's suppose that we want to edit the liquor store inventory record for quarts of Auld Country Scotch. If we happen to know that this item is stored as Record 1, we can start the editing process with:

```
. EDIT 1
```

The monitor presents the display shown in Screen 7-3. The record can be changed by moving the cursor to the desired field and typing the new information over the old. The cursor is moved by using the arrow keys.

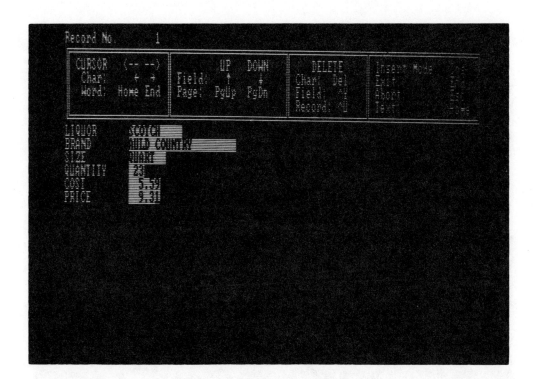

Screen 7 - 3

To illustrate EDITing, let's change the QUANTITY from 23 to 33, the COST to 5.75, and the PRICE to 10.98. Press the down arrow key three times to move the cursor to the QUANTITY field. Type 33 and press <RETURN>. This changes the value stored in QUANTITY to 33, and moves the cursor to the COST field. Type in 5.75 and press <RETURN>. This changes the value to 5.75 and moves the cursor to the PRICE field. Type 10.98 and press <RETURN>. This changes the value to 10.98, and advances to the next record, in this case, Record 2. Press <PgUp>. This will return you to Record 1. The changed record appears as shown in Screen 7-4.

152

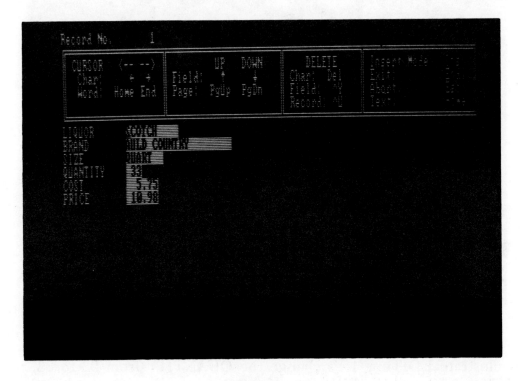

Screen 7 - 4

There are a number of special keys that can be used with EDIT. These are described in Figure 7-2. Adjacent records may be selected by <PgUp> (the previous record) and <PgDn> (the next record). The editing operation may be aborted by pressing <Esc>. Aborting the changes can be convenient if you find that you have been editing the wrong record. The changes are saved by moving to another record, or by pressing <Ctrl-

MODIFYING AND MAINTAINING YOUR DATABASE

End>. The special keys are described by the Help Menu shown at the top of the entry screens. If your computer does not display the Help Menu as shown, press the special function key <F1> and it will.

KEY	EFFECT
←	Moves cursor 1 character left
→	Moves cursor 1 character right
↑	Moves cursor 1 field back
↓	Moves cursor 1 field forward
^Y	Erases field contents
^U	Toggle — deletes/undeletes record
Ins	Toggle — turns character insert mode on/off
^End	Save new file information
Esc	Abort the change operation
PgUp	Edits previous record
PgDn	Advances EDIT to next record

Figure 7-2. Special Key Functions for EDIT

153

If you don't happen to know the record number, as is nearly always the case, it can be acquired in a number of ways, such as:

```
. DISPLAY FOR LIQUOR='SCOTCH' .AND. BRAND='AULD COUNTRY'
. LOCATE FOR SIZE='QUART' .AND. BRAND='AULD COUNTRY'
```

Each of the above will provide the desired record number. The LOCATE command also positions the database to the desired record. In this case, the record can then be edited by:

```
. EDIT
```

CHAPTER SEVEN

EDIT used alone edits the current record.

CHANGE is similar to EDIT. Both are full-screen commands. CHANGE can be more flexible than EDIT. Let's suppose we wanted to change the records for Auld Country Scotch.

```
. CHANGE FOR LIQUOR = 'SCOTCH' .AND. BRAND = 'AULD COUNTRY'
```

The screen display would be identical to Screen 7-4. Pressing <PgDn> will bring up the next record that meets our criteria. Pressing <PgUp> will return us to the original record.

CHANGE has the added advantage that you can specify the fields to be edited and the order in which they will be displayed.

```
. CHANGE FIELDS QUANTITY,BRAND FOR LIQUOR = 'SCOTCH'
```

This allows us to edit only the fields QUANTITY and BRAND for those records where the LIQUOR field contains SCOTCH.

All of the special keys shown in Figure 7-2 are used in the same manner with CHANGE.

Another full-screen command which allows you to view as well as change the contents of a database is BROWSE. A graphic description of BROWSE may be provided by cutting a section from a piece of paper. Now place the paper with the hole cut in it over this page. This is a window opening onto the page. By moving this window about, you can view the entire contents of the page a little at a time. BROWSE is a window onto the database. It allows you to view a section of the database at a time and make changes wherever you desire. The first part of our liquor store inventory is shown as Screen 7-5.

154

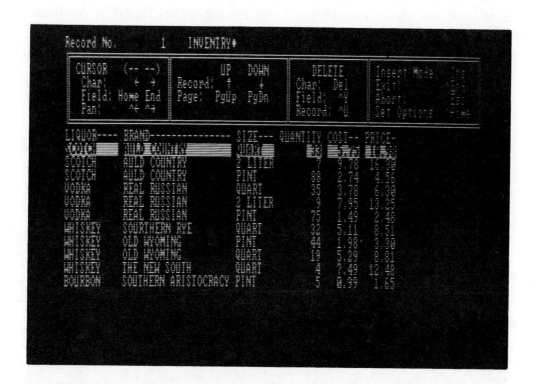

Screen 7 - 5

In BROWSE, each record is displayed on a single row. If the record is too long to fit on a single row, only as much as will fit is displayed. To view the remainder of the record, press <Ctrl> right (or left) arrow. This "pans" the database record one field at a time in the direction of the arrow. The up and down arrows move the cursor a record at a time in the direction of the arrow. The <PgUp> and <PgDn> keys scroll through the database a screenful at a time. When the Help Menu is on (the function key <F1> toggles it on and off), eleven records at a time are in view. Otherwise, seventeen records are visible.

CHAPTER SEVEN

BROWSE has a Special Options Menu (Screen 7-6) that allows you to reset the beginning of BROWSE to the beginning of the database (the TOP), the end of the database (the BOTTOM), or any record number. The Special Options Menu is selected by pressing <Ctrl-Home>. An item on the menu is chosen by using the arrow keys. Each time an arrow key is pressed, a different option is highlighted. Press the <RETURN> key to select the highlighted option.

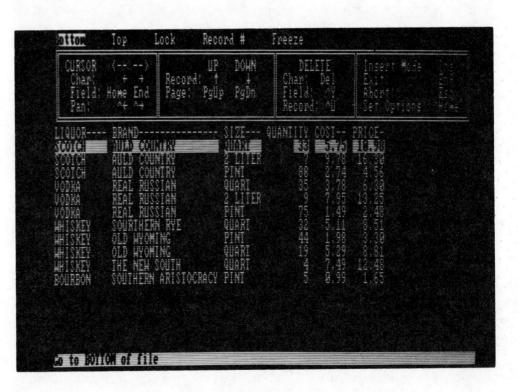

Screen 7 - 6

Other features of this Options Menu are LOCK and FREEZE. The LOCK option allows you to "hold" one or more of the leftmost fields on the screen when panning the database. This is most useful when a record is too long to be displayed on a single line. Then we can hold a "key item" (such as a name) in view while we pan to the field off screen. For this reason, it is advisable to make key fields the first items in the database.

The FREEZE option limits cursor movement to a single field—although the rest of the record will be visible. This is ideal for making changes in a single field such as quantities in our Little Liquor Store database.

BROWSE also allows you to specify the fields to be BROWSEd and the order in which they are used.

```
. BROWSE FIELDS BRAND,SIZE,QUANTITY,LIQUOR
```

ADDING AND DELETING RECORDS

157

A far more common change operation than changing the structure or contents of a database involves adding records to or deleting records from a database. New employees are hired, others quit or retire. Adding and deleting records is ordinarily straightforward. The process of adding a record to a database has been described in Chapters Two and Five. In dBASE, this is the APPEND process. Whenever a record is appended, it is placed at the end of the database, the BOTTOM.

Occasionally, it may be desirable to insert a record into the middle of a database. In dBASE, this is accomplished by the command INSERT. This command is similar to APPEND, except that it adds the new record wherever you desire in the database. To use this command you must first position yourself in the database with the GOTO command.

```
. GOTO RECORD 127
. INSERT
```

FEATURING dBASE III

The use of INSERT places a blank record at record location 128. All of the records after record 127 are renumbered and moved down one record position. The old Record 128 becomes Record 129, the old Record 129 becomes Record 130, and so on. Once this re-ordering has been completed, the screen is erased and the blank Record 128 is presented for data entry exactly as in APPEND.

Records are removed by a two-step process. First, a record is marked for deletion. Examples of commands which mark a record for deletion are:

```
. DELETE RECORD 216
. DELETE FOR NAME='BRONCO,BILLY'
. DELETE FOR LIQUOR='IRISH MALT'.AND.BRAND='KILARNY GREEN'
```

Each time there is a delete command, the computer should respond with the number of records that have been deleted. This allows you to take corrective action and "undelete" those records that were inadvertently deleted. The dBASE command to "undelete" records is RECALL. Examples of RECALL are:

```
. RECALL ALL
. RECALL RECORD 216
. RECALL FOR NAME='BRONCO,BILLY'
```

The actual removal of the record(s) is done with a second command. In *dBASE III*, that command is PACK. PACK permanently removes those records you have marked by DELETE.

If the database is used in conjunction with tables such as INDEX files, the database may require re-indexing whenever records are added or removed. Relational database management systems normally allow adding or removing records while an index file is in use. When this is the case, as with *dBASE III,* the index file is automatically updated when each record is added or removed. This is normally the case with the Hierarchical and Network (CODASYL) database systems.

MODIFYING AND MAINTAINING YOUR DATABASE

When a record is appended while an index file is in use, the record will appear to be inserted into the database. If, for example, the database is indexed on NAME, the records will appear to be in alphabetical order. Though a new record appears to be placed in its proper alphabetical location, it is actually added to the end of the database just as it is without an index file.

The database system must also provide for changing several records at once because a *condition* has changed. One example of this occurs when a school teacher leaves and is replaced by a new teacher. Using EDIT or BROWSE would require typing the new teacher's name for each record being changed. An easier approach for this situation is to use the *dBASE III* command REPLACE. If the new teacher is Mrs. Jones and the old teacher is Mr. Smith and the room number is 21, you can use either command shown below.

```
. REPLACE TEACHER WITH 'Mrs. Jones' FOR ROOM='21'
. REPLACE TEACHER WITH 'Mrs. Jones' FOR TEACHER='Mr. Smith'
```

When REPLACE is used for a condition, every record that meets the condition will be changed. Database applications that require frequent changing can benefit from the kinds of procedures illustrated in the last chapter: descriptive prompts and menus. The use of procedures can be an effective substitute for your memory. Procedures also allow a database to be manipulated by less skilled (hence less costly) help. The two techniques can be combined to provide very powerful and versatile aids to changing a database.

Screen 7-7 illustrates changing a hypothetical elementary school database using a combination of descriptive prompts and menus to help the person entering the data. This particular example will add records, delete records, and provide the capability of changing records. The records contain the NAME, ROOM, GRADE, TEACHER and fields containing other information about each student.

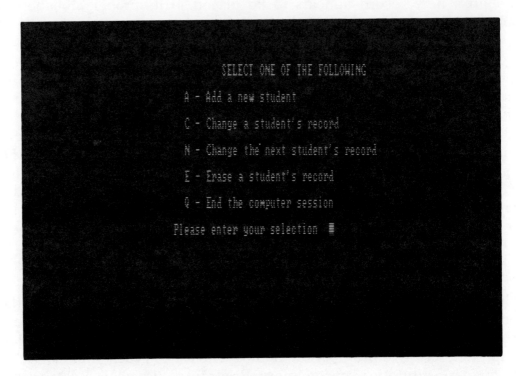

160

Screen 7 - 7

If selection C is chosen, the computer can be set up to provide a new display Screen 7-8.

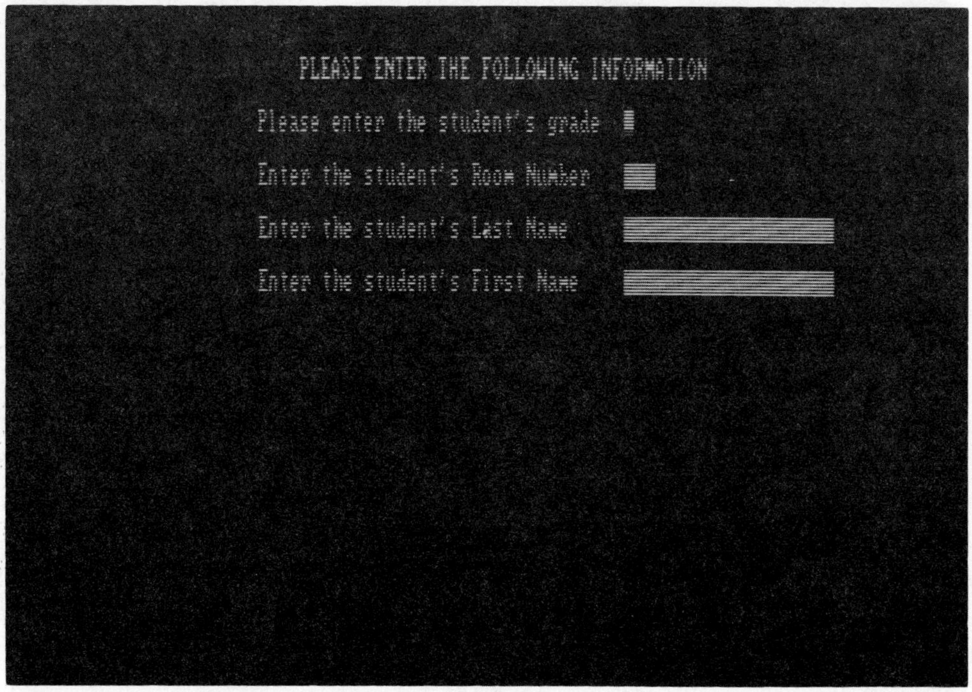

PLEASE ENTER THE FOLLOWING INFORMATION

Please enter the student's grade

Enter the student's Room Number

Enter the student's Last Name

Enter the student's First Name

Screen 7 - 8

When the information above has been provided to the computer, there will be a short delay while the computer locates the student of interest. The computer will then display the student's record as in Screen 7-9.

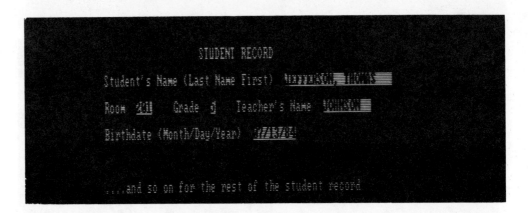

STUDENT RECORD

Student's Name (Last Name First) ▓▓▓▓▓▓▓▓▓ ▓▓▓▓▓

Room ▓▓▓ Grade ▓ Teacher's Name ▓▓▓▓▓▓

Birthdate (Month/Day/Year) ▓▓▓▓▓▓▓

....and so on for the rest of the student record

Screen 7 - 9

An operator could select information to be changed by moving the cursor to the field to be changed and typing in the new information. When the changes have been completed, the operator is returned to the first (main) menu. A new change operation is selected and the process is repeated. The menu option A would go directly to the last student record. The new record displayed would, of course, be all blank. Menu option S would provide a means of moving from record to record, as when entering test scores, without the necessity of entering unnecessary information. Menu option D would use Screen 7-8 requesting information about the student. If the delete option were selected, the procedure should always provide the operator a display like that in Screen 7-10.

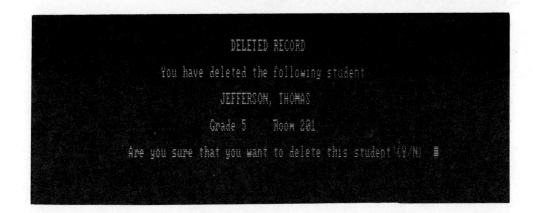

DELETED RECORD

You have deleted the following student

JEFFERSON, THOMAS

Grade 5   Room 201

Are you sure that you want to delete this student (Y/N) ▮

Screen 7 - 10

This example shows how the use of menus and descriptive prompts can aid the person who must enter new information into the computer. It is somewhat analogous to the use of paper forms by clerical help wherein a written procedure tells the clerk which form to use. In the case of the computer, a procedure tells the computer which "form" to use. If the operator using the computer is not familiar with the computer, the procedure should contain at least one menu selection for operator assistance or HELP.

For most database applications it is imperative that the database not contain errors. One of the additional values of using procedures is that the process of changing a database is formalized while the effort required by the operator is minimized. If the data entry process can be made interesting, if not entertaining, the likelihood of error is reduced. Some menu operations minimize both the effort required and the chance of spelling errors. Remember here that while you might know that "scocth" means "scotch", the computer doesn't.) The opportunity still exists, however, for the entry of "gin" instead of "scotch". Though a procedure can provide safeguards against these possibilities, it does require additional effort on the part of the person writing the procedure.

163

CHAPTER SEVEN

MAINTAINING A DATABASE

Maintaining can be defined as "safeguarding" a database. If you have a database which consists of a bunch of records on paper, there are some problems to safeguarding those paper records: coffee can be spilled on part of a record; a single piece of paper can be inadvertently thrown away. However, few things short of absolute calamity (fire, flood, hurricane, etc.) are catastrophic to a whole paper database. This is not true with a computer database. A database contained on a thin sheet of magnetized mylar can be damaged by a finger inadvertently placed on the mylar film. A cigarette will destroy it completely. One piece of film is more vulnerable than a filing cabinet full of paper. All of the things that work to make the database convenient to use also work to make it susceptible to disaster.

Much of the foregoing gloom can be avoided by maintaining and protecting one or two backup copies of the database. This is one very good reason for having at least two disk drives on your computer system. If you have more than two disk drives you can make the copy easily by placing a fresh disk in one of the additional drives and using the copy command. For instance, if your database is located on the C disk drive and a fresh disk has been placed in the B drive, the copy can be made by:

```
. COPY ALL TO B:BACKUP
```

If you have only two disk drives, your database is located on the B disk drive, and there is enough space available on the A drive to contain the database, then the copy can be made by:

```
. COPY ALL TO A:BACKUP
```

If you have only two disk drives, your database is located on the B disk drive and there is insufficient space available on the A drive to contain the database, use the command QUIT. QUIT will return you to your computer's operating system.

```
.  QUIT
END RUN      dBASE III
A>
```

The following procedure will provide you with a backup copy of your database. Remove the disk from the A disk drive. Insert a fresh disk into the A drive. Type in Copy B:*.*. This will copy and verify all of the contents of disk drive B to disk drive A. Then remove the database disk and the backup copy.

One approach to backup of your files is to have two copies and to use them on alternate days. Properly used, two copies protect against loss of all except, perhaps, one day's work. If you can limit the liability to this, you have done about as well as you can do.

It's actually possible to protect against major disasters to a higher degree than is possible with paper records. While it is not reasonable to maintain two sets of paper records in two separate locations, this is not the case with computer databases. Since you can copy the database onto floppy disks or tape, copies can be dispersed and stored at remote locations—providing some reasonable protection for disasters short of war.

165

CHAPTER EIGHT

USING YOUR DATABASE

There are really two parts to using the database. The first, keeping it current (updating), was covered in the last chapter. The second, getting it to do something for you, is the subject of this chapter.

TWO BASIC USES OF THE DATABASE

There are two basic database uses:

(1) To perform standard services such as generating payroll reports, tax reports, current inventory.
(2) To obtain specific information whenever necessary.

Our database management system, *dBASE III*, has a report writer suitable for producing a variety of standard reports. You may also write procedures that allow you to produce specialized custom reports suited to your needs. Specific information necessary to a non-routine process is obtained from the computer keyboard using a "query language." We will first discuss reports, which we encountered briefly in Chapter Two, and move on later in the chapter to query languages and processes.

CHAPTER EIGHT

REPORT

In Chapter One, we used the liquor store inventory example to introduce the report writing concept. Most modern database systems provide a capability for easily generating reports based on the contents of a database. REPORT's standard capabilities can be exploited from the keyboard, providing you, the user, with information extracted from the database. In Chapter Two, we learned that a simple dialogue with the computer sets up a reporting process the computer can remember. We can use this report over and over again. The process is initiated by:

```
. CREATE REPORT
```

An existing report can be easily changed by:

```
. MODIFY REPORT
```

The ensuing dialogue with the computer is identical to CREATE REPORT except that the existing information is already there—to be changed. If you want the resulting report to be printed by your printer, the command is:

```
. REPORT FORM TO PRINT
```

The report for the database B:INVENTRY (from Chapter Two) is reproduced for your convenience as Figure 8-1.

This report works well because kinds of liquor are grouped together in the database. If they were not grouped, the result would be a shambles. If we had been unsure whether or not the liquors were blocked, we would first index the database to group the data—ensuring a coherent report.

```
PAGE NO. 00001
09/15/81
                        LIQUOR STORE INVENTORY

            BRAND            SIZE      QTY     COST    INVEST

*  SCOTCH
AULD COUNTRY               QUART       23      5.59    128.57
AULD COUNTRY               1/2 LIT      7      9.78     68.46
AULD COUNTRY               PINT        88      2.74    241.12

** SUBTOTAL **                        118             438.15
*  VODKA
REAL RUSSIAN               QUART       35      3.78    132.30
REAL RUSSIAN               1/2 LIT      9      7.95     71.55
REAL RUSSIAN               PINT        75      1.49    111.75

** SUBTOTAL **                        119             315.60
*  WHISKEY
SOUTHERN RYE              QUART        32      5.11    163.52
OLD WYOMING              PINT          44      1.98     87.12
OLD WYOMING              QUART         19      5.29    100.51
THE NEW SOUTH            QUART          4      7.49     29.96

** SUBTOTAL **                         99             381.11
*  BOURBON
SOUTHERN ARISTOCRACY     PINT           5      0.99      4.95
SOUTHERN ARISTOCRACY     FIFTH         22      1.78     39.16
SOUTHERN ARISTOCRACY     QUART         21      3.50     73.50
SOUTHERN ARISTOCRACY     1/2 GAL        3      6.89     20.67
SOUTHERN ARISTOCRACY     1/2 LIT        5      6.47     32.35

** SUBTOTAL **                         56             170.63

** TOTAL **                           392            1305.49
```

Figure 8-1. Computer Report on Liquor Store Inventory

169

```
. INDEX ON LIQUOR TO B:LIQUOR
. USE B:INVENTRY INDEX B:LIQUOR
```

One report prompt which we answered "no" to was "SUMMARY REPORT ONLY." With a "yes" to this prompt, we get a different report than the one shown in Figure 8-1. Such a summary report is shown below in Figure 8-2. Note there is no information in the cost column. The only values printed are the category subtotals.

PAGE NO. 00001
09/15/81

LIQUOR STORE INVENTORY

BRAND	QTY	COST	INVEST
* SCOTCH	118		438.15
* VODKA	119		315.60
* WHISKEY	99		381.11
* BOURBON	56		170.63
** TOTAL **			
	392		1305.49

Figure 8-2. Computer Prepared Summary Of Liquor Store Inventory

The lack of information in the cost column is a result of our "no" to the prompt "SUBTOTALS IN REPORT?"

Using the original example, we request a detailed report on bourbon:

```
. REPORT FORM FOR LIQUOR='BOURBON'
```

This provides the report presented as Figure 8-3. This particular report gives "bourbon only" information. Since the database is so small, the example result is valuable only because it illustrates the ability to report on any identifiable subset of a database. This capability is invaluable if the database is large. With a large database, you might first obtain a printout on the summary only. Subsequent reports, such as Figure 8-3, are selected based on information in the summary.

171

```
PAGE NO. 00001
09/15/81
                        LIQUOR STORE INVENTORY
        BRAND                 SIZE        QTY     COST    INVEST

*   BOURBON
SOUTHERN ARISTOCRACY          PINT          5     0.99      4.95
SOUTHERN ARISTOCRACY          FIFTH        22     1.78     39.16
SOUTHERN ARISTOCRACY          QUART        21     3.50     73.50
SOUTHERN ARISTOCRACY          1/2 GAL       3     6.89     20.67
SOUTHERN ARISTOCRACY          1/2 LIT       5     6.47     32.35
** SUBTOTAL **
                                           56             170.63

** TOTAL **
                                          392            1305.49
```

Figure 8-3. Computer Prepared Report For Bourbons Contained In The Liquor Store Inventory

172

If we want an even quicker, if somewhat less elegant response, we can use two *query language processor* commands. Though we will discuss query languages and processes later in the chapter, this example is included here to show side-by-side results of the two major ways you go about using your database. This process of QLP commands and responses is shown in Screen 8-1.

Screen 8 - 1

You can see from our rather extensive use of the liquor store inventory example that extracting information from a database via report is really simple. For a business environment, it would be easy, as well as pertinent, to develop many special applications reports from your database. These might include accounts payable, accounts receivable, payroll, personnel, and so forth, in addition to an inventory system such as the one for our liquor store. There is great value in keeping a database as the foundation for all these applications activities. Each separate application can be easily

173

accommodated with its own custom procedure or report. At the same time, however, everything originates in a common database—a common pool of information that can be accessed for specific, non-routine tasks in addition to the standard structure you have up and running on its own regular cycle.

An example. Suppose a company is considering a new union contract. Management would like to know the impact of the contract before agreeing to the terms. If, as is often the case even in large, professionally designed and managed systems, the personnel and payroll systems are separate, it might take considerable effort to determine the impact of the proposed contract, if it is even possible. With separate systems, there is much duplication of effort and information. For example, a computer system for doing payroll needs employee name, number, number of dependents, salary rate, and so on. A computer personnel system needs similar information. When the systems are separate, the information stored by one cannot always be used by another.

On the other hand, if personnel and payroll systems use a common database system, the information might be available directly from the keyboard with a simple query.

This separateness of related information is one of the things that led to the development of databases. In a database, unlike in an accounts payable program, as far as the computer is concerned the stored information is independent of the application. It is up to the user to impose the desired application when requesting use of the database. This brings us to something mentioned a couple of times: information available by query.

EXTRACTING INFORMATION (QUERY)

Database systems respond to user requests for information (queries). The part of the database system that does this is called the query language processor (QLP). *dBASE III's* query language processor is called *applications development language* (ADL).

You use the *query language* to tell the computer what to do. Most contemporary query languages are like ordinary English. In some systems, the only function of the QLP is to extract information from the database. In this case, it is said that the QLP is a *"read-only"* function. In dBASE, ADL is also used to update the database. This means it can "write" as well as "read."

QUERY LANGUAGES

There are two kinds of query languages: procedural and non-procedural.

● Procedural is the traditional computer language. With this language, you tell the computer, step by step, what you want it to do to produce a desired result. Examples of procedural languages are BASIC, FORTRAN, PL/1 and COBOL. In all of these, you tell the computer how to find an answer—not what the problem is.
● Non-procedural language allows you to state the problem and the computer figures out how to get the answer.

From the personal telephone book example, if you want to know how many of the entries are in Glendale,

```
. COUNT FOR'Glendale'$ADDRESS
```

is an example of a non-procedural command. Here you have told the computer what you want and it figures out how to do it.

Some query languages have features of both. The dBASE ADL is both a procedural and non-procedural query language. Procedural and non-procedural features of relational database system query languages are sometimes referred to in technical terms. Procedural features are called the relational algebra; non-procedural are called the relational calculus. It isn't clear that these terms have any particular value other than to attempt to intimidate the non-professional.

FEATURING dBASE III

CHAPTER EIGHT

Specific information necessary for a non-routine process is obtained from the computer keyboard using the query language. If the database has a lot of fields, you may need to keep and use a data dictionary (Chapter Five). To make use of a database—under any conditions—you must know the fieldnames and what is contained in the fields.

A query language that allows you to make very high-level requests from the keyboard has three parts to a command. These are:

- the name
- the scope
- the condition

The command name is normally representative of the function required. Examples of dBASE command names are: DISPLAY, SUM, COUNT, LOCATE, and LIST. Scope determines how much of the database the command applies to. Condition means that the command applies if the database record meets the condition stated. Examples of possible requests are:

```
. SUM QUANTITY FOR LIQUOR='BOURBON'
. COUNT FOR 'Robert'$NAME
. DISPLAY QUANTITY FOR LIQUOR='SCOTCH'.AND.SIZE='FIFTH'
. DISPLAY QUANTITY,BRAND FOR LIQUOR='SCOTCH'.AND.SIZE='FIFTH'
```

In the first of the four examples above, the command means "tell us how many bottles of bourbon we have." Specifically, it means that the contents of the field QUANTITY should be added whenever the contents of the field LIQUOR are 'BOURBON'. If we omit QUANTITY from the command, all numeric fields are summed for the condition.

In the second example, the command means: count the records that contain the sequence of letters "Robert" in the NAME field. The third sample request asks to display the quantity (only) for each kind of fifth of scotch. In the fourth, the brand name is also displayed.

EVERYMAN'S DATABASE PRIMER

In each of these, the command is remarkably like ordinary English. This is partly because we have given each field a good descriptive fieldname.

In dBASE, the entire record is normally displayed by the command DISPLAY. If less than that is desired, entering a list of fieldnames separated by commas (as in the fourth example) tells the computer to display only the fields listed. By the way, separating items by commas is known as "comma delimiting."

The fourth example uses the word "and" in a somewhat odd manner. Here we have said to the computer—if the contents of the field LIQUOR is SCOTCH, and the contents of the field SIZE is FIFTH, display the brand and its quantity. This request will extract exactly what we want.

Suppose that we enter this request:

```
. DISPLAY FOR LIQUOR='SCOTCH'.AND.LIQUOR='BOURBON'
```

177

We want the computer to display all the records where the LIQUOR is SCOTCH and where the LIQUOR is BOURBON. The computer's response to the command is a dot prompt. There is no display. This means that it found none. How can this be? We know that there are entries for both bourbon and scotch, and yet the computer says there are none. This answer actually does make sense: there is no record where the liquor is both scotch and bourbon. If we rewrite the English sentence as follows— "We want the computer to display all of the records where the kind of liquor is either scotch or bourbon"—we get the idea. Though we think of the entire database when we ask for information, the computer works with only one record at a time. Rewriting the command as:

```
. DISPLAY FOR LIQUOR='SCOTCH'.OR.LIQUOR='BOURBON'
```

will get the desired result.

BOOLEAN OPERATORS

The .AND. and the .OR. in the example above are called *Boolean operators*. The Boolean operators are often called *logical* operators. As we have seen, .AND. and .OR. are almost the same as "and" and "or" in everyday English. These operators are written with periods at each end to distinguish them from their ordinary English counterparts. You must be careful when using Boolean operators, or you can get a strange result. You can get a technically correct, but nonetheless wrong answer. It is of no small importance that you understand the logical operators. This is where the computer does exactly what you tell it to do, not what you wanted it to do. Another Boolean operator used in dBASE is .NOT., which is described further in Chapter Eleven.

A BIT MORE ON QUERIES

Queries are appropriate to a wide range of user needs. We might want—for one reason or another—to manipulate data contained in a database, but not to actually change it. We already encountered an example of this, when we copied a database so that the structure could be modified. Part of a database can be copied to a new database for any desired purpose.

Let's make a copy of that part of B:INVENTRY containing only the fields BRAND, SIZE, and PRICE. To further constrain this new database, we will copy only for the scotch. This operation is accomplished with a single command.

```
. COPY FIELD BRAND,SIZE,PRICE TO B:SCOTCH FOR LIQUOR='SCOTCH'
```

This produces your "Scotch only" database. To digress briefly into specialist terminology, this copy operation is called "the projection of the relation B:INVENTRY onto B:SCOTCH as restricted by the predicate LIQUOR='SCOTCH'. Would you recognize that as a description of our little copying operation?

Let's think of another random need. Say we're desperate to know what item the liquor store has the most of, and what item it has the least of. We can do this either by sorting or indexing. An index provides a list of the records ordered by quantity.

```
. INDEX ON QUANTITY TO B:QTY
15 records indexed
```

To go to the beginning of the indexed database, use the *dBASE III* command, GO TOP. To go to the end of the database, use GO BOTTOM.

```
. GO TOP
. DISPLAY OFF BRAND,SIZE,QUANTITY
BRAND                           SIZE          QUANTITY
SOUTHERN ARISTOCRACY            1/2 GAL       3

. GO BOTTOM
. DISPLAY OFF BRAND,SIZE,QUANTITY
BRAND                           SIZE          QUANTITY
AULD COUNTRY                    PINT          88
```

From the keyboard we have in a straightforward manner answered our question. The item we have least of is half gallons of Southern Aristocracy, and the one we have most of is pints of Auld Country.

These query examples are a tiny random sampling of kinds of things you can ask your database. The possibilities are really unlimited. The important thing is understanding enough about the process to make query use sensible and usable in light of your own needs.

YOUR OWN ELECTRONIC SCRATCHPAD

There is another very useful activity available to you, a kind of accessory to all the larger things possible with your database and computer. Data from a single field in a record can be brought for your

179

convenience into a special space in the computer's main memory. This temporary storage capability is provided through a microcomputer database system's query language processor. It is convenient when performing manual operations from the keyboard and invaluable when writing procedures for automatic operations. It's very much like having an electronic scratchpad available for use.

The scratchpad works a lot like the memory system in an electronic calculator. In *dBASE III*, you are allowed to have:

- 256 separate items stored in this scratchpad memory at any one time.
- a maximum number of 254 bytes (characters or numeric digits) allowed for any one item.
- total bytes allowed for all 256 items is 6000 bytes.

Each item stored in memory is a *memory variable.* When an item (memory variable) is stored into memory, it must be given a name. Naming the memory variable makes it convenient to use and keep track of. Each system uses some key word to tell the computer to accept an item as a memory variable. In dBASE, this key word is STORE.

To illustrate how this "scratchpad" memory works, we will store the number 6 into a memory variable that we name EXAMPLE.

```
. STORE 6 TO EXAMPLE
```

Alternately we can just use

```
. EXAMPLE=6
```

Remember:

- Within limits, you can store 256 separate items in memory at any one time.
- Each time you store an item, give it a name.

● If you assign the same name to two different items, only the second entry will be stored.

● To change what is stored in a memory variable, just store the new item to the old name, i.e., . STORE 7 TO EXAMPLE will put a 7 in EXAMPLE instead of the 6 we started with above.

● You cannot have two items with the same name at the same time.

Memory variables can be character strings, dates, numbers, or logical data.

```
. STORE 'ALPHABET' TO SOUP
. STORE .T. TO ANSWER
```

You are allowed to use the memory for nearly any purpose. You can combine character strings into a sentence:

```
. STORE 'ALPHABET' TO A
. STORE 'SOUP' TO B
. STORE A+B TO SOUP
```

To see what is contained in a memory variable, after the dot prompt, use a question mark followed by the name of the item.

```
.? SOUP
ALPHABET SOUP
```

Memory variables can be used to perform arithmetic.

```
. STORE 6 TO X
6
. STORE 7 TO Y
7
. STORE X+Y TO Z
13
. STORE Y-X TO W
```

181

```
1
. STORE X*Y TO Z      (remember * means multiply)
42
. STORE X/Y TO D      (the / indicates division)
0.86
```

To give you a better idea of the scratchpad memory's usefulness, let's look at the computerized checkbook. We enter the following field information: NUMBER, PAIDTO, AMOUNT, CANCELLED, and DEPOSIT. To determine the balance in the account, we make the following keyboard entries:

```
. SUM AMOUNT FOR DEPOSIT TO DEP
17434.53
. SUM AMOUNT FOR.NOT.DEPOSIT TO SPENT
15997.18
. STORE DEP-SPENT TO BALANCE
1437.35
```

Here we have obtained a useful result, the current account balance, directly from the keyboard with three inquiries. To check the computer accounts against the bank's monthly statement, we have:

```
. SUM AMOUNT FOR DEPOSIT.AND.CANCEL TO BANKDEP
16621.21
. SUM AMOUNT FOR.NOT.DEPOSIT.AND.CANCEL TO CANCELLED
15793.23
. STORE BANKDEP-CANCELLED TO BANKBAL
827.98
```

Thus, with only three instructions to the computer, we have another useful result: a check on the bank's assessment of our account balance. The last result can be compared against the bank statement.

In the last two examples, we could have obtained the sums as requested without storing them. Then we could have calculated the result with a pencil and paper or a hand calculator. That would have introduced a chance for error—the hand copying of the numbers. The scratchpad memory gives us direct use of the computer to perform operations using data from the database. If the data in the database is correct, the chance of error is nearly zero.

In the event you get the feeling that all this is just too easy— that you must be overlooking something vital—please rest assured: it really is easy.

Much of today's literature on computers contributes substantially to the notion that computers should be difficult. Textbooks address the subject from a technical person's frame of reference. In such textbooks, discussion of an example command containing the .OR. would be considerably different from our discussion. The computer-generated display in response to some such example command might be described in a technical textbook as "the relation B:INVENTRY restricted by the predicate LIQUOR='SCOTCH' .OR. LIQUOR='BOURBON'." A predicate, in case you simply must know, is a "relationship among the values of the domains."

183

There are times when it may seem as though professionals use specialized jargon in order to justify their positions and salaries. This really isn't true. The jargon allows specialists to communicate better among themselves.

But, put the barrier that such technical language creates for people unfamiliar with the "computer profession" together with the general sense that computers are strange, inaccessible, and difficult, and you have a good part of the reason a lot of people are haunted by "it just can't be this easy." In reality, most of the difficulty is simply due to unfamiliarity. Computers aren't just for computer professionals. They have incredible capabilities that are easily accessible to anyone with a need to store and disseminate information.

CHAPTER EIGHT

The database stores data. The database management system allows you to extract information from that data. If we have a liquor store, we can easily learn we are dangerously low on tequila and scandalously overstocked on scotch. If we combine the sample inventory database with a database which records the stock received, we can determine annual sales of each kind and size of liquor. Over a period of time, we can learn to manage the stock more efficiently. This, in turn, results in a more efficient use of money and a better return on our investment. There are, of course, many other uses for database management systems in business, education, and government. The point is this: a DBMS is easy to use. It can provide real support for whatever you endeavor. It can be fun. It can release you to do more interesting kinds of activities. It may even broaden your perspective, enabling you to see your entire operation from one source.

184

SECTION THREE

Section Three discusses various types of databases, examining the nature of each system and recognizing the differences among them. Chapter Eleven discusses computer logic, which may seem at first glance a potentially complicated or difficult topic.

Though technical and complex terminology may sometimes make computers seem mysterious or difficult, this impression is inaccurate and misleading. Computers are really very understandable and a lot of fun besides. Section Three attempts to fill in some of the gaps and answer some common questions people ask about computers. This will increase our understanding of the computer world and help us make further progress with our computer databases.

CHAPTER NINE

THINGS YOU MIGHT WANT TO KNOW ABOUT

A number of questions are often asked about microcomputer database systems. In this and the following chapters, we will attempt to answer some of the most common questions like: What is an assembly language system? What is a hierarchical database? What is a network database? What is CODASYL? What are . . .?

Assembly language is the computer's "native" language. Often mistakenly called machine language, it is the language the computer uses internally. Beyond assembly language are higher-order languages such as FORTRAN, COBOL, Pascal and *dBASE III*'s application development language (ADL). Each command or instruction in these languages is built out of many assembly language instructions.

When the computer executes a command such as DISPLAY, it is actually executing a large number of assembly language instructions. Very high-level languages such as BASIC and ADL use an average of 50 to 100 assembly language instructions for each high-level language command.

CHAPTER NINE

Many commercial software packages are written in a high-level language such as Pascal or BASIC. This is done because it is normally easier to write the package in a high-level language, and because it is *portable*, which means that the same package can be adapted for use on different kinds of microcomputers. An assembly language program is only usable on one kind of microcomputer. To be used on other kinds, it must be specifically rewritten for each kind. *dBASE III* and many of the newer software packages are written in a language called "C." C is an intermediate level language that provides an excellent compromise between the execution speed of assembly language and the portability of a high-level language.

It is often assumed that an assembly language program makes more efficient use of a machine's resources than a higher-order language program such as BASIC. This is probably true if you are comparing a well-written assembly language program with a well-written program in a higher-order language.

Since it is difficult to judge whether or not two systems are equally well written, this shouldn't be a consideration in selecting a commercial system. There are advantages to each approach for a software system. Since you will almost never see vendors advertising their systems as "mediocre" or "average to good," you should probably discount how well written a program might be as a factor in your selection. What is really important to you is: Will it do your job?

SEQUENTIAL AND RANDOM ACCESS

A set of terms often found in articles on databases and occasionally in advertisements is *sequential access* and *random access*. These terms refer to the way that a computer gets to data. Sequential access means that the computer starts with the first record and goes through the entire database file in sequence until it finds the record that you want. Random access means that the computer has "direct" access to every record.

```
. DISPLAY FOR NAME='Byers,Robert'
```

```
. LOCATE FOR NAME='Byers, Robert'
```

Query language commands such as DISPLAY and LOCATE use the sequential approach. When DISPLAY is used in this way, the computer examines every record in the database—starting with record one—in the order of their record numbers (sequentially). When LOCATE is used, the computer will examine each record in the database starting with record one and proceeding sequentially until it comes to the record containing Byers, Robert in the NAME field. This is sequential access for a particular record. *Note*: The time it takes the computer to find a particular record depends on where the record is in the database. If the database is large and the desired record is near the end, it could take several seconds for the computer to find the record. If the computer can read the entire database in one minute, the average access time will be thirty seconds.

The term random access is somewhat misleading. It does not mean that the computer leafs through the database in a haphazard manner until it finds the desired record. It really means that the computer has direct access to every record in the database. The word "random" really comes from the concept that if you choose any record at random, the computer can get to that record as quickly as to any other.

A rough example of a paper database that is designed for random (direct) access is the telephone book. The telephone directory is printed in alphabetical order. When you are looking for a particular person's telephone number, you use the alphabetical nature of the book to find the person's name and hence the number you desire. If you were to attempt to find the number by sequential access, you would begin with the first name in the directory and go through it name by name until you found the name you desire. Sequential access is simple, reliable, and relatively slow. Direct (random) access can provide a much quicker method of getting to a particular record.

PRIMARY AND SECONDARY KEYS

If the computer is to have random (direct) access to a particular record, it needs a little help. The specific help usually given the computer is a special *primary key* tacked on the front of the record by the computer when the record is created. The computer uses this key to go directly to a record, either keeping track of or calculating exactly where the record is on the disk. Then when the record is requested, the computer goes directly to the record's physical location and reads it into main memory.

In *dBASE III*, the *record number* is the primary key added by the computer. If you know a record number, you can go directly to that record. Locating a record by key is very fast, but the user must first know the key. In the case of *dBASE III*, knowing the key means knowing the record number. The primary key must be unique. It is not likely that you can remember the primary key for each record in a computer database. That may be possible if the database is very small. However, if it is that small, direct access isn't necessary.

A *secondary key* is the solution to the problem of how to make the primary key useful. Keys that are used by the computer are generally not useful to us, and keys meaningful to us are generally not useful to the computer. In trying to gain direct access, secondary key(s) provide the link.

A database can have one or more secondary keys. Secondary keys do not provide true direct access, but they come close. Access is much faster than the average access time for the sequential approach. Tables provide "translation" between primary and secondary keys.

An ordinary cookbook provides a good everyday example of primary and secondary keys.

The primary key is the page number. The secondary key(s) are the names of the dishes and the ingredients. The index is the table that translates the name of the food into a page number. The page number directs you to the item you want. If you knew the recipe you wanted was on page 123, that would be quicker than using the index. If you can't remember the page number, however, using the index is a lot quicker than leafing through the whole cookbook. You might observe more than one page number next to some of the entries. These entries are examples of non-unique keys. Secondary keys do not need to be unique.

Let's suppose that we have a database of students. Each record has the student's name, address, telephone number, room, and grade. We would like to be able to access student records by name or grade or room number. In order to do this we identify these three fields as secondary keys. We have three tables, one of each of the three keys. When we want a particular student's record, we use the name key and request the student by name. The computer finds the name in the table, takes the record number and uses the record number to get the record from the database.

Because the tables are for a special purpose, they can be constructed to provide nearly direct access to the desired data item. In *dBASE III*, direct access is provided by using index files for the tables. The system will build the tables for you if the command INDEX is used. The three tables can be established like this:

```
. USE B:SCHOOL
. INDEX ON NAME TO B:NAME
. INDEX ON ROOM TO B:ROOM
. INDEX ON GRADE TO B:GRADE
```

These commands have built three tables which allow you to use the three fields NAME, ROOM, and GRADE as secondary keys. The three tables have filenames B:NAME, B:ROOM, and B:GRADE. The database system adds .ndx to the end of the filename to tell the computer this is an INDEX FILE to be used for record access by the secondary key. If you need to find records according to the student's name,

```
. USE B:SCHOOL INDEX B:NAME
```

You can now directly access any student record by using only the student's name with the command FIND.

```
. FIND Aardvark,Anthony
```

Incidentally, if Anthony was the only student in the school whose last name began with Aa, we could have used . FIND Aa which would have accomplished the same result. The computer has found the record for Anthony. To see the record, just type the word DISPLAY. If you are interested in the sixth grade, you would

```
. USE B:SCHOOL INDEX B:GRADE
. FIND 6
```

These two commands will get you to the first record for a sixth grade student. All of the sixth grade students will be grouped together in the order of their record numbers. Because they are grouped together, you can display all sixth graders with the command

```
. DISPLAY WHILE GRADE='6'
```

When using a database with an index file (using secondary keys), the computer's execution of a command such as DISPLAY FOR GRADE='6' will be significantly slower than when using the database without the index file. Because they can be used to sort records into groups, index files can be used instead of commands such as SORT which physically rearrange the database. In addition to not affecting the physical arrangement of the database, the indexing operation is much faster than sorting.

You can also index on more than one field at a time. For example, suppose that you want to have students grouped by class (room and grade), and that you want them to be alphabetical within a class. You can use the three fields strung together as a secondary key. As an example:

```
. USE B:SCHOOL
. INDEX ON GRADE+ROOM+NAME TO B:CLASS
```

The "+" signs link the three fields together to form one key. If you were to display the entire database with the command DISPLAY ALL, the students would appear in grade order, by room within the grade, and alphabetically within the room. The computer keeps these files on the disk so that they can be used again without having to re-index. Re-indexing can take some time, particularly if the key has several characters and the database is large. Re-indexing is necessary only if records are added or deleted, or if any record has a key field changed.

Some database management systems do provide for automatic re-indexing. In dBASE this is handled by using the index files while you are adding, changing, or erasing records. In our example

193

```
. USE B:SCHOOL INDEX B:CLASS,B:NAME,B:ROOM,B:GRADE
```

will cause the index files B:CLASS, B:NAME, B:ROOM, AND B:GRADE to be updated each time a record is added, one of the key fields is changed, or records are erased with the DELETE and PACK commands.

There are disadvantages to this. Updating multiple index files (multiple secondary keys) can be very slow. This is not unique to dBASE. Updating multiple secondary keys tables in any database management system is time consuming. For this reason it is usually recommended that multiple keys (multiple index files) be avoided if at all possible. A related disadvantage is that a change made to the database without incorporating the change into an index file can invalidate the table and any computer processing done with the use of that table.

Secondary key tables (index files), of course, require space on a disk. If you have more than one disk drive, you may place an index table on a separate disk drive than the database. Though tables do not need to be on the same disk as the database, they must be on-line. This means that the computer must have simultaneous access to the database and the index file that you are using. An index file, like a database, must be entirely contained on a single disk for most microcomputer database systems. You should consider this fact in planning your database system, as well as when selecting computer hardware to support your database system.

PHYSICAL RECORDS AND LOGICAL RECORDS

In Chapter One we used the operation of an automotive parts store as an analogy to explain the concept of a database management system. In the analogy, the clerk, his parts catalogs, and the storage bins to hold the auto parts are analogous to the DBMS. The actual parts are analogous to the information that is stored in the database. As you begin to read more about database systems, you will find references to *physical records* and *logical records*. Physical records are the actual data records—they correspond to the auto parts in the analogy. Logical records are the entries in the secondary key tables (index files) that tell the computer where the physical record is located on the disk. These records correspond to the entries in the clerk's catalogs that tell him where the auto parts are located.

In Chapter One we also used a library as an analogy to a database management system. In the library example, the physical records correspond to the books. The logical records correspond to the cards in the library card catalog.

RECORD LOCKOUT

In our library example, there is also another set of logical records used to keep track of the books. These are the book checkout cards. There are times when a book that you want is out. The librarian can consult the

194

checkout cards to tell you when the book is due to be returned. If you so desire, the book can be reserved, and you will be notified when the book has been returned. It will be held a limited period of time for you.

As in the library example, in a computer database more than one person may want or need to use a physical record at the same time. It is usually not desirable for more than one person to use a database record at any one time. To illustrate, suppose the database contains the seating availability on an airline flight. If two ticket agents were to use that flight information at the same time, it would be possible for them to sell two separate customers the last seat on the flight. To guard against this sort of thing happening, the DMBS "checks out" the record to the first requestor. A second requestor will be informed that the record is currently in use. The DBMS will reserve the record for the second requestor's use as soon as it becomes available. All requestors of this record are said to be "locked out" from access to that record until it has been released by the first user. The technical term for this is *record lockout*.

It is, at present, unusual for a microcomputer database management system to provide the capability for record lockout. Most current microcomputer systems are designed to be used by only one person at a time. There is a growing tendency, however, for microcomputers to be shared by more than one person at a time. This allows relatively expensive and normally under-utilized peripherals, such as a printer, to be shared. As database management systems become more widely used on microcomputer systems, they too will contribute towards encouraging the use of multi-user microcomputers, providing an organization with the ability to share information. The ability to share information rapidly and inexpensively is of enormous value, and is the basic reason behind the development of database management systems for large mainframe computers. It is likely to become the reason for the development of affordable hardware systems to support pooled information for the smaller organization as well.

CHAPTER TEN

THINGS YOU MIGHT WANT TO KNOW, PART II

There are three basic kinds of database systems:

- Relational
- Hierarchical
- Network

Think of data in tables, with rows and columns, as in a relational system. The stacking hierarchy of a corporate organization chart is the picture we see in a hierarchical system. In imagining a network system, think of the organization charts of two companies which have just merged. Most new database management systems are either *relational* or a version of the network system called CODASYL.

THE RELATIONAL DATABASE

This book focuses on the relational database system because it relates so easily to everyday experience. Most microcomputer database management systems are variations on the relational idea. The relational database system is exactly what it appears to be: data is handled and stored in what, to most people, is a natural way. When using a relational system, a person inexperienced and unfamiliar with computer systems can produce useful work with relative ease.

An example of a simple relational database (taken from our liquor store inventory in Chapter Two) is shown in Figure 10-1.

198

LIQUOR	BRAND	SIZE	QTY	COST	PRICE
SCOTCH	AULD COUNTRY	QUART	23	5.59	9.31
SCOTCH	AULD COUNTRY	2 LITER	7	9.78	16.30
SCOTCH	AULD COUNTRY	PINT	88	2.74	4.56
VODKA	REAL RUSSIAN	QUART	35	3.78	6.30
VODKA	REAL RUSSIAN	2 LITER	9	7.95	13.25
VODKA	REAL RUSSIAN	PINT	75	1.49	2.48
WHISKEY	SOUTHERN RYE	QUART	32	5.11	8.51
WHISKEY	OLD WYOMING	PINT	44	1.98	3.30
WHISKEY	OLD WYOMING	QUART	19	5.29	8.81
WHISKEY	THE NEW SOUTH	QUART	4	7.49	12.48
BOURBON	SOUTHERN ARISTOCRACY	PINT	5	0.99	1.65
BOURBON	SOUTHERN ARISTOCRACY	FIFTH	22	1.78	2.96
BOURBON	SOUTHERN ARISTOCRACY	QUART	21	3.50	5.83
BOURBON	SOUTHERN ARISTOCRACY	1/2 GAL	3	6.89	11.48
BOURBON	SOUTHERN ARISTOCRACY	2 LITER	5	6.47	10.78

Figure 10-1. Example of A Relational Database

199

Each record in a relational database has a fixed length, and each field within the record is always the same size. This relational database looks just as it would if you were to take inventory using pencil and paper.

THE HIERARCHICAL DATABASE

Hierarchical database systems require you to think of the data as being arranged in subordinate segments (a hierarchy). A diagram of a hierarchical database resembles an organization chart. Since they resemble upside-down trees, hierarchical structures are often called tree structures. The liquor store database could be represented as shown in Figure 10-2.

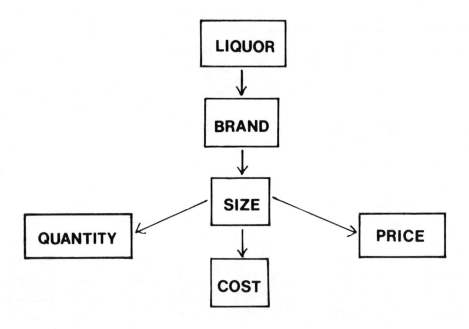

Figure 10-2. Hierarchical Representation Of Liquor Store Inventory

When represented in this way, the hierarchical structure becomes apparent. Each data item is subordinate to another data item (except of course for that in the topmost box). Instead of being a simple collection of fields, the "record" is a collection of subrecords or segments. Each box in the example is a segment or piece of the record. A segment may contain more than one field. The bottom three boxes, for example, might be grouped together to form a single segment.

The use of the word "record" is somewhat unfortunate, since it is difficult to separate one kind of record from another in our thinking. In this particular version of our liquor store database, we have four records: one for each of the four different kinds of liquor represented in the relational database B:INVENTRY: (scotch, vodka, whiskey, and bourbon). The hierarchical whiskey record corresponding to the whiskey entries in our relational database is shown in Figure 10-3.

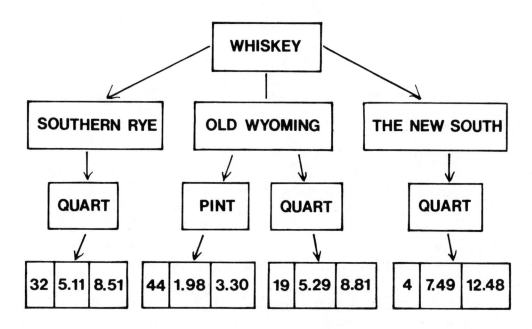

Figure 10-3. A Hierarchical 'Whiskey' Record

In these systems, each segment must belong to another segment, and no segment may belong to more than one segment. However, a segment may "own" more than one segment. Owners are often called parents, and subordinate segments referred to as children. In the example of Figure 10-3, whiskey is the parent of Old Wyoming, Southern Rye, and The New South. Each of these, in turn, is the parent (or owner) of various SIZE segments, also the "children" of whiskey.

Now let's see how this might work. Each segment has an identification code attached to it. That code is unique for each segment or primary key. It identifies the kind of segment and the sequence number, which is similar in concept to *dBASE III*'s record number.

Each of the four LIQUOR segments contains several pointers. Pointers allow the computer to go directly from segment to segment to assemble the entire record. Each LIQUOR pointer directs the computer to a BRAND segment that belongs to that LIQUOR segment. Each of these BRAND segments, in turn, contains pointers which direct the computer to each of the SIZE segments belonging to that BRAND. Each of these, in turn, contain pointers which direct the computer to the segments which contain QUANTITY, COST, and PRICE. These segments may contain no pointers.

On the surface, this appears to be a complicated way of doing a simple job. In a relational database system we don't use these pointers to put each record together. In our relational example, however, we use four records for the "whiskey" inventory. In the hierarchical version we need only one 'Whiskey' segment, plus some pointers. Then if our liquor store inventory has a thousand entries and there are only ten kinds of liquor, we avoid a great deal of duplication with the hierarchical system.

Saving a lot of duplication seems like a good idea. Where's the rub? First of all, duplication is reduced at the expense of simplicity. While many applications fit easily into a hierarchical structure, many do not. In addition, you need to decide up front what your applications will be. The fact that a segment can belong to only one parent is one rather obvious drawback to the hierarchical system.

Let's suppose that we have a personnel database that is hierarchical. Two of our employees marry each other and have a child. The database record segment for that child cannot belong to the personnel records of both parents. Though many artifices have been worked out to cope with such a situation, it illustrates a classic shortcoming of the hierarchical system.

Telephone directory yellow pages provide a rough analogy from the paper database world to a hierarchical database. If we represent the yellow pages as shown in Figure 10-4, their hierarchical nature becomes evident.

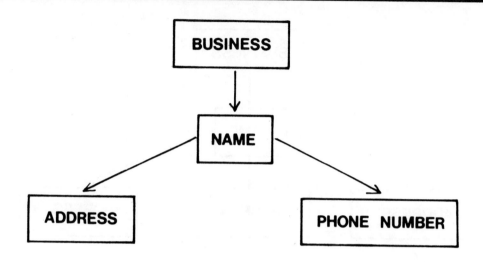

Figure 10-4. Hierarchical Representation Of The Yellow Pages

203

ADDRESS and PHONE NUMBER belong to the name; the NAME, in turn, belongs to the BUSINESS. Starting from the other end, BUSINESS is the owner of NAME. NAME, in turn, is the owner of both ADDRESS and PHONE NUMBER. A segment cannot belong to more than one owner. An owner, however, may own many other segments. For businesses that have more than one address and/or phone number, the structure might be diagrammed as shown in Figure 10-5.

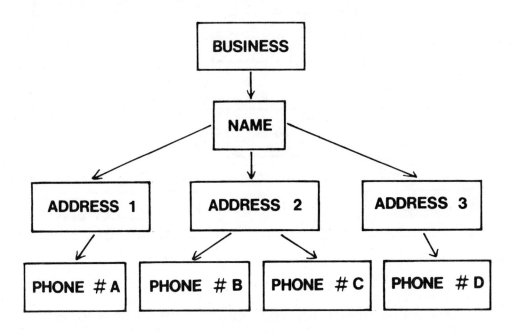

Figure 10-5

204

Unlike in a relational database, records in a hierarchical database can be of varying sizes. Some records, for example, might have several telephone numbers while others have only one. Though this situation can be handled by a relational database, it requires that you either waste memory or become clever.

To get a better idea of this, suppose we have a record of new car dealers. The BUSINESS segment contains the title "New Car Dealers," plus pointers to direct the computer to all of the segments that contain names of new car dealers. One such dealer is "Vroom Vroom Motors." The segment for Vroom Vroom Motors contains the company's name, as well as a set of pointers leading the computer to the addresses of the company's facilities. The database system may use the segment ID to keep order within a record (for example, to keep company names in alphabetical order). Each address segment contains the address and pointers for the phone numbers. A segment will always contain pointers that direct the computer to segments belonging to it. A segment *might* contain a pointer to lead the computer to its owner segment.

There are some possible shortcomings to the hierarchical database system—from the user's viewpoint. First of all, to get an alphabetical listing of all the names in the database would, most likely, require a substantial effort. Second, it is quite possible that a company would belong to more than one business category. Vroom Vroom Motors might very well have a repair shop, a body shop, a parts department, and a used car lot in addition to its new car dealership. In a hierarchical system, a "child" can have only one parent. So to list our sample car dealer under four business categories, the dealership must be entered four times, once in each category.

THE NETWORK DATABASE

Network database management systems are similar to hierarchical systems. One major difference is that, under certain conditions, a child can have more than one parent. Another is that a parent-child relationship such as BUSINESS-NAME can be switched. Finally, the terminology is different from both the relational and hierarchical systems.

205

The term *network* is often used interchangeably with CODASYL. This is because the most common network database systems are based upon a proposed national standard for databases, a standard developed by the Data Base Task Group (DBTG) of the COnference on DAta SYstems Languages. CODASYL is the organization that developed the computer language COBOL. The network database is based on the new math concept of sets. The network database is even more complex than the hierarchical, but it does provide greater flexibility.

In the network database system, the database is made up of a collection of sets. A set is a group of like items. Each set consists of a collection of records similar to those in a relational system, except that the length need not be fixed. A record can belong to more than one set. Several businesses (NAMES) belong to each business category set (BUSINESS). In the phone book, the new car dealers such as Vroom Vroom Motors belong to, or are members of, the new car dealer set. The "owner" record is thus New Car Dealers. Every set must have an owner record. A set can consist of only one record. A record cannot belong to two occurrences of the same set type. Therefore, the situation below is not allowed.

206

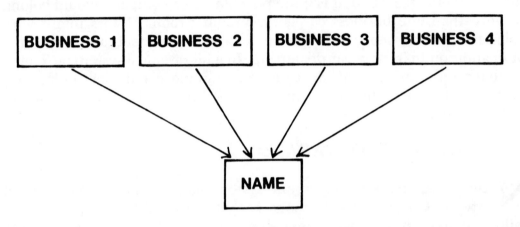

Figure 10-6

Now of course this is nonsense because we all know that a company name can show up under many business categories in the yellow pages. The problem here is that we have a situation where the number of possible relationships is enormous. It can become so enormous as to overwhelm even the largest computer. The network database is comfortable when dealing with one to many relationships. The problem is to restructure the sets so that all relationships are one to many.

A particular characteristic of the hierarchical database system was that if NAME belonged to BUSINESS, an alphabetical listing of all of the names might be difficult to do. This is because the NAMES are alphabetized within each business category and can only be accessed by business category. In the network system, NAME can belong to BUSINESS and at the same time the BUSINESS can belong to NAME.

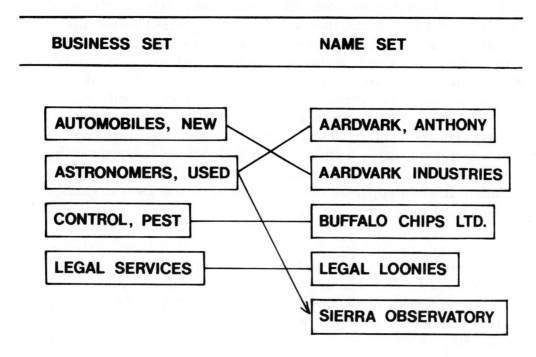

Figure 10-7

As you might have expected, the network database uses an entirely different terminology from either the hierarchical or the relational database systems. The data item is similar to what we have been calling a field. In the hierarchical database example, there might be several phone numbers belonging to an address. This is called a "vector data aggregate." There might also be several addresses belonging to a name. Each of the addresses has a phone number. The address-phone number is called a group. If there is more than one group, it is a repeating group.

Hierarchical and network database systems are substantially different in structure from the relational systems. The way that data records are structured in these systems is much more complex than in relational systems. These systems are well suited to large, complex database applications. Because of this, they are used extensively on large computers. This is because they can be very efficient in the use of the computer resources—CPU time and main memory. The potential efficiency they offer can become extremely important when the database contains tens or hundreds of thousands of records. Since the cost of operating a large mainframe computer system can easily amount to several hundred dollars an hour, the value of efficiency is readily apparent. The cost of professional programmers to work with these database systems is easily justified when their efforts can reduce the cost of using a database management system on this kind of computer installation. It is not apparent that this kind of efficiency is as valuable for databases used on microcomputers.

As was stated earlier, each of the three database systems can accommodate all of the required database functions. Each has its strengths and weaknesses. The hierarchical/network systems offer the user efficiency and speed. They are conservative in the use of the computer's resources. They are, however, complex and relatively inflexible. They were developed for use on large mainframe computer systems where billions of bytes of on-line disk storage are not uncommon. A billion bytes represents one to four thousand eight-inch floppy disks. Just reading that much storage at floppy disk read speed could take a half-million seconds. That is *days*. If your database needs are truly this large, a microcomputer database system may not be for you. It is not at all inconceivable that you need either a hierarchical or network database system and a large computer.

Each of the three kinds of database systems has things that it does best. Each can perform any database task. The hierarchical and network approaches to database systems require that you represent the data as either a hierarchy or a network by designing your database to satisfy a particular way of using the data. What this means to you is that when you create the database you must have already decided how you will use it.

208

With a relational approach, you represent the data in terms of tables of rows and columns and the ways in which the data is used can be determined later.

209

CHAPTER ELEVEN

A LITTLE LOGIC

Computers and database management systems are built on the use of logic. Most microcomputer database systems are designed so this use of logic occurs in a very natural way: it isn't difficult— in fact it's kind of fun. However you feel about it, understanding computer logic allows you to get far more from your computer and your database management system.

There are three commonly used logical terms, referred to as *logical operators*.

. AND .
. OR .
. NOT .

As we mentioned earlier in this book, these are very similar to their ordinary English counterparts. The periods at each end of the word are part of the logical operator.

To illustrate the use of these terms, we will use the liquor store inventory from the example in Chapter Two. The database is shown in Figure 11-1.

LIQUOR	BRAND	SIZE	QTY	COST	PRICE
SCOTCH	AULD COUNTRY	QUART	23	5.59	9.31
SCOTCH	AULD COUNTRY	2 LITER	7	9.78	16.30
SCOTCH	AULD COUNTRY	PINT	88	2.74	4.56
VODKA	REAL RUSSIAN	QUART	35	3.78	6.30
VODKA	REAL RUSSIAN	2 LITER	9	7.95	13.25
VODKA	REAL RUSSIAN	PINT	75	1.49	2.48
WHISKEY	SOUTHERN RYE	QUART	32	5.11	8.51
WHISKEY	OLD WYOMING	PINT	44	1.98	3.30
WHISKEY	OLD WYOMING	QUART	19	5.29	8.81
WHISKEY	THE NEW SOUTH	QUART	4	7.49	12.48
BOURBON	SOUTHERN ARISTOCRACY	PINT	5	0.99	1.65
BOURBON	SOUTHERN ARISTOCRACY	FIFTH	22	1.78	2.96
BOURBON	SOUTHERN ARISTOCRACY	QUART	21	3.50	5.83
BOURBON	SOUTHERN ARISTOCRACY	1/2 GAL	3	6.89	11.48
BOURBON	SOUTHERN ARISTOCRACY	2 LITER	5	6.47	10.78

Figure 11-1. Liquor Store Inventory

Suppose you wanted to see all the entries for whiskey and bourbon. The natural tendency is to write the query command as:

```
. DISPLAY FOR LIQUOR='BOURBON'.AND.LIQUOR='WHISKEY'
```

Unfortunately this won't work. This command tells the computer to display all the records where the LIQUOR field contains WHISKEY and

BOURBON. There are none. Computer logic applies to one record at a time—not the entire database. The correct command is:

```
. DISPLAY FOR LIQUOR='BOURBON'.OR.LIQUOR='WHISKEY'
```

The section of the example database this applies to is shown by the non-crosshatched area in Figure 11-2.

LIQUOR	BRAND	SIZE	QTY	COST	PRICE
SCOTCH	AULD COUNTRY	QUART	23	5.59	9.31
SCOTCH	AULD COUNTRY	2 LITER	7	9.78	16.30
SCOTCH	AULD COUNTRY	PINT	88	2.74	4.56
VODKA	REAL RUSSIAN	QUART	35	3.78	6.30
VODKA	REAL RUSSIAN	2 LITER	9	7.95	13.25
VODKA	REAL RUSSIAN	PINT	75	1.49	2.48
WHISKEY	SOUTHERN RYE	QUART	32	5.11	8.51
WHISKEY	OLD WYOMING	PINT	44	1.98	3.30
WHISKEY	OLD WYOMING	QUART	19	5.29	8.81
WHISKEY	THE NEW SOUTH	QUART	4	7.49	12.48
BOURBON	SOUTHERN ARISTOCRACY	PINT	5	0.99	1.65
BOURBON	SOUTHERN ARISTOCRACY	FIFTH	22	1.78	2.96
BOURBON	SOUTHERN ARISTOCRACY	QUART	21	3.50	5.83
BOURBON	SOUTHERN ARISTOCRACY	1/2 GAL	3	6.89	11.48
BOURBON	SOUTHERN ARISTOCRACY	2 LITER	5	6.47	10.78

Figure 11-2

Proper use of the .AND. operator finds the common area of two groups. For example, to determine what records contain pints of whiskey, the command is:

```
. DISPLAY FOR LIQUOR='WHISKEY'.AND.SIZE='PINT'
```

The order of the fields doesn't matter. The same result is obtained by:

```
. DISPLAY FOR SIZE='PINT'.AND.LIQUOR='WHISKEY'
```

If we used .OR. instead of .AND. in this last example, we would obtain an entirely different result.

```
. DISPLAY FOR SIZE='PINT'.OR.LIQUOR='WHISKEY'
```

The non-crosshatched area of Figure 11-3 indicates records that would display based on this command construction.

LIQUOR	BRAND	SIZE	QTY	COST	PRICE
SCOTCH	AULD COUNTRY	QUART	23	5.59	9.31
SCOTCH	AULD COUNTRY	2 LITER	7	9.78	16.30
SCOTCH	AULD COUNTRY	PINT	88	2.74	4.56
VODKA	REAL RUSSIAN	QUART	35	3.78	6.30
VODKA	REAL RUSSIAN	2 LITER	9	7.95	13.25
VODKA	REAL RUSSIAN	PINT	75	1.49	2.48
WHISKEY	SOUTHERN RYE	QUART	32	5.11	8.51
WHISKEY	OLD WYOMING	PINT	44	1.98	3.30
WHISKEY	OLD WYOMING	QUART	19	5.29	8.81
WHISKEY	THE NEW SOUTH	QUART	4	7.49	12.48
BOURBON	SOUTHERN ARISTOCRACY	PINT	5	0.99	1.65
BOURBON	SOUTHERN ARISTOCRACY	FIFTH	22	1.78	2.96
BOURBON	SOUTHERN ARISTOCRACY	QUART	21	3.50	5.83
BOURBON	SOUTHERN ARISTOCRACY	1/2 GAL	3	6.89	11.48
BOURBON	SOUTHERN ARISTOCRACY	2 LITER	5	6.47	10.78

Figure 11-3

214

Suppose we want to extract those records that are pints of either whiskey or bourbon. The way to set up the command is:

```
. DISPLAY FOR(LIQUOR='WHISKEY'.OR.LIQUOR='BOURBON');
.AND.SIZE='PINT'
```

The records that qualify under this criteria are shown in the unshaded areas of Figure 11-4.

215

LIQUOR	BRAND	SIZE	QTY	COST	PRICE
SCOTCH	AULD COUNTRY	QUART	23	5.59	9.31
SCOTCH	AULD COUNTRY	2 LITER	7	9.78	16.30
SCOTCH	AULD COUNTRY	PINT	88	2.74	4.56
VODKA	REAL RUSSIAN	QUART	35	3.78	6.30
VODKA	REAL RUSSIAN	2 LITER	9	7.95	13.25
VODKA	REAL RUSSIAN	PINT	75	1.49	2.48
WHISKEY	SOUTHERN RYE	QUART	32	5.11	8.51
WHISKEY	OLD WYOMING	PINT	44	1.98	3.30
WHISKEY	OLD WYOMING	QUART	19	5.29	8.81
WHISKEY	THE NEW SOUTH	QUART	4	7.49	12.48
BOURBON	SOUTHERN ARISTOCRACY	PINT	5	0.99	1.65
BOURBON	SOUTHERN ARISTOCRACY	FIFTH	22	1.78	2.96
BOURBON	SOUTHERN ARISTOCRACY	QUART	21	3.50	5.83
BOURBON	SOUTHERN ARISTOCRACY	1/2 GAL	3	6.89	11.48
BOURBON	SOUTHERN ARISTOCRACY	2 LITER	5	6.47	10.78

Figure 11-4

Suppose you inadvertently omitted the parentheses in the last example. The command would have read

```
. DISPLAY FOR LIQUOR='WHISKEY'.OR.LIQUOR='BOURBON';
.AND.SIZE='PINT'
```

The resulting display—which is entirely different—is shown in Figure 11-5. This happens because the .AND. operator takes precedence over the .OR. operator.

LIQUOR	BRAND	SIZE	QTY	COST	PRICE
SCOTCH	AULD COUNTRY	QUART	23	5.59	9.31
SCOTCH	AULD COUNTRY	2 LITER	7	9.78	16.30
SCOTCH	AULD COUNTRY	PINT	88	2.74	4.56
VODKA	REAL RUSSIAN	QUART	35	3.78	6.30
VODKA	REAL RUSSIAN	2 LITER	9	7.95	13.25
VODKA	REAL RUSSIAN	PINT	75	1.49	2.48
WHISKEY	SOUTHERN RYE	QUART	32	5.11	8.51
WHISKEY	OLD WYOMING	PINT	44	1.98	3.30
WHISKEY	OLD WYOMING	QUART	19	5.29	8.81
WHISKEY	THE NEW SOUTH	QUART	4	7.49	12.48
BOURBON	SOUTHERN ARISTOCRACY	PINT	5	0.99	1.65
BOURBON	SOUTHERN ARISTOCRACY	FIFTH	22	1.78	2.96
BOURBON	SOUTHERN ARISTOCRACY	QUART	21	3.50	5.83
BOURBON	SOUTHERN ARISTOCRACY	1/2 GAL	3	6.89	11.48
BOURBON	SOUTHERN ARISTOCRACY	2 LITER	5	6.47	10.78

Figure 11-5

To go back to the previous example, the logical arrangement resulting in the unshaded areas of Figure 11-4 is due to the command structure

```
. DISPLAY FOR(LIQUOR='WHISKEY'.OR.LIQUOR='BOURBON');
.AND.SIZE='PINT'
```

Now suppose you really want everything else. This can get messy if you try to write out the logic. However, you can handle this with ease by using the .NOT. operator. The command becomes

```
. DISPLAY FOR.NOT.((LIQUOR='WHISKEY'.OR.LIQUOR='BOURBON');
.AND.SIZE='PINT')
```

The entire logical expression is placed in parentheses to tell the computer that the .NOT. applies to everything. The result is shown in the unshaded areas of Figure 11-6.

217

LIQUOR	BRAND	SIZE	QTY	COST	PRICE
SCOTCH	AULD COUNTRY	QUART	23	5.59	9.31
SCOTCH	AULD COUNTRY	2 LITER	7	9.78	16.30
SCOTCH	AULD COUNTRY	PINT	88	2.74	4.56
VODKA	REAL RUSSIAN	QUART	35	3.78	6.30
VODKA	REAL RUSSIAN	2 LITER	9	7.95	13.25
VODKA	REAL RUSSIAN	PINT	75	1.49	2.48
WHISKEY	SOUTHERN RYE	QUART	32	5.11	8.51
WHISKEY	OLD WYOMING	PINT	44	1.98	3.30
WHISKEY	OLD WYOMING	QUART	19	5.29	8.81
WHISKEY	THE NEW SOUTH	QUART	4	7.49	12.48
BOURBON	SOUTHERN ARISTOCRACY	PINT	5	0.99	1.65
BOURBON	SOUTHERN ARISTOCRACY	FIFTH	22	1.78	2.96
BOURBON	SOUTHERN ARISTOCRACY	QUART	21	3.50	5.83
BOURBON	SOUTHERN ARISTOCRACY	1/2 GAL	3	6.89	11.48
BOURBON	SOUTHERN ARISTOCRACY	2 LITER	5	6.47	10.78

Figure 11-6

218

Now let's suppose we need to see all whiskey and bourbon records for all sizes except quarts. This is accomplished by

```
. DISPLAY FOR(LIQUOR='WHISKEY'.OR.LIQUOR='BOURBON');
.AND..NOT.SIZE='QUART'
```

The records affected are shown in the unshaded areas of Figure 11-7.

LIQUOR	BRAND	SIZE	QTY	COST	PRICE
SCOTCH	AULD COUNTRY	QUART	23	5.59	9.31
SCOTCH	AULD COUNTRY	2 LITER	7	9.78	16.30
SCOTCH	AULD COUNTRY	PINT	88	2.74	4.56
VODKA	REAL RUSSIAN	QUART	35	3.78	6.30
VODKA	REAL RUSSIAN	2 LITER	9	7.95	13.25
VODKA	REAL RUSSIAN	PINT	75	1.49	2.48
WHISKEY	SOUTHERN RYE	QUART	32	5.11	8.51
WHISKEY	OLD WYOMING	PINT	44	1.98	3.30
WHISKEY	OLD WYOMING	QUART	19	5.29	8.81
WHISKEY	THE NEW SOUTH	QUART	4	7.49	12.48
BOURBON	SOUTHERN ARISTOCRACY	PINT	5	0.99	1.65
BOURBON	SOUTHERN ARISTOCRACY	FIFTH	22	1.78	2.96
BOURBON	SOUTHERN ARISTOCRACY	QUART	21	3.50	5.83
BOURBON	SOUTHERN ARISTOCRACY	1/2 GAL	3	6.89	11.48
BOURBON	SOUTHERN ARISTOCRACY	2 LITER	5	6.47	10.78

Figure 11-7

219

You can often use characteristics of the language to help you avoid some of the more complicated logic. For example,

. DISPLAY FOR LIQUOR$ 'BOURBON   ,WHISKEY

will produce the same result as

. DISPLAY FOR LIQUOR='BOURBON'.OR.LIQUOR='WHISKEY'

The dollar sign is a shorthand way of saying "contained in." It is sometimes called a string operator. The first statement tells the computer to display each record where the content of the field LIQUOR is contained in the "character string," 'BOURBON   ,WHISKEY   '. The blank spaces are there because the computer will compare the entire field LIQUOR with the character string. Since the field has ten characters, if you had omitted the blank spaces, the computer would not find a match with any field content. Blank spaces have as much meaning to the computer as any other character. The comma is not necessary in this case because we have used up all ten spaces in our LIQUOR field, but it is usually good practice to separate possible matches with some character (such as a comma) that is not a possible match.

If you want to see everything except BOURBON or WHISKEY, the proper command is

```
. DISPLAY FOR.NOT.LIQUOR$'BOURBON    ,WHISKEY        '
```

The use of the logical operators—.AND., .OR., and .NOT.—allows you to specify to the computer exactly what conditions apply to the commands. They improve your efficiency by having the computer screen the database records to locate the specific ones you are interested in. Later in the book we will discuss procedures which provide you with even more help from the computer. Logical operators then become more important as you begin to describe to the computer exactly what you want it to do automatically.

CHAPTER TWELVE

DATE AND MEMO FIELDS

One of the special data types is DATE. This data type is specially designed to make working with dates straightforward and easy. Although a DATE type may seem to be a natural part of a database management system, it is not available with all database systems. *dBASE III* offers a date data type, though *dBASE II* does not.

To specify a field as a date type, press the space bar until the type column indicates "Date." Then press the <RETURN> key. A field width of eight is automatically selected—all dates take eight bytes (character spaces). An alternative method for selecting DATE is to press the "D" key when the cursor is positioned to the first character of the field type entry area.

Dates are normally entered as MM/DD/YY. This is the American style for dates. The European style is DD/MM/YY. *dBASE III* can accept dates entered in the European style by using the *picture* function.

To illustrate working with dates, let's use the following four-record database:

Record#	NAME	DEPARTED	RETURNED
1	Jim Jones	12/15/83	01/02/84
2	Ed Smith	03/17/84	03/21/84
3	Frank Brown	04/05/84	04/12/84
4	Bill Adams	05/27/84	06/03/84

The data entry screen that *dBASE III* uses for this database is shown as Screen 12-1. Note that the slashes are already a part of the date fields, so you do not have to enter them. You must, however, enter leading zeroes for day and month entries.

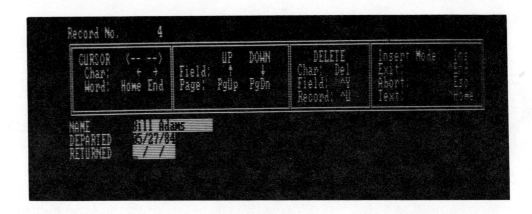

Screen 12 - 1

dBASE III validates dates. If you enter a non-existent date such as 15/27/84 (there is no fifteenth month), an error message will be displayed at the upper righthand corner of the screen, and you will be prevented from proceeding until you have entered a legitimate date. Note that there is no test for a "correct" date. 07/04/76 would have been just as acceptable as the correct date of 05/27/84.

A date may be subtracted from a date. The answer is given as the number of days between the two dates. For example, we subtract the field

222

DEPARTED from the field RETURNED for the first record in the sample database.

```
.  GO TOP
.  ? RETURNED — DEPARTED
      18
```

Note that the answer takes into account changes in both month and year. A date may *not* be added to another date. The result is meaningless (just as it is without a computer). When the addition of dates is attempted, an error message will be displayed.

A number may be added to (or subtracted from) a date. This number is treated as a number of days. The result of the addition (or subtraction) is a new date. For example, let's add eighteen to the field DEPARTED:

```
.  ? DEPARTED
12/15/83

.  ? DEPARTED + 18
01/02/84
```

The query commands SUM and AVERAGE can also be used with date fields. To determine the sum of the difference between the RETURNED and DEPARTED dates for all four records:

```
.  SUM RETURNED — DEPARTED
    4 records summed
 RETURNED — DEPARTED
                36
```

To determine the average of the difference between the RETURNED and DEPARTED dates:

```
.  AVERAGE RETURNED — DEPARTED
```

223

```
          4 records averaged
RETURNED — DEPARTED
                    9
```

To sort on a date field, just use the name of the date field directly in the SORT command. To illustrate, we want to sort our database chronologically by the contents of the field DEPARTED to the new database file DATESORT. The command is:

```
. SORT ON DEPARTED TO DATESORT
100% sorted   4 records sorted
```

To index on a date field, we again use the name of the field as the item to be indexed on.

```
. INDEX ON DEPARTED TO DEPART
4 records indexed
```

Once the database is indexed on a date field, you can go directly to the first record for a particular date by means of the SEEK command and the CTOD (character to date) function. For example, to position the indexed database to the first record where the content of the DEPARTED field is 04/05/84, use the command:

```
. SEEK CTOD("04/05/84")
```

The entire date must be specified when using the SEEK command.

The CTOD (character to date) function is only one of several date functions. The date functions are:

FUNCTION	DESCRIPTION	EXAMPLE
CTOD	Character To Date	
DTOC	Date To Character	
Day	Day of Month	21
Month	Month of Year	10
Year	Year	1984
DOW	Day of Week	3
CDOW	Calendar Day of Week	Tuesday
CMONTH	Calendar Month	January
Date	Current System Date	MM/DD/YY

Figure 12-1

225

These functions make it more convenient for us to work with dates. CTOD, as we have seen, allows us to use a character string as a date. DTOC allows us to use a date in a character string. One use of this function is to embed dates in a text string.

```
.? 'He left on '+DTOC(DEPARTED)+' and returned ';
+DTOC(RETURNED)
He left on 05/27/84 and returned 06/03/84
```

The Day, Month, and Year functions make it convenient for us to specify dates to be used as conditions of *dBASE III* commands. Examples of the use of these functions are shown by the three DISPLAY commands below:

```
. DISPLAY FOR YEAR(DEPARTED) = 1984
. DISPLAY FOR YEAR(DEPARTED) = 1984 .AND.;
MONTH(DEPARTED) = 9
. DISPLAY FOR YEAR(DEPARTED) = 1984 .AND.;
MONTH(DEPARTED) = 9 .AND. DAY(DEPARTED) = 21
```

The DOW (day of week) function returns a number code for each day of the week beginning with Sunday (1). To display all departing dates that were Tuesdays:

```
. DISPLAY FOR DOW(DEPARTED) = 3
```

CDOW (calendar day of week) and CMONTH (calendar month) allow us to transform dates into forms that are more convenient for us to use in text. As an example, let's use the DEPARTED field from record one.

```
. ? DEPARTED
12/15/83
```

```
. ? CDOW(DEPARTED)
Thursday
```

```
. ? CMONTH(DEPARTED)
December
```

The system date allows us to read the PC's internal calendar clock.

```
. ? DATE()
07/04/84
```

dBASE III cannot change the system date directly. If your computer has more than the required minimum of 256 kilobytes, and the file COMMAND.COM is on the dBASE disk, the date can be changed by:

```
. RUN DATE
```

This command calls the operating system command DATE. When the date has been entered, you will return to where you were in dBASE automatically.

It may well be that you would like to print the contents of date fields in the form "calendar month, day, year" (for example, April 9, 1984) from reports and procedures. To do this, use the following instead of the simple fieldname:

```
CMONTH(FIELDNAME)+STR(DAY(FIELDNAME),3)+',';
+STR(YEAR(FIELDNAME),5)
```

The above will convert a date such as 04/09/84 to the more convenient form April 9, 1984.

MEMO FIELDS

Another special data type allows you to work with variable length text. In *dBASE III*, the field type used for this kind of data is MEMO. Examples of the kind of data stored in memo fields would be memoranda, abstracts, general comments, etc.

To specify a field as a memo type, press the space bar until the type column indicates "Memo." Then press the <RETURN> key. A field width of ten is automatically assigned to a memo field. An alternative method for selecting MEMO is to press the "M" key when the cursor is positioned to the first character of the field type entry area.

Any or all of the 128 fields in a *dBASE III* database file can be memo fields. If a database file has one or more memo fields, the contents of the memo fields are actually stored in an auxiliary file to the database file. The text information stored in this auxiliary file is connected to the data record by means of a ten byte *pointer* in the database file. The auxiliary file has the same name as the database file. It has the file extension .DBT to distinguish it from the .DBF database file.

During data entry into the main database file, the data entry area of a memo field is indicated by the word "memo" as shown in Screen 12-2.

227

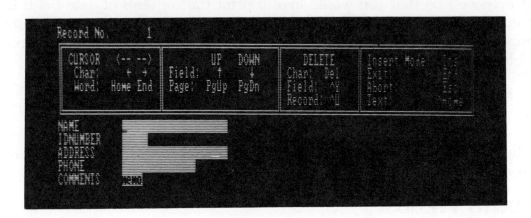

Screen 12 - 2

To enter data into a memo field, place the cursor on the "m" of "memo." Then press <Ctrl-Home>. (The <Ctrl> key is held down while the <Home> key is pressed). The screen will clear, and display the current contents of the memo field. The cursor will be positioned to the beginning of any text already in the field.

Data is entered by simply typing in the desired text. When the text has been completely entered, press <Ctrl-End> to save it (or <Esc> to abandon the entry).

No space is taken in the auxiliary text file until data is actually entered into a memo field. Once data is entered, space is allocated, as needed, in 512 byte chunks. The maximum size for memo fields is normally 4,096 bytes.

A word processor is provided to help with data entry and editing of memo fields. When the memo field is entered, the word processor is automatically activated. An external disk file can be read into a memo field by using <Ctrl-KR>. The contents of a memo field can be copied to an external disk file with <Ctrl-KW>. Other functions that can be performed by use of the <Ctrl> key and/or the special keys are:

228

KEY	DESCRIPTION
PgUp	Scroll toward the beginning of the text
PgDn	Scroll toward the end of the text
↑	Move one line toward beginning of text
↓	Move one line toward end of text
←	Move one character space left
→	Move one character space right
Ctrl-←	Move to beginning of the current line
Ctrl-→	Move to end of the current line
Home	Move one word left
End	Move one word right
Ctrl-T	Delete word to right of cursor
Ctrl-Y	Delete current line
Ctrl-N	Insert blank line
Ins	Insert characters
Del	Delete the character cursor is on
Backspace Arrow	Delete character to left of cursor
Ctrl-KR	Read in external disk file
Ctrl-KW	Write memo field to external disk file
Esc	Abort changes and return to data entry
Ctrl-End	Save and return to data entry mode

Figure 12-2

229

The memo field can only be entered via one of the *dBASE III* full screen data entry commands: APPEND, INSERT, CHANGE or EDIT. The memo field cannot be entered from the full screen command BROWSE.

CHAPTER TWELVE

When entry or editing of a memo field is completed, you will be returned to the data entry screen that was used to enter the field.

The content of a memo field can be viewed using the DISPLAY, LIST, ?, and REPORT commands only. When these commands are used, the contents of the specified memo field will be displayed in a fifty character wide format. The memo field must be explicitly named in any of the above commands. The use of DISPLAY or LIST alone will show the word "memo" under the name of the field.

There are severe restrictions as to the use of memo fields. They can be changed only manually via one of the four full screen data entry commands APPEND, INSERT, CHANGE, and EDIT. They can be viewed only via these commands or DISPLAY, LIST, ?, or REPORT. They cannot be searched automatically for content and they cannot be used as part of a condition for a command.

If your computer has sufficient memory in addition to the 256 kilobytes required for *dBASE III*, a commercial word processor (such as *WordStar*) can be used instead of the *dBASE III* internal word processor for editing the contents of memo fields. To do so, enter the commands

```
. SET DEFAULT TO
. MODIFY COMMAND CONFIG.DB
```

The command SET DEFAULT TO is used exactly as is to insure that the disk drive that *dBASE III* is on will be the default disk drive. The disk file CONFIG.DB must be on the disk that *dBASE III* is on. If CONFIG.DB is on the *dBASE III* disk, it will be read when *dBASE III* is loaded. Any specifications—such as which word processor to be used for memo fields—will be incorporated into *dBASE III* at that time. The CONFIG.DB file can be changed at any time.

MODIFY COMMAND CONFIG.DB allows us to change CONFIG.DB if it already exists, or create it if it does not exist. To use *WordStar* as the word processor for *dBASE III* memo fields WordStar.Com and its associated overlay files must be on the *dBASE III* disk.

To change CONFIG.DB to incorporate *WordStar* as the internal word processor, move the cursor to the end of the file CONFIG.DB and enter the line

```
WP = WORDSTAR.COM
```

Press <Ctrl-End> to save the file. The *next* time that *dBASE III* is loaded, *WordStar* will be the internal word processor for memo fields.

231

SECTION FOUR

Section Four is about power, speed, and ease. The computer's capability can be dramatically enhanced by teaching it some new tricks. It is not hard to teach the computer tricks—and it is really great how closely you can customize these tricks to support your specific information storing and reporting needs.

Again we use familiar database examples to define menu options, utilize *DO WHILE* clauses, and automate routine activities that customize our system, giving us a greater "reach" and saving us time and energy. The customization gives us a very important thing: the ability to produce specific reports.

CHAPTER THIRTEEN

THE FINE ART OF PROCEDURES

Most database management systems have a Query Language Processor and a Report Writer. These two DBMS pieces can probably satisfy most, if not all, of your needs. Any further need is easily accommodated using simple procedures. In previous chapters, we discussed several examples of procedure-generated special processes. There are lots of things you can do using procedures to construct exactly what you want the computer to do for you in a specific circumstance. This process not only makes custom, deluxe, "designed-for-you" computer output, but also is a very practical way to save you work.

To illustrate how a procedure can save you effort, we will work through a simple example of a check register database. This sample database, B:CHECKREG, has a plan which is shown as Figure 13-1.

FIELD	FIELD DESCRIPTION	FIELDNAME	TYPE	WIDTH	DECIMALS
1	Check Number	CHECKNO	N	4	
2	Paid To	PAIDTO	C	20	
3	Amount of Check or Dep	AMOUNT	N	7	2
4	Deposit or Check	DEPOSIT	L	1	
5	Deductible (Y/N)	DEDUCT	L	1	
6	Cancelled (Y/N)	CANCEL	L	1	
7	Date (mm/dd/yy)	DATE	D	8	

Figure 13-1. Check Register Database Plan

236

In this particular example we have chosen to have a logic field indicate whether the amount is for a check or a deposit. A "Y" indicates that the amount is a deposit.

To calculate the account balance, proceed with the query language dialogue in Screen 13-1.

Screen 13 - 1

Note the memory variable which stores the sum of the deposits is called MDEPOSIT. The temptation to name the variable DEPOSIT is unfortunate: a data field and a memory variable should not have the same name. It will confuse the computer.

Note: In this example we add all of the checks and all of the deposits each time we calculate the balance. In a conventional checkbook, we usually keep a running balance. With the computer it is often easier to calculate the balance all at one time than to keep a running balance.

As you can see, there are three instructions required to determine the bank balance. We will likely want to know the bank balance often. To save ourselves the work and nuisance of typing three instructions each time we want to know the balance, we will create a means for the computer to "remember" the instructions. A procedure is our means for getting the computer to do this remembering.

The way we get the computer to remember a procedure is by placing the instructions in a special kind of file. The file is then placed on a disk and available whenever we want to use it. In dBASE, this special file is called a

237

command file. A command file provides the capability to "save" a group of commands so that we can use them, as a group, without retyping them each time.

To get the computer to remember a procedure, you must first tell it that you are going to write one. In dBASE, this is accomplished by the command MODIFY COMMAND.

```
.MODIFY COMMAND
```

The computer responds with a request for a filename. The same filename rules apply as have applied for database files and report files. A filename must have eight or fewer letters and must begin with a letter. You should also identify which disk drive the procedure is to be stored on by using a disk drive identifier. In this example we will call the command file BALANCE, and place it on the B drive.

```
Enter filename:  B:BALANCE
```

The video screen then clears and displays

```
dBASE Word Processor
```

in the upper left-hand corner of the screen. There will be no dot prompt. There is nothing wrong—this is just the way the designer implemented the command.

Type in the instructions one after another just as though you were typing on a blank sheet of paper. The typed instructions appear as shown in Screen 13-2.

238

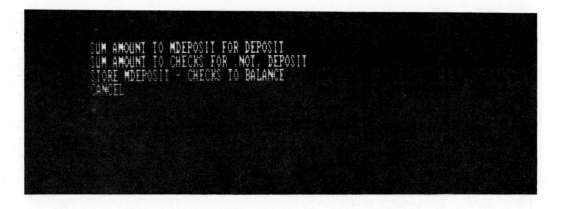

Screen 13 - 2

Note that an extra line has been added to the end of the procedure. This line contains the single word CANCEL. This is to return control of the computer to the keyboard after the computer has completed the procedure.

The computer will not execute the instructions while you are writing a procedure. Since most of us are not perfect typists, the system provides a limited editing capability through use of the control and arrow keys. Editing capabilities and the associated control keys are shown in Figure 13-2.

239

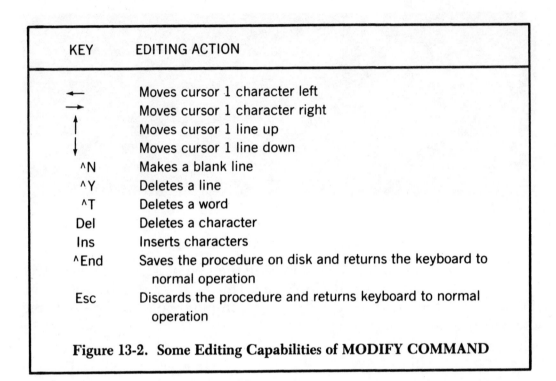

KEY	EDITING ACTION
←	Moves cursor 1 character left
→	Moves cursor 1 character right
↑	Moves cursor 1 line up
↓	Moves cursor 1 line down
^N	Makes a blank line
^Y	Deletes a line
^T	Deletes a word
Del	Deletes a character
Ins	Inserts characters
^End	Saves the procedure on disk and returns the keyboard to normal operation
Esc	Discards the procedure and returns keyboard to normal operation

Figure 13-2. Some Editing Capabilities of MODIFY COMMAND

240

When commands have been typed in as shown in Screen 13-2, simply press <Ctrl-End>. This causes the COMMAND FILE named BALANCE to be written on the B disk: you can use it as often as you desire.

You can use the procedure in B:BALANCE any time the check register database is in use. To have the computer do the procedure B:BALANCE, type DO followed by B:BALANCE, as shown in Screen 13-3. This is certainly easier than typing the instructions each time we want the balance. Note that the result of each instruction is displayed—the instructions themselves are not.

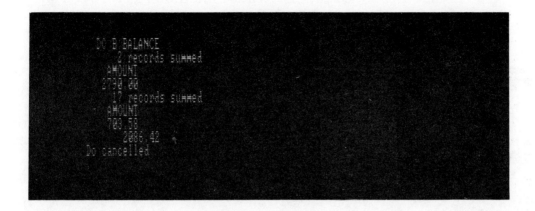

Screen 13 - 3

This is terrific. We only have to type in a couple of words (DO: B:BALANCE) and the answer appears. The only problem might be remembering which number is which. The solution is easy: we simply have the computer display the instructions as well as the answers. The instructions are displayed by using the command SET ECHO ON.

241

So, we want to add to our procedure this request to see the instruction sequence. We insert SET ECHO ON into our existing procedure B:BALANCE by using the command MODIFY COMMAND.

```
.MODIFY COMMAND
Enter filename: B:BALANCE
```

The screen will be erased and the existing file, B:BALANCE, will be displayed. The cursor will be positioned at the upper left corner of the screen directly on the "S" of the first SUM. The command SET ECHO ON is placed on the first line by pressing <Ctrl-N> which provides a blank line—and then typing SET ECHO ON. Move the cursor to the first C of the word CANCEL. Press <Ctrl-N> which provides you with a blank line,

FEATURING dBASE III

then type in SET ECHO OFF (the normal condition). The screen should appear as shown in Screen 13-4.

Screen 13 - 4

242

Press <Ctrl-End> to save the new command file BALANCE on disk drive B. Now, whenever you have the computer execute the procedure B:BALANCE, the results will appear as shown in Screen 13-5.

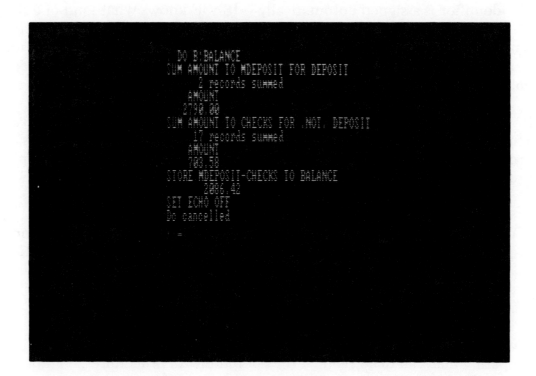

Screen 13 - 5

243

Writing a procedure uses the same "mechanics" as writing a letter. The difference, of course, is that a procedure is written on the computer using a language the computer understands. Most microcomputer database management systems allow you to write procedures in two ways: via an internal feature of the DBMS, or using a word processing system separate from the DBMS.

A word processing system is a special software system designed specifically for working with text. When you use a word processing system to write a procedure, you must type in a FILE IDENTIFIER in addition to the filename and disk drive identifier. A FILE IDENTIFIER consists of a period followed by three letters. When working "inside" *dBASE III*, this file identifier is assigned automatically—dBASE knows what kind of a file you're making by the commands you give it and attaches the file identifier for you. When working from a word processing system, the file identifier must be typed in as part of the name. The word processing system does not know about kinds of files.

In *dBASE III*, the file identifier for procedures (command files) is .PRG. This file identifier lets the database system know that the file is a procedure. When prepared on a word processing system, our sample procedure (command file) would be named B:BALANCE.PRG.

Even if the procedure can be written from within the database system, it is often advantageous to write it with a word processing system. Word processing systems generally offer significantly greater editing capabilities than are available with a DBMS. After all, editing is what word processing systems are for, and editing features are of great value when writing lengthy procedures.

Word processing systems usually provide a special mode for use when preparing material to be read by the computer. All procedures, command files, and computer programs prepared on a word processing system must be written using this mode. The normal word processing mode for preparing letters and documents adds symbols to the text that you cannot see. These are for its internal use in editing, and subsequently printing, the letters and documents. These extra symbols can cause problems if they are inadvertently included in a procedure. If you are not sure which mode to use, consult the user's manual for the word processing system you are using.

SAVE YOURSELF SOME TIME AND MINOR IRRITATION

When the computer executes an instruction such as SUM, it must read the entire database from the disk. The time it takes to read the database depends primarily on the size of the database and the kind of disk drive. A typical floppy disk drive might read the database at 2,300 characters per second. A very small database of 23,000 characters will take ten seconds each time that it is read. A database of 230,000 characters will take 100 seconds.

If you are entering commands manually, you will find that the short delay for the computer to read the database becomes very annoying if the delay is more than about five seconds. Because of this "read" time, it is beneficial to group commands. Whenever entering a number of manual commands, it is often convenient to place the commands into a procedure. This frees you from the annoying short waits of a few to several seconds for each instruction.

245

The idea behind establishing a procedure is to have the computer do all (or at least most) of the work. You give it a list of single instructions, and it does them for you all at once. You are the boss; it is the uncomplaining, loyal slave. If you normally sit at a computer keyboard and interrogate the computer about the contents of your database, you can save yourself a lot of time if you write a procedure that has the computer do what you want it to.

For instance, suppose you want to acquire a lot of information about scotch and gin from our liquor store inventory database. You can sit at the keyboard and enter a series of commands *or* you can write a procedure that is a list of those commands and have the computer run through the commands for you.

```
COUNT FOR LIQUOR='SCOTCH'
COUNT FOR LIQUOR='GIN'
```

```
COUNT FOR LIQUOR='SCOTCH'.AND.SIZE='FIFTH'
```

If you enter these commands from the keyboard, it takes the computer a few seconds to respond to each of them. If the database is large, it may take many seconds for each response. If you enter the commands as a procedure, you can relax and have a cup of coffee while the computer gets you the answers you want. The time it takes the computer might not be any less, but *you* aren't sitting around twiddling your thumbs in between commands while the computer searches for the answers.

A computer follows the set of instructions you give it explicitly. If the computer is to be able to follow the procedure, we must write the instructions in a way the computer can understand. Remember, the computer may be very, very fast, but it isn't very bright. A computer procedure must be written very clearly. You may not assume that the computer "knows" anything.

246

To really get a feeling for this, consider the following example. If we ask a very small child to count to three, he or she can probably manage to do it. To get the computer to count to three is something else. The computer can only count to three if we give it a procedure to count to three. Even after it's done it once, it won't be able to do it again unless the procedure is used.

To illustrate this, an ordinary English version of a computer procedure to count to three is shown below. This procedure is very similar to the procedure a person might follow if using a hand calculator with a memory.

Step 1.   Store a zero in memory
Step 2.   Add one to the contents of the memory and store the
              result in memory
Step 3.   Display the contents of the memory
Step 4.   Add one to the contents of the memory and store the
              result in memory
Step 5.   Display the contents of the memory
Step 6.   Add 1 to the contents of the memory and store the
              result in memory
Step 7.   Display the contents of the memory

When we want the computer to perform this procedure, it must be written differently. The translation of our English to a computer language will be different for each computer language, just as it would differ if we were translating into some other human language such as French or German. In dBASE it will look like this.

```
Step 1.           STORE 0 TO X
Steps 2 and 3.    STORE X + 1 TO X
Steps 4 and 5.    STORE X + 1 TO X
Steps 6 and 7.    STORE X + 1 TO X
```

247

(The procedure itself contains only the terms starting with the word STORE. The step numbers are shown so that you can easily see the correspondence between the two versions of the procedure.)

You should notice two things about this sample procedure.

● We are doing the same thing over and over.
● This approach wouldn't be very practical for doing the same thing a large number of times—like counting to a thousand.

The English version can be rewritten like:

CHAPTER THIRTEEN

Step 1.   Store a zero in memory
Step 2.   Add one to the contents of the memory and store the
            result in memory
Step 3.   Display the contents of the memory
Step 4.   Repeat step 2
Step 5.   Repeat step 3
Step 6.   Repeat step 2
Step 7.   Repeat step 3

In A. A. Milne's book, *Winnie The Pooh*, Winnie and Piglet discover footprints in the snow in front of Piglet's house. Dreaming of great adventure, the two set out to follow the tracks and see where they might lead and what sort of creature might have made them. They follow these footprints on and on until, at last, they find themselves back at Piglet's house. There they find three sets of footprints leading away from Piglet's house. One set is much smaller than the other two. After some debate, they speculate that they are tracking a woozle and a wizzle. Off they go again following the footprints. After a time they find two more sets of footprints have joined the first three. Piglet becomes quite concerned over his safety and discovers he has work to do at home. He leaves. Winnie the Pooh finally determines the footprints are their own . . . they have been going in circles.

In the case of Winnie the Pooh and Piglet, going in circles might have been high adventure, but it really got them nowhere. In our case, however, it turns out that going in circles will get us farther faster. Circles facilitate writing simple procedures.

DO WHILE. . .ENDDO

Simplification #1
Step 1.   Store a zero in memory
Step 2.   Add one to the content of the memory and store the
            result in memory
Step 3.   Display the content of the memory
Step 4.   If memory is less than 3, go to step 2

Simplification #2
Step 1.   Store a zero in memory
Step 2.   Do steps 3 and 4 as long as the content of the memory
            is less than 3
Step 3.   Add one to the content of the memory and store the
            result in memory
Step 4.   Display the content of the memory

The first example is typical of the way you might write a procedure in one of the "traditional" computer languages such as FORTRAN, COBOL, or BASIC. The latter is representative of the "modern" languages such as Pascal, PL/1, and dBASE. Writing our simple counting example (Simplification #2) in dBASE, we get:

249

```
STORE 0 TO X
DO WHILE X<3
STORE X+1 TO X
ENDDO
```

The sideways arrow "<" is arithmetic shorthand meaning "less than." The statement beginning with DO is read as "do while X is less than 3." The arrow turned around (">") means "greater than." The statement could be written "DO WHILE 3>X" which reads "do while 3 is greater than X." The two statements DO WHILE X<3 and DO WHILE 3>X mean exactly the same thing.

FEATURING dBASE III

This new example has just as many instructions as the original did. There is one important difference, however—we can cause the computer to count to a hundred or a thousand or a million just by changing the "3" to the desired counting goal. The command DO WHILE X<3 tells the computer that you want it to keep repeating the following instructions as long as the value of X is less than three. ENDDO signifies the end of the group of instructions begun by DO WHILE. Each DO WHILE must have an ENDDO. DO WHILE—ENDDO is one way of telling the computer to perform the same set of instructions over and over as long as some condition (such as X<3) is valid. The group of statements beginning with DO WHILE and ending with ENDDO is called a *loop*.

INITIALIZING THE LOOP

Immediately in front of the loop we used an instruction that stored the value zero in the memory variable X. You know if you count to three, you begin at one. The computer doesn't know where to begin. It must be told where to begin—as well as how to count. This single instruction—STORE 0 TO X—does two things:

- It stores the value of 0 to X
- It also creates the memory variable X

You are not allowed to use a memory variable in a procedure until the variable has been created. Also, you are not allowed to create the memory variable without giving it an initial value. In this case the variable was created and assigned an initial value with the instruction STORE 0 TO X. The statement "initialized" the loop by providing the starting place and creating the variable X.

ACCUMULATOR: A BASIC CONCEPT

A simple little counting procedure is an accumulator. The accumulator forms the basis of the ordinary adding machine and the hand-held electronic calculator. The basic concept is often used in procedures in database systems business applications.

To accomplish more complex tasks, you use a group of simple procedures. As an example, suppose you want to count by ones to ten and then by tens to one hundred. One way to do this is to use two simple counting loops in succession.

```
STORE 0 TO X
DO WHILE X<10
STORE X+1 TO X
ENDDO

DO WHILE X<100
STORE X+10 TO X
ENDDO
```

AN ALTERNATIVE PROCEDURE: "IF"

251

Another way to achieve exactly the same result is to have the computer take different actions for different values of X. This is, of course, what occurs above, however this procedure takes advantage of the fact that we know everything about X, and about what we want to happen. The computer is capable of making decisions—albeit limited ones. We can take advantage of this capability and write an equivalent procedure.

```
STORE 0 TO X

DO WHILE X<100

  IF X<10
   STORE X+1 TO X
  ENDIF

  IF X>=10
```

```
   STORE X+10 TO X
ENDIF
```

```
ENDDO
```

"IF" is the word we use when we want the computer to make a decision about whether or not to do something. It's used in exactly the same way we ordinarily use the word "if." If it's raining, take an umbrella; if the gas tank is getting low, stop and get gasoline. We use IF when the action to be taken (or conclusion to be drawn) depends on some condition.

In the example, the action is to add one number to another. The condition is the value stored in X. When the computer makes each decision, it doesn't know about the other IF. Each IF must have an ENDIF just as each DO WHILE must have an ENDDO. The information after IF (X is less than ten, X is greater than or equal to ten) is the condition the computer must make a decision about. The decision that it makes after the first IF is whether or not X is less than ten. If it is, the IF applies, and the computer will execute the instruction STORE X + 1 TO X. If it isn't, the computer won't store X + 1 to X.

DO WHILE and IF are the basic tools that can be used for a procedure. These examples employ the specific terminology of dBASE. The concepts, however, are universal and are used in all computer languages. This terminology is similar to that used by modern languages such as PL/1 and Pascal.

To give you a better idea of how you can use DO WHILE and IF, we will write a procedure using these two features that accomplishes the same things as B:BALANCE. We will also take this opportunity to demonstrate how you can exert more control over the displays produced by the computer. The new B:BALANCE is shown as Screen 13-6. The original results of the procedure (Screen 13-1) are reproduced here for your convenience.

```
SUM AMOUNT TO MDEPOSIT FOR DEPOSIT
    2 records summed
   AMOUNT
  2790.00
SUM AMOUNT TO CHECKS FOR .NOT. DEPOSIT
   17 records summed
   AMOUNT
   703.58
STORE MDEPOSIT-CHECKS TO BALANCE
   2086.42
```

In our example, we use instructions which may be unfamiliar to you:

SET TALK OFF/ON
SKIP
DO WHILE.NOT.EOF()
?

253

254

```
USE B:CHECKREG
SET TALK OFF
STORE 0 TO MDEPOSIT,CHECKS
DO WHILE .NOT. EOF()
 IF DEPOSIT
    STORE AMOUNT+MDEPOSIT TO MDEPOSIT
 ENDIF
 IF .NOT. DEPOSIT
   STOR AMOUNT+CHECKS TO CHECKS
 ENDIF
SKIP
ENDDO
? 'TOTAL DEPOSITS ',MDEPOSIT
? 'TOTAL CHECKS  ',CHECKS
? '  BALANCE    ',MDEPOSIT-CHECKS
SET TALK ON
CANCEL_
```

Screen 13 - 6

SET TALK OFF/ON

You may have noticed that many commands—like STORE and SUM— display a response each time they are used. This is one of the ways the computer "talks" to you. Though this is desirable when you are working from your keyboard, it may not be so desirable when using procedures. It clutters up the screen (and/or the printer). In dBASE, the computer's visual response to a command can be turned on and off. SET TALK ON and SET TALK OFF are the commands that do this.

SKIP

The database management system actually works with only one record at a time. When the USE statement is made, the DBMS is positioned to the very top of the database—Record 1. SKIP advances the DBMS one record. When the last record is reached, the next use of SKIP will alert the DBMS that the end of the file has been reached.

DO WHILE.NOT.EOF()

As we have seen in previous examples, the DO WHILE command applies as long as some condition is true. EOF( ) is read as "end of file." The command literally means "computer—do the following until you come to the end of the database." This is probably the most commonly used version of DO WHILE. This will automatically stop the "DO" loop when the end of the database is reached.

255

?

The question mark is a versatile command providing the ability to display specific information. The apostrophes at each end of the text—such as 'TOTAL DEPOSITS'—are called delimiters. Their presence indicates that the enclosed characters are text to be displayed. The memory variable names (DEPOSIT, CHECKS) indicate that the contents of the memory variables are to be displayed. The comma is used to separate items to be displayed. Each question mark produces one line of display.

Our new sample procedure, B:BALANCE, is just a little more complicated than our original version. On the other hand, a few moments of work have produced a result much more tailored to our needs. When we have the computer execute this command file, the display shown in Screen 13-7 is produced.

Screen 13 - 7

Procedures enable you to get more work out of your computer. In this chapter we introduced some basic concepts: the accumulator, the DO loop, the decision (IF), as well as some of the *dBASE III* commands frequently used in procedures. Procedures like the ones in this chapter are fun to write, and ultimately save you both time and effort. In addition, they reduce the chance of error. Once a procedure is correctly written, it enables the computer to perform a function over and over without mistake.

CHAPTER FOURTEEN

MAKING A PROCEDURE WORK FOR YOU

Procedures not only save you time, effort, and money, they also often provide a more satisfactory result. Automating routine activities is one of the more useful things you can make the computer do for you. After all, computers are supposed to make life easier. In this chapter, we will explore a fairly comprehensive example of what a computer plus a database management system can do. Again, we stay in the realm of universal familiarity and "computerize" an ordinary checkbook. The resulting check register process can be used to demonstrate numerous ideas.

The plan for our example database B:CHECKREG is shown in Figure 14-1.

FIELD	FIELD DESCRIPTION	FIELDNAME	TYPE	WIDTH	DECIMALS
1	Check Number	CHECKNO	N	4	
2	Paid To	PAIDTO	C	20	
3	Amount of Check or Dep	AMOUNT	N	7	2
4	Deposit or Check	DEPOSIT	L	1	
5	Deductible (Y/N)	DEDUCT	L	1	
6	Cancelled (Y/N)	CANCEL	L	1	
7	Date (mm/dd/yy)	DATE	D	8	

Figure 14-1. Check Register Database Plan

258

The fields in this plan correspond to an ordinary check register with one major exception: there is no field provided for a running account balance. In a conventional checkbook, it is vital to keep a running balance. With the computer, however, this isn't true, as it is perfectly reasonable to do all of the bookkeeping each time we use the checkbook. This was demonstrated in Chapter Thirteen.

MAKING A MENU

There are a number of routine tasks involved in keeping any checkbook up to date. Among these are:

1.   Entering a check
2.   Entering a deposit
3.   Changing an entry to correct a mistake
4.   Checking to see if you wrote a particular check
5.   Listing deductible checks at tax time
6.   Determining current balance
7.   Comparing balance to bank statement)

Some of these activities are performed as needed. Others are done regularly, that is, daily, monthly, or yearly. All can be accomplished from your computer keyboard using a database and query language. In the long run it is more efficient—and you will feel more confident—if your checkbook maintenance is done using procedures. The procedure establishes an appropriate

In Chapter Thirteen we discussed the basic concept of a procedure as well as the tools used in implementation. In the remainder of this chapter, we will use those tools to write a set of procedures to manage our checkbook. *This set of procedures is intended to illustrate the concept, **not** to be a comprehensive checkbook management package.*

259

To accomplish our objective and accommodate our routine checkbook tasks, we need a total of seven procedures. We have one of these already (number six—Determine Current Balance). Each of the seven is about the same size as our example B:BALANCE. And, because they are all part of the same process—managing a checkbook—it is reasonable to make them items on a menu.

Making a menu is even simpler than our example procedure B:BALANCE. To give a very quick and straightforward treatment to this process, we will take our list of routine tasks and make the menu directly from it. The menu procedure B:BANKMENU is shown in Figure 14-2.

```
USE B:CHECKREG
INDEX ON CHECKNO TO B:CHECKNO
SET TALK OFF
DO WHILE .T.

CLEAR
TEXT


                    CHECK REGISTER MENU

        1.   Enter a Check
        2.   Enter a Deposit
        3.   Changing an entry to correct a mistake
        4.   Seeing if you wrote a particular check
        5.   Listing deductible checks at tax time
        6.   Determine Current Balance
        7.   Balancing (Compare to Bank Balance)
        8.   EXIT

ENDTEXT
WAIT 'Press the number for your selection ' TO SELECTION
CLEAR
IF SELECTION='1'
    DO B:CHECKENT
ENDIF
IF SELECTION='2'
    DO B:DEPOSITS
ENDIF
IF SELECTION='3'
    DO B:CHANGES
ENDIF
IF SELECTION='4'
    DO B:LOOK
ENDIF
```

```
    IF SELECTION='5'
        DO B:DEDUCT
    ENDIF
    IF SELECTION='6'
        DO B:BALANCE
    ENDIF
    IF SELECTION='7'
        DO B:CHKBANK
    ENDIF
    IF SELECTION='8'
        SET TALK ON
        CANCEL
    ENDIF
    ENDDO
```

Figure 14-2. Check Register Menu

Once again we have introduced a few new instructions. These are:

```
DO WHILE.T.
CLEAR
WAIT <PROMPT> TO SELECTION
TEXT/ENDTEXT
```

DO WHILE.T./ENDDO
This literally means "do forever." The DO WHILE statement usually means "do while the following condition is true." In this case .T. (for true) is always true. Since we really don't want to go through this loop forever, we have included menu item 8, which provides an escape from the loop back to the database management system.

CLEAR
This instruction erases any existing text from the screen.

WAIT <PROMPT> TO SELECTION
The WAIT command causes a procedure to pause. You can restart a procedure by pressing any character. WAIT <PROMPT> TO SELECTION means to store whatever number you press for your selection in the memory variable SELECTION. The contents of SELECTION then tell the computer which procedure to do. The prompt is an optional text message that will be displayed on the screen. In Screen 14-1 and Figure 14-2, the prompt is "Press the number for your selection."

TEXT. . .ENDTEXT
This pair of commands is used to display the text appearing between them.

262

The menu procedure works like this. Entering the command DO B:BANKMENU will cause the menu to appear on the screen as shown in Screen 14-1. Figure 14-2 creates Screen 14-1.

Press the number key that corresponds to your selection. This is another case where you do not need to use the <RETURN> key. The number you press is stored in the memory variable SELECTION as a character. The IF instruction that matches your selection causes the computer to execute a procedure. For example, if you choose item 6, "Determine current balance," the computer will execute the command file B:BALANCE.

The first set of instructions in the menu procedure (Figure 14-2) will index the database according to check number. You would not normally put the commands to INDEX the database into this program. The indexing operation is shown only to point out that the procedure is based on using an indexed database.

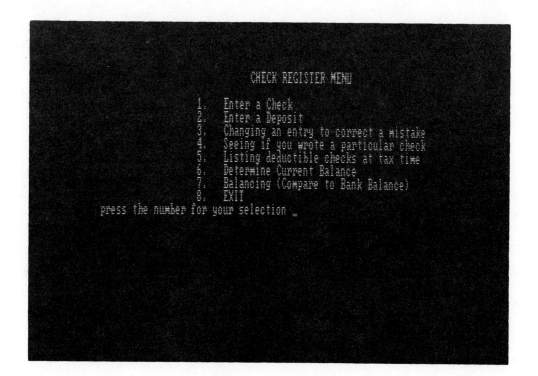

```
                    CHECK REGISTER MENU
              1.   Enter a Check
              2.   Enter a Deposit
              3.   Changing an entry to correct a mistake
              4.   Seeing if you wrote a particular check
              5.   Listing deductible checks at tax time
              6.   Determine Current Balance
              7.   Balancing (Compare to Bank Balance)
              8.   EXIT
         press the number for your selection _
```

Screen 14 - 1

MENU OPTION #1

Pressing the "1" key selects menu option 1, entry of a new check into your computerized checkbook. This could, of course, also be accomplished by the command APPEND, but in this example we want to illustrate a means of accomplishing the results of APPEND while providing fully descriptive prompts for each data item.

One procedure that allows entry of a new check is shown in Figure 14-3.

FEATURING dBASE III

```
APPEND BLANK
INPUT 'Enter Check Number   ' TO MCHECKNO
ACCEPT 'Paid to the Order of   ' TO MPAIDTO
INPUT 'Enter Amount of Check   ' TO MAMOUNT
ACCEPT 'Enter Date (mm/dd/yy)   ' TO MDATE
INPUT 'Is This Check Deductible (.Y./.N.)   ' TO MDEDUCT
REPLACE CHECKNO WITH MCHECKNO, PAIDTO WITH MPAIDTO, AMOUNT;
   WITH MAMOUNT, DATE WITH CTOD(MDATE), DEDUCT WITH MDEDUCT,;
   DEPOSIT WITH .N., CANCEL WITH .N.
RETURN
```

Figure 14-3. A Preliminary Procedure for Check Entry

264

Again, we introduce a few new commands:

    ACCEPT
    INPUT
    RETURN
    APPEND BLANK

ACCEPT And INPUT

ACCEPT and INPUT offer a means for the computer to "ask" you to enter data from the keyboard during a procedure. INPUT is used to enter numeric or logical data. ACCEPT is used to enter character data. Otherwise they are the same. The command form is demonstrated by the examples in Figure 14-3. The command displays the desired text, creates a memory variable such as MCHECKNO, and waits for you to enter the data. A weakness of this approach is that INPUT requires that you enter "Y" as .Y. and "N" as .N. .

RETURN

RETURN is similar to CANCEL in that it terminates the procedure— in this case, the check entering procedure—returning control of the computer to the main menu program B:BANKMENU. CANCEL would terminate the entire operation, returning computer control to the dot prompt.

APPEND BLANK

APPEND BLANK, often used with procedures, is a variation of the APPEND command. APPEND is used to add a record to the database. APPEND BLANK adds a blank record, but does not display the record for data entry. In this example, a blank record is created, data is entered into memory variables with ACCEPT and INPUT commands, and then the data is transferred from the memory variables into the blank record using the REPLACE command. Notice that it is not necessary to SET TALK OFF, since that has already been accomplished by the main menu procedure B:BANKMENU (Figure 14-2).

265

In this particular example, the prompts are displayed and the data entered one instruction at a time. From this standpoint, the procedure is not as effective as APPEND, since the cursor cannot be moved back to correct a previous data item. Since the date is entered here using the ACCEPT command, MDATE is a character variable. To convert it to a date variable, use the CTOD (Character to date) function.

A computer display similar to APPEND with more descriptive prompts replacing the fieldnames would be far more desirable. In addition, for more relaxed data entry, the cursor should be movable backwards one or more fields to correct errors. This is accomplished within dBASE using special commands provided for exactly this purpose.

ALTERNATE MENU OPTION #1

The general form of the *dBASE III* command is:

FEATURING dBASE III

```
@ ROW,COLUMN SAY 'Whatever You Want' GET FIELDNAME
READ
```

The first of these, the "@" command, allows data positioning control on the screen. Most computer terminals have a video screen with 24 rows of 80 characters each. The rows are numbered from top to bottom, 0 to 23. The columns (character positions) are numbered from left to right, 0 to 79. To display the words THIS IS AN EXAMPLE on line row, beginning with column ten, the command reads

```
@ 5,10 SAY 'THIS IS AN EXAMPLE'
```

The text, THIS IS AN EXAMPLE, will be displayed in standard video just as the fieldnames are in APPEND.

Similarly, the contents of a field named PAIDTO could be displayed by

```
@ 5,10 GET PAIDTO
```

This example displays the current contents of the field PAIDTO in reverse video—as when using the EDIT command.

The two examples can be combined as

```
@ 5,10 SAY 'THIS IS AN EXAMPLE' GET PAIDTO
READ
```

The command READ allows you to change the field contents identified with GET, in this case, the contents of the field PAIDTO. An example procedure to enter checks using these commands is shown in Figure 14-4.

This procedure will cause the computer to behave in a manner very similar to APPEND, except that descriptive prompts replace the

266

```
APPEND BLANK
@ 5,10 SAY 'Enter Check Number' GET CHECKNO
@ 7,10 SAY 'Paid to the Order of' GET PAIDTO
@ 9,10 SAY 'Enter the Amount of Check' GET AMOUNT
@ 11,10 SAY 'Enter Date (mm/dd/yy)' GET DATE
@ 13,10 SAY 'Is This Check Deductible (Y/N)' GET DEDUCT
READ
REPLACE DEPOSIT WITH .N., CANCEL WITH .N.
RETURN
```

Figure 14-4

267

fieldnames. All the control keys for moving the cursor behave just as in APPEND. Note that all the fields in our database are not displayed—only those relevant to this procedure.

The display produced by this procedure, and specifically by the READ command, is shown as Screen 14-2. The cursor is in the first character position of the CHECKNO field—ready to enter data.

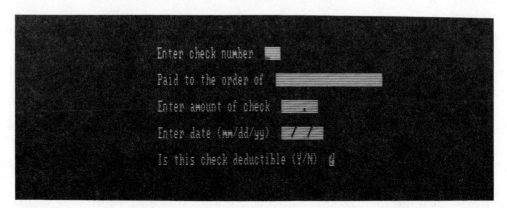

Screen 14 - 2

Since check numbers are usually sequential, you can save a small amount of bother by having the computer enter the check numbers for you. The revised procedure to accomplish this is shown in Figure 14-5.

```
GO BOTTOM
STORE CHECKNO+1 TO NEXTCHECK
APPEND BLANK
REPLACE CHECKNO WITH NEXTCHECK, DEPOSIT WITH .N., CANCEL WITH .N.
@ 5,10 SAY 'CHECK NUMBER' GET CHECKNO
CLEAR GETS
@ 7,10 SAY 'PAID TO THE ORDER OF' GET PAIDTO
@ 9,10 SAY 'ENTER AMOUNT OF CHECK' GET AMOUNT
@ 11,10 SAY 'ENTER DATE (mm/dd/yy)' GET DATE
@ 13,10 SAY 'IS THIS CHECK DEDUCTIBLE (Y/N)' GET DEDUCT
READ
RETURN
```

Figure 14-5. Procedure for Check Entry B:CHECKENT

The command GO BOTTOM positions the record pointer to the last record in the database. This record contains the last check number used. The check number you want to enter must be the number following that one. This new check number is temporarily stored to the memory variable NEXTCHECK by STORE CHECKNO+1 TO NEXTCHECK. A blank record is added to the database. The new check number is written in the blank record by REPLACE CHECKNO WITH NEXTCHECK.

The instruction CLEAR GETS prevents cursor movement to the fields displayed by GET commands prior to the CLEAR GETS. The display produced by this procedure is shown as Screen 14-3. Note that this display is almost the same as Screen 14-2, except that the cursor is positioned to the first character of PAIDTO and the check number is already filled in.

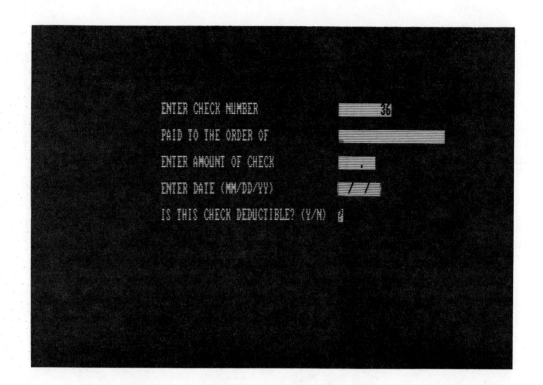

Screen 14 - 3

MENU OPTION #2

Our next procedure allows you to enter deposits in your electronic
bankbook. Figure 14-6 illustrates the deposit entry procedure, named
B:DEPOSITS.

```
APPEND BLANK
REPLACE DEPOSIT WITH .Y., PAIDTO WITH '*DEPOSIT*'
@ 9,10 SAY 'ENTER AMOUNT OF DEPOSIT' GET AMOUNT
@ 11,10 SAY 'ENTER DATE' GET DATE
READ
RETURN
```
Figure 14-6. Procedure For Entering A Deposit

It is similar to, but much simpler than B:CHECKENT, the procedure for entering checks. Screen 14-4 is the display produced by B:DEPOSITS.

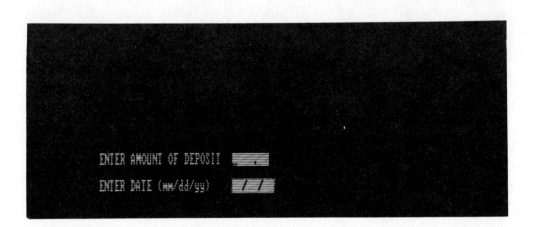

Screen 14 - 4

Again, the procedure is similar to APPEND, except for added detail in the descriptive prompts and the fact that all fields are not displayed.

MENU OPTION #3

The third menu selection allows "error correction," change of a previously entered record. In dBASE, this could be accomplished with either the EDIT or BROWSE commands. As you may suspect, you can write a procedure similar to EDIT, except prompts will be descriptive text rather than fieldnames.

A procedure that will do this is shown as Figure 14-7.

Our first problem is how to find the record we want. If we want to change a check entry, this is pretty simple—we have the computer find the record containing the check number for the check entry we want to change. If we have a deposit, however, we have to find the record some other way, because there is no check number field entry when entering a deposit.

In our example database, there is no unique deposit record identification (except, of course, for the record number). This points out the need for planning. Our lack of planning leads us to seek a work-around solution. Though it is tempting to use the date as our change criteria, even if we never have more than one deposit per day, we can err when entering a deposit such that there will appear to be two deposit entries per day. Our solution will be to use the record number as well as the date as the identifying criteria. Displaying all records for a particular date enables access to the appropriate record number.

The procedure has two sections, selected according to whether or not the record we wish to change is a check:

(1)   If it is a check, we find the record containing the desired check number and then produce the same display we used to enter data into a check record. The record is found by the SEEK command and the memory variable FINDER. SEEK VAL(FINDER) means to find the record corresponding to the check number stored in FINDER.

272

```
WAIT 'PRESS C FOR CHECK, D FOR DEPOSIT:' TO TYPE

IF TYPE='C'
    CLEAR
    STORE SPACE(4) TO FINDER
    @ 5,10 SAY 'ENTER CHECK NUMBER:' GET FINDER
    READ
    SEEK VAL(FINDER)
    IF EOF( )
      RETURN
    ENDIF
    @ 5,10 SAY 'CHECK NUMBER:' GET CHECKNO
    CLEAR GETS
    @ 7,10 SAY 'PAID TO THE ORDER OF:' GET PAIDTO
    @ 9,10 SAY 'ENTER AMOUNT OF CHECK:' GET AMOUNT
    @ 11,10 SAY 'ENTER DATE (mm/dd/yy):' GET DATE
    @ 13,10 SAY 'IS THIS CHECK DEDUCTIBLE (Y/N):' GET DEDUCT
    READ
ENDIF
IF TYPE='D'
    STORE DATE() TO FINDER
    @ 5,10 SAY 'ENTER DATE OF DEPOSIT:' GET FINDER
    READ
    DISPLAY FOR DEPOSIT .AND. DATE=FINDER
    STORE 0 TO FINDER
    INPUT 'ENTER RECORD NUMBER TO BE EDITED: ' TO FINDER
    GOTO FINDER
    CLEAR
    @ 9,10 SAY 'ENTER AMOUNT OF DEPOSIT:' GET AMOUNT
    @ 11,10 SAY 'ENTER DATE (mm/dd/yy):' GET DATE
    READ
ENDIF
RETURN
```

Figure 14-7. A Procedure For Changing A Record

(2)   The second section deals with the need to change a deposit record, not a check record. The computer first asks for the date, displays the deposit records for that date, and then asks for the record number of the deposit to be changed. GOTO FINDER positions the database to the record with the record number stored in FINDER. The change display is the same as that used to enter information into a deposit record.

MENU OPTION #4

The fourth menu item provides for looking at the check register contents to determine whether or not you wrote a particular check. Figure 14-8 is a simple procedure providing a cursory "look through" capability.

273

```
USE B:CHECKREG
INPUT 'ENTER MONTH ' TO MO
INPUT 'ENTER YEAR (19XX) ' TO YR
DISPLAY FOR MONTH(DATE)=MO .AND. YEAR(DATE)=YR
USE B:CHECKREG INDEX B:CHECKNO
WAIT
RETURN
```

Figure 14-8. A Procedure To Look Through The Check Register

This procedure provides for display of all records from a particular month. In this case we use the database without the index file, because the index file separates the deposit records and check records and we would ordinarily want to see them displayed together in time sequence.

CHAPTER FOURTEEN

The procedure displays (in record order) the records for a designated month and year. The records are displayed one screenful at a time. (This is the way DISPLAY works.) After each screenful is displayed, the message "Press any key to continue . . ." will appear. Don't press the <Esc> key; it will take you out of the procedure.

The DISPLAY command compares the month entered to the month stored in DATE, and the year entered to the year stored in DATE.

When the procedure is complete, the indexed file is again selected for use.

This menu item is a good candidate for a second menu, although we will not include one here. The second menu would include a selection of possible displays, in many cases the kind of REPORTS used in the liquor store inventory example of Chapter Two.

MENU OPTION #5

Menu item five—listing deductible checks—allows the opportunity to use a REPORT FORM within a command file. Figure 14-9 shows the deductible check listing procedure.

```
ACCEPT 'DO YOU WANT A PRINTED COPY (Y/N)   ' TO QUERY
IF QUERY='Y'
   REPORT FORM B:DEDUCT TO PRINT FOR DEDUCT
ENDIF
IF QUERY='N'
   REPORT FORM B:DEDUCT FOR DEDUCT
ENDIF
RETURN
```

Figure 14-9. A Procedure That Uses A Report As Output

The resulting report is shown as Figure 14-10. Reports are a convenient way to display data.

```
PAGE NO. 00001
02/01/82
                                   DEDUCTIBLE EXPENSES

 CHECK
   NO          PAID TO            DATE          AMOUNT

  208      WRACKING PAIN HOSP     6/22/81          98.50
  227      QP COMPUTERS           8/14/81        4011.04
  234      DR DENTAL,DDS (KEN)    8/21/81          91.00
  267      QP COMPUTERS          10/24/81         486.38
  289      COMPUTE-AWHILE        11/27/81          79.50
  323      LEMON MICRO           01/23/82        1257.16
  324      QP ELECTRONICS        01/23/82         344.50

** TOTAL **                                      6368.08
```

Figure 14-10

MENU OPTION #6

Menu item six determines the current account balance. This procedure is nearly identical to B:BALANCE, Screen 13-6, developed in the previous chapter. Figure 14-11 shows this variation.

```
USE B:CHECKREG
STORE 0 TO MDEPOSIT, CHECKS
DO WHILE .NOT.EOF()
  IF DEPOSIT
    STORE AMOUNT+MDEPOSIT TO MDEPOSIT
  ELSE
    STORE AMOUNT+CHECKS TO CHECKS
  ENDIF
SKIP
ENDDO
@ 5,15 SAY 'TOTAL DEPOSITS' GET MDEPOSIT
@ 7,15 SAY 'TOTAL CHECKS' GET CHECKS
STORE MDEPOSIT-CHECKS TO BALANCE
@ 9,15 SAY 'BALANCE' GET BALANCE
CLEAR GETS
WAIT
USE B:CHECKREG INDEX B:CHECKNO
RETURN
```

Figure 14-11. Procedure To Calculate The Current Account Balance

Here we use the dBASE @ command for the display as shown in Screen 14-5. Another difference from the original B:BALANCE is the use of the RETURN command instead of the CANCEL command.

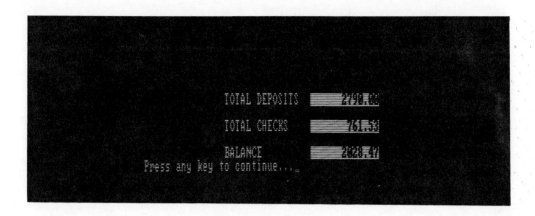

Screen 14 - 5

Because it takes less time to calculate the balance using the unindexed B:CHECKREG, we do not use the indexed database for this procedure. This time efficiency results from reading the records sequentially instead of jumping back and forth according to the index. An indexed database requires movement back and forth; and, hence, the disk read head must also move back and forth.

MENU OPTION #7

The seventh menu entry checks up on the bank. You need a way to monitor how well the bank is taking care of your account. This procedure is one way to do that.

Balancing a checking account is sometimes called "reconciliation." Whatever it's called, it always consists of four parts:

(1) Checking off cancelled checks
(2) Checking off cancelled deposits
(3) Entering bank charges

(4)   Take your final balance
       add outstanding checks
       subtract outstanding deposits
       compare the result to the bank's balance

The procedure to reconcile your account is shown in Figure 14-12. This procedure is also a menu, allowing you to undertake each of the four parts and deal with each until you are satisfied.

```
STORE '   ' TO CHOICE
DO WHILE .NOT. CHOICE = '5'
CLEAR
@ 5,15 SAY '(1) Check off cancelled Checks'
@ 7,15 SAY '(2) Check off cancelled Deposits'
@ 9,15 SAY '(3) Enter bank charges'
@ 11,15 SAY '(4) Compare bank balance to your balance'
@ 13,15 SAY '(5) Return to the main menu'
@ 20,15 SAY 'Enter your selection' GET CHOICE
READ
DO CASE
CASE CHOICE='1'
     DO B:BALMENU1
CASE CHOICE='2'
     DO B:BALMENU2
CASE CHOICE='3'
     DO B:BALMENU3
CASE CHOICE='4'
     DO B:BALMENU4
ENDCASE
ENDDO
RETURN
```

Figure 14-12. A Checkbook Balancing Menu

If you compare this menu with the main check register menu, you find a few differences. These differences illustrate the principle that you can often accomplish the same result in different ways.

DO WHILE .T. is replaced by DO WHILE .NOT.CHOICE='5'. Entering 5 terminates the DO loop and returns you to the first (main) menu. Selection of a character which is not a menu choice will redisplay the menu.

A new command, DO CASE is introduced in this example. Similar in concept to IF, DO CASE is often used where there are a number of choices for action and the choices are exclusive. Only one of the possible cases is acted on—even if several apply. The first case to satisfy the condition is acted on. In a string of IFs, it is possible that more than one would satisfy some condition and be acted on—even if the choice is undesirable.

The way the procedures are named in this construction is preferable to that used for the main menu example. Choice of a procedure name should allow easy identification of that specific procedure, if you come across the name in some other context.

CHECKING OFF CANCELLED CHECKS

The first menu item of this submenu allows cancellation of checks that have cleared the bank. In the example procedure shown in Figure 14-13, the check record is found and the pertinent data is displayed on the screen so you can be sure it's what you want. If the record displayed is the one you want, you cancel the record. A representative display from this procedure is shown in Screen 14-6.

```
STORE '    ' TO ENABLE
STORE 0 TO NUMBER,TOTAL
DO WHILE .NOT. ENABLE = 'X'
   CLEAR
   STORE 0 TO FINDER
   @ 5,10 SAY 'Enter Check Number' GET FINDER
   READ
   SEEK FINDER
   IF .NOT. EOF()
      @ 7,10 SAY 'Check Paid To' GET PAIDTO
      @ 9,10 SAY 'The Amount Is' GET AMOUNT
      @ 7,50 SAY 'Dated' GET DATE
      CLEAR GETS
      @ 9,50 SAY 'Cancel (Y/N)' GET CANCEL
      READ
      IF CANCEL
         STORE TOTAL+AMOUNT TO TOTAL
         STORE NUMBER+1 TO NUMBER
         @ 12,1 SAY 'Number of Checks Cancelled' GET NUMBER
         @ 12,40 SAY 'Totaling' GET TOTAL
      ENDIF
      CLEAR GETS
      @ 15,10 SAY 'Enter X When Finished – RETURN To Continue' GET ENABLE
      READ
   ENDIF
ENDDO
RETURN
```

Figure 14-13. A Procedure For 'Cancelling Checks'

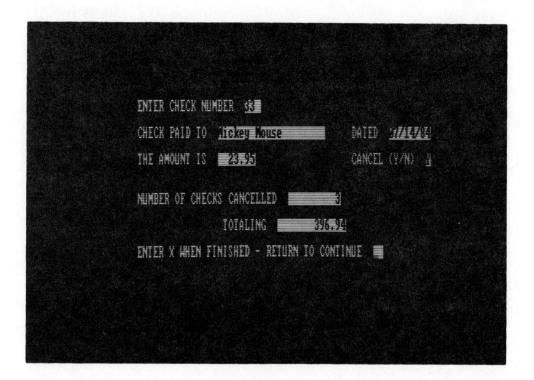

Screen 14 - 6

When you have finished entering cancelled checks, the number of checks cancelled and their total value should agree with the bank's statement. If not, you need to determine why the totals do not agree. The procedure can be repeated if necessary.

CHECKING OFF CANCELLED DEPOSITS

Having completed the check cancelling procedure, you move on to deposit "cancelling." The procedure to accomplish this is B:BALMENU2, which is shown in Figure 14-14.

```
STORE .T. TO ENABLE
STORE 0 TO NR,DEP
DO WHILE ENABLE
   CLEAR
   ? 'When finished enter - STOP - for the record number'
   ?
   DISPLAY AMOUNT,DATE FOR DEPOSIT.AND..NOT.CANCEL

   ACCEPT 'Enter Record Number to be cancelled    ' TO F1
   IF UPPER(F1) = 'STOP'
      STORE .F. TO ENABLE
   ELSE
      STORE VAL(F1) TO FINDER
      GOTO FINDER
      STORE NR+1 TO NR
      STORE DEP+AMOUNT TO DEP
      REPLACE CANCEL WITH .Y.
   ENDIF
ENDDO
CLEAR
@ 10,10 SAY 'Number of cancelled deposits' GET NR
@ 15,10 SAY 'Total value was' GET DEP
WAIT
RETURN
```

Figure 14-14. A Procedure to Cancel Deposits

In this example we "turn off" the DO loop from within the procedure. This loop operates as long as the memory variable ENABLE is true. Note that the .T. and .F. do not need to be enclosed in delimiters because the computer assumes them to be LOGICAL values, .T. stands for true and .F. for false.

Note also that the record number was stored as a character set. (ACCEPT is a way to tell the computer the data entered are characters.) If we use INPUT, we cannot enter the word "stop" into the memory variable F1.

Since we stored the record number as a character string, we need to convert it back to a number if we are to use the command GOTO. Accomplish this with the command STORE VAL(F1) TO FINDER. This means store the value of F1 to the memory variable FINDER. As you might expect, numbers can also be converted to characters.

ENTERING BANK CHARGES

The third procedure in this menu allows you to enter bank charges into the database. The procedure for accomplishing this is shown as Figure 14-15.

```
CLEAR
APPEND BLANK
@ 5,5 SAY 'ENTER BANK CHARGES' GET AMOUNT
@ 7,5 SAY 'ENTER DATE (mm/dd/yy)' GET DATE
READ
REPLACE DEPOSIT WITH .N.,PAIDTO WITH 'BANK CHARGE', ;
  CANCEL WITH .Y.
RETURN
```
Figure 14-15. A Procedure to Enter Bank Charges

Since charges and checks are both debits against the account, the charges were treated as checks so the arithmetic works correctly. Charges are also cancelled at the time of entry, because they are part of the statement.

Menu item four provides for comparison of your version of the account balance to the bank's conclusion. A procedure to accomplish this is shown as Figure 14-16.

```
CLEAR
BANKBAL = 0.00
SUM AMOUNT TO SPENT FOR CANCEL .AND..NOT.DEPOSIT
SUM AMOUNT TO EARNED FOR CANCEL .AND. DEPOSIT
@ 5,10 say "Enter bank's version of balance" GET BANKBAL;
            picture '@Z ##,###.##'
READ
STORE EARNED-SPENT TO MYBALANCE
STORE BANKBAL-MYBALANCE TO BANKSERROR

@ 10,10 SAY 'My version of balance . . . . . . . . . .' GET MYBALANCE;
            picture '##,###.##'
@ 15,10 SAY "The bank's error is . . . . . . . . . ." GET BANKSERROR;
            picture '##,###.##'
CLEAR GETS
WAIT
RETURN
```

Figure 14-16. Procedure For Monthly Balancing

In this example we did not need to consider outstanding checks and deposits. You do this normally in a paper checkbook because of the running balance. In the computer checkbook we ignore outstanding entries and work with the same set of data the bank uses. If all of the data is entered correctly, the resulting display should be like that shown in Screen 14-7.

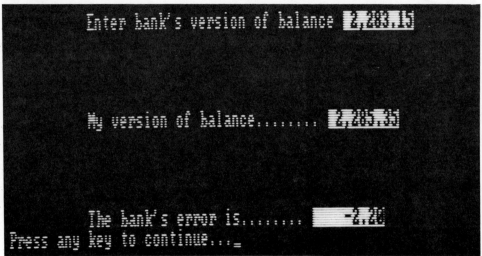

Screen 14 - 7

In this chapter we have attempted to describe a complete database system for maintaining a check register. Some details were overlooked in the interest of describing the basic concepts involved. Also, many banks today offer interest-paying checking accounts. Because of this, a real check register menu should also include an entry for bank credits. In any case, a menu system is a convenient way of using the computer for routine tasks to be accomplished on a daily, weekly, or other periodic basis. The menu may contain submenus for more complex tasks. As a rule, the more frequently used menu items would be on the highest or main menus and those least frequently used would be on the lowest or submenus.

CHAPTER FIFTEEN

SPECIAL REPORTS

You can use procedures to prepare special reports in just about any format you desire. Procedures can be used to prepare reports that cannot normally be obtained from the DBMS's Report Writer. Though procedures may take a little more effort than is required to obtain a report from the Report Writer, the result will be worth it.

To illustrate the use of procedures to prepare special reports, we will work through an example of a typical report that cannot easily be accommodated by the standard report writer.

An elementary school uses a database management system for student record keeping. At the beginning of the school year, and periodically thereafter, it is desirable to provide copies of class lists to staff members such as the school nurse, the librarian, the school secretary, and the classroom teacher.

The school database contains, among other items, fields which record each student's progress in reading and mathematics, room number, grade, teacher's name, and whether or not the student was retained in grade. The relevant parts of the database structure are shown in Figure 15-1.

FIELDNAME	FIELDTYPE	WIDTH
NAME	C	20
ROOM	C	3
GRADE	C	1
TEACHER	C	15
RETAINED	L	1
READING	N	2
MATH	N	2
SEX	C	1

Figure 15-1. School Database Structure (Partial)

The school wants to print and distribute class rosters which look like the one shown in Figure 15-2.

```
                        SPECTACULAR SCHOOL

TEACHER: WISEMAN                              9 SEPTEMBER 1982
ROOM:    101
GRADE:   6

          CLASS ROSTER FOR THE 1982/1983 SCHOOL YEAR
```

NAME	READING	MATH	
Aardvark, Anthony	21	88	
Anerson, Hann	43	29	
Apple, Wise	87	29	RETAINED
.	.	.	
.	.	.	
Zachary, Abram	34	19	

```
CLASS SIZE: 28
BOYS:     14
GIRLS:    14

READING AVERAGE: 43.32
MATH AVERAGE:    62.67
```

Figure 15-2. Example Of Special Report

This particular example cannot be prepared in this format using *dBASE III*'s standard report writer. The bulk of the report can be handled by REPORT, of course. It is the special annotation of

TEACHER	BOYS
ROOM	GIRLS
GRADE	READING AVERAGE
CLASS SIZE	MATH AVERAGE

that cannot be readily accommodated by REPORT.

```
SET TALK OFF
USE B:SCHOOL
INDEX ON GRADE+ROOM+NAME TO B:ROSTER
GO TOP
SET MARGIN TO 15
STORE STR(DAY(DATE()),2)+' '+CMONTH(DATE()) ;
      +STR(YEAR(DATE()),5) TO CALDATE
SET PRINT ON
DO WHILE .NOT. EOF()
?
?
?
?
?
? '                    SPECTACULAR SCHOOL'
?
? 'TEACHER: ',TEACHER,'                              ',CALDATE
? 'ROOM    : ',ROOM
? 'GRADE   : ',GRADE
?
? '        CLASS ROSTER FOR THE 1984/1985 SCHOOL YEAR'
? '-----------------------------------------------------------------',
? ' NAME                  READING                 MATH'        ,
? '-----------------------------------------------------------------'
?
STORE ROOM TO MROOM
STORE GRADE TO MGRADE
STORE 0 TO BOYS,GIRLS,XREADING,XMATH
```

```
DO WHILE ROOM=MROOM .AND. GRADE=MGRADE .AND..NOT. EOF()
   STORE '   ' TO RET
   IF RETAINED
      STORE 'RETAINED' TO RET
   ENDIF
   ? NAME, '     ',READING, '                    ',MATH, '                ',RET
   IF SEX='M'
      STORE BOYS+1 TO BOYS
   ELSE
      STORE GIRLS+1 TO GIRLS
   ENDIF
   STORE READING+XREADING TO XREADING
   STORE MATH+XMATH TO XMATH
   SKIP
ENDDO
?
?
?  ' CLASS SIZE:',STR(BOYS+GIRLS,2)
?  ' BOYS:      ',STR(BOYS,2)
?  ' GIRLS:     ',STR(GIRLS,2)
?
?  ' READING AVERAGE:  ',STR(XREADING/(BOYS+GIRLS),6,2)
?  ' MATH AVERAGE:      ',STR(XMATH/ (BOYS+GIRLS),6,2)
EJECT
ENDDO
SET PRINT OFF
SET TALK ON


CANCEL
```

Figure 15-3

This procedure will provide a set of printed reports with each class roster printed on a separate page. It is completely tailored to the needs and desires of the people who want it. In the following paragraphs we will go over this procedure and describe each step in some detail.

To accomplish this we will start out with the basic element of this procedure. Then we will add new elements and continue to iterate, or repeat, until we arrive at the final procedure. At each iteration we will add the new or changed statements in bold faced type. The most basic element is to do a loop that produces a continuous listing of all of the students in the school (this is nothing more than a procedural version of the command LIST).

```
SET TALK OFF
DO WHILE .NOT. EOF()
   ? NAME, READING, MATH
   SKIP
ENDDO
SET TALK ON
CANCEL
```

Figure 15-4. Procedural Version of dBASE Command List

SET TALK OFF/ON
Nearly all procedures will begin and end with the command. Though it may be desirable for the computer to respond to you each time you issue a command from the keyboard, this is not true when using procedures. You will wish to inhibit the computer from "talking" except when you want it to. In this case, we want to see field contents, but we don't want to have the computer echo the record number from the command SKIP.

SKIP

This command will advance the database one record each time it is used. If we had not SET TALK OFF, the computer would display the record number each time SKIP was used.

If SKIP is used with a database that is not indexed, the records will be advanced in the order of the record numbers. If an indexed database is used, the records will be advanced in their "logical" order.

DO WHILE.NOT.EOF()

This command tells the computer to repeat the commands DISPLAY and SKIP until the end of the database file is reached.

In our next step of explaining the example special report procedure, we will:

- Tell the computer which database to use
- INDEX the database by class
- Tell the computer to use the indexed database
- Display only the fields that we desire

```
SET TALK OFF
USE B:SCHOOL
INDEX ON GRADE+ROOM+NAME TO B:ROSTER
GO TOP
DO WHILE .NOT. EOF ()
   ? NAME,READING,MATH
   SKIP
ENDDO
SET TALK ON
CANCEL
```

Figure 15-5. Modified Procedural Version of dBASE Command LIST

This procedure now produces a screen display with the students displayed alphabetically by grade and room. The ? prevents the record number from being displayed, and requires less typing than DISPLAY OFF. Only the contents of the fields NAME, READING, and MATH will be displayed.

For our next step we will add the commands to produce a simple printout of the class rosters. At this step in our development of this procedure, the resulting printout would be very crude. Each class roster would be just a list of student name, reading level and math level—beginning at the very top of the page. There would not be any left margin.

```
SET TALK OFF
USE B:SCHOOL
INDEX ON GRADE+ROOM+NAME TO B:ROSTER
USE B:SCHOOL INDEX B:ROSTER
SET PRINT ON
DO WHILE .NOT. EOF()
    STORE ROOM TO MROOM
    STORE GRADE TO MGRADE
    DO WHILE ROOM=MROOM.AND.GRADE=MGRADE.AND..NOT.EOF()
    ? NAME,READING,MATH
    SKIP
    ENDDO
    EJECT
ENDDO
SET PRINT OFF
SET TALK ON
CANCEL
```

Figure 15-6. Elementary Version Of Class Roster Procedure

295

SET PRINT ON/OFF
This turns the printer on and off. You should usually turn the printer on after you SET TALK OFF. Similarly, turn the printer off before you SET TALK ON.

STORE ROOM TO MROOM
STORE GRADE TO MGRADE
These two commands allow you to set up the DO loop for listing each class separately. They allow the computer to automatically establish the beginning and end of a class grouping.

DO WHILE ROOM=MROOM.AND.;
GRADE=MGRADE.AND..NOT.EOF()
Here we have a DO loop within a DO loop. The inner DO loop is fully contained within the outer loop. As long as each record meets the conditions:

- The room number is the same as MROOM
- The grade is the same as MGRADE
- The end of file is not encountered

the procedure will continue to print out each student name, reading level, and math level. Note the double period between AND and NOT. Though this may look odd, this is the correct way to enter the condition.

EJECT
This causes the printer paper to be advanced to the next sheet.

This procedure is relatively straightforward. The outer loop allows the entire database to be listed. Once we enter the outer loop DO WHILE .NOT. EOF() the room and grade of the first record will be stored to the memory variables MROOM and MGRADE. Then we enter the inner loop. This inner loop will be repeated until the database is advanced to a record where ROOM and GRADE do not equal the contents of the memory variables MROOM and MGRADE. When this occurs, the paper is ejected and we go back to the beginning of the outer loop, store the new room and grade to the memory variables, and continue. If we encounter the end of file marker, we turn the printer off and we are through. Note that the inner loop also has .NOT.EOF() as a part of its condition.

At this point we are ready to add the commands that perform the actions necessary to:

- Count the boys
- Count the girls
- Add the contents of the reading and math fields for each class

```
SET TALK OFF
USE B:SCHOOL
INDEX ON GRADE+ROOM+NAME TO B:ROSTER
GO TOP
SET PRINT ON
DO WHILE .NOT. EOF()
   STORE ROOM TO MROOM
   STORE GRADE TO MGRADE
   STORE 0 TO BOYS,GIRLS,XREADING,XMATH
DO WHILE ROOM=MROOM .AND. GRADE=MGRADE .AND..NOT. EOF ()
   ? '            ',NAME,READING,MATH
  IF SEX='M'
    STORE BOYS+1 TO BOYS
  ELSE
    STORE GIRLS+1 TO GIRLS
  ENDIF
  STORE READING+XREADING TO XREADING
  STORE XMATH+MATH TO XMATH
 SKIP
ENDDO
 EJECT
ENDDO
SET PRINT OFF
SET TALK ON
CANCEL
```

Figure 15-7

STORE 0 TO BOYS,GIRLS,XREADING,XMATH

This command creates the four memory variables BOYS, GIRLS, XREADING, and XMATH and sets their initial values to zero.

```
IF SEX='M'
   STORE BOYS+1 TO BOYS
ELSE
   STORE GIRLS+1 TO GIRLS
ENDIF
```

In the inner loop we increment the value of BOYS by one if the content of SEX is M. Otherwise, we increment GIRLS by one.

```
STORE XREADING+READING TO XREADING
STORE XMATH+MATH TO XMATH
```

In addition, we add the contents of the reading field to the memory variable XREADING, and the contents of the math field to the memory variable XMATH.

At this point we have set up the procedure to be able to print this specially formatted information at the bottom of each class roster:

CLASS SIZE
BOYS
GIRLS
READING AVERAGE
MATH AVERAGE

This is accomplished by the commands:

```
?
? 'CLASS SIZE: ',STR(BOYS+GIRLS,2)
? 'BOYS:       ',STR(BOYS,2)
? 'GIRLS:      ',STR(GIRLS,2)
```

```
?
? 'READING AVERAGE:',STR(XREADING/(BOYS+GIRLS),6,2)
? 'MATH AVERAGE:    ',STR(XMATH/(BOYS+GIRLS),6,2)
```

The question mark (?) when used alone will produce a blank line on the screen and/or the printer. The command line

```
? 'CLASS SIZE:',STR(BOYS+GIRLS,2)
```

will produce a printed line which looks like the one shown in the example.

```
STR(BOYS+GIRLS,2)
```

This part of the command will take the sum of the memory variables BOYS and GIRLS and print the result as a two-digit character string. In this case we know that the result cannot contain more than two characters. If we were to just use the command line as:

```
? 'CLASS SIZE:',BOYS+GIRLS
```

The sum would be printed as a ten-digit field. This would put eight blank spaces between the text "CLASS SIZE" and the printed sum.

```
? 'READING AVERAGE:',STR(XREADING/(BOYS+GIRLS),6,2)
```

This particular version of the command is similar except that the ",2" tells the computer that we want two decimals displayed.

Now we are ready to add the commands to print the page heading and properly format the page.

```
STORE STR(DAY(DATE()),2)+' ';
+CMONTH(DATE())+STR(YEAR(DATE()),5) TO CALDATE
```

CHAPTER FIFTEEN

The date is printed in calendar form by using the date functions DATE(), DAY, CMONTH, and YEAR. DATE() returns the system date, DAY extracts the day of the month from a date, CMONTH produces the calendar month, and YEAR gives the year as 19XX. DAY and YEAR are numbers. The STR function is used to "convert" these numbers to characters.

Page Heading

The page heading is printed by the use of the ? command. The ? used alone will cause a blank line to be printed and/or displayed. The text enclosed by apostrophes (delimiters) will be printed as shown in the example. (The delimiters don't get printed.) Contents of memory variables or data fields will be printed when the variable name or the fieldname is used as shown.

```
? NAME,'            ',READING,'                    ',MATH,'          ',RET
```

This produces the basic display format for each printed record. The blank spaces are used to position the column entries on the page. RET is a memory variable indicating whether or not the student was retained. The variable must be created and contain the proper information prior to this command line.

```
STORE' 'TO RET
IF RETAINED
   STORE 'RETAINED'TO RET
ENDIF
```

These commands show one way to set up the memory variable RET for its later use. This process must be repeated for each data record.

As you can see, there is nothing difficult about developing a procedure to prepare a special report. All that you need to do is be careful and methodical. Each step in the process must be entered into the computer. One very good approach is to add the SET PRINT ON command *after* you have the procedure working. This allows you to check out your procedure on the terminal without wasting paper.

301

SECTION FIVE

303

Now that we are expert programmers (and you thought programming was for computer people only), Section Five illustrates how our database applications work in a practical business situation.

The "Video Store" example allows us to apply our database methods to the many procedures encountered when running a business. Our database management system accommodates a variety of services, from mailing lists and inventory needs to specialized transaction recording.

BUSINESS USES

305

The whole idea of the microcomputer and database management is to help you. One area in which they can help is in the conduct of a small business. According to a recent report, there are over three million businesses with gross revenues of less than $500,000 which employ less than ten people.

A video store is a prime example of this type of small business. A video store specializes in the sale and rental of TV-related items, primarily video cassette recorders (VCRs), video taped movies, and related accessories. In addition to the sale and rental of goods, these stores often sponsor "video clubs" which entitle members to reduced rates on rentals and equipment.

There are several video store operations areas that can be appropriately supported by a database management system.

- Payroll and Accounting
- Standard Tax Reporting
- Inventory Management
- Flooring Charges

CHAPTER SIXTEEN

- Mailing Lists
- Daily Cash Register Tally
- Transaction Recording

This list is certainly not all-inclusive. However, it is fairly representative of areas easily supported by a DBMS, support that helps owners manage their operations better and with less effort. We discuss the video store because it is particularly well suited to examples which explain the support concepts. There are very few specialized skills involved.

THE VIDEO STORE

Renting out pre-recorded movies is a major part of the video store's business. The shop either purchases or leases movies for subsequent rental. Since each tape represents an investment and takes up valuable shelf space, it is important to the owner to know which movies rent well and which don't. A movie which doesn't move should be disposed of, either by placing it "on sale" or by returning it to the owner. It is also important to monitor how many times a popular movie is rented. Tapes do wear, and worn out movies can result in unhappy (and probably, former) customers. A database management system can help monitor the number of times each tape is rented.

Many video stores operate video clubs which benefit both the store and the customer. This scheme involves a fixed membership fee paid for significant discounts to members on movie rentals and other merchandise. A club member's list often forms the basis of a mailing list. A database management system can simplify mailing list maintenance and print out mailing labels. It can also offer further support such as reminding the shop when a membership is due for renewal.

There are various other levels of record keeping which, without a computer, are done with pencil and paper. To be of value, a computer system must perform additional services and/or reduce the amount of paperwork. For example, receipt of new merchandise requires the addition of the items to the inventory and accounts payable systems. Sale of an item requires a record of the sale as well as inventory system modifications. A database system easily accommodates inventory management as well as helps with most routine bookkeeping tasks such as accounts payable.

"Flooring" merchandise, which is similar to having goods on consignment, is a common business arrangement. A shop would have merchandise for a period of time (often ninety days) before payment is due. Payment is due immediately if the merchandise is sold prior to the due date. Often a nominal flooring charge is paid each month on unsold flooring. Such flooring arrangements require careful record keeping—a task easily supported with a database management system.

What starting point might become a good basis for a computer system? Since a pencil and paper database is familiar and useful to everyone, let's start there. We will exactly replace our old style database with a computer system database. Think first in terms of an overview of the work involved.

On a typical business day, several things might happen:

- Movies and equipment are rented
- Club memberships are sold
- Stock is sold
- Movies and equipment are returned
- Cash register transactions are balanced
- New stock is received

Each of these activities requires paperwork. For example, a "Cash Register Tally Sheet" summarizing the day's business activity and accounting for all the money must be completed each day. Such a form is shown as Figure 16-1.

CASH REGISTER TALLY SHEET

Day _____ Date _____

Person _____

COUNT MONEY FIRST AT OPENING

1. Beginning Total (Starting cash in drawer) $ _____

S A L E S

2. Rentals (Pre-recorded movies & equipment) $ _____

3. Memberships (Lifetime_____ Year _____ Other _____) $ _____

4. Services (Equipment repair & installation) $ _____

5. NON-TAXABLE Equipment & Accessories $ _____

6. Deposits (Prepayments) $ _____

7. TAXABLE Equipment & Accessories (Sales Tax included) $ _____

8. Total Sales (2+3+4+5+6+7) $ _____

9. Total Cash Paid Out (attach receipts) $ _____

10. Total Sales less Paid Out (8 minus 9) $ _____

COUNT MONEY IN REGISTER AT END OF DAY

11. Cash (15+16) $ _____

12. Checks (number of checks _____) $ _____

13. Charges (MasterCard and VISA) $ _____

14. Total Money in Register (11+12+13) $ _____

17. TOTAL (1+10) $ _____

18. Total Register (14) $ _____

Difference if any between #17 and #18   ☐ Short ☐ Extra $ _____

Z PRINT OUT AT END OF DAY $ _____

TOTAL CASH $ _____

Less starting cash for drawer $ _____

Amount for deposit $ _____

$ 1	
$ 2	
$ 5	
$ 10	
$ 20	
$ 50	
$100	

1¢	
5¢	
10¢	
25¢	
50¢	
$1	

15. TOTAL BILLS _____

16. TOTAL CHANGE _____

Figure 16-1

308

Since the activities summarized on this form constitute a large part of the store's day-to-day paperwork, the demonstration of appropriate database management support can begin here. As with all our previous processes, the first step is *planning*.

Planning must begin with a solid understanding of what is to be accomplished. So far we have identified several daily activities, represented by several pieces of paper, involved in operating the store. Duplicating each piece of paper with "electronic paper" is an uncomplicated and useful way to get started. It allows you to build the system one piece at a time. You can easily check the results against the actual paperwork, thus providing a test of your computer system operation.

In our example, the clerk beings by selecting from a menu of possible "electronic forms." The beginning menu is shown in Screen 16-1.

309

310

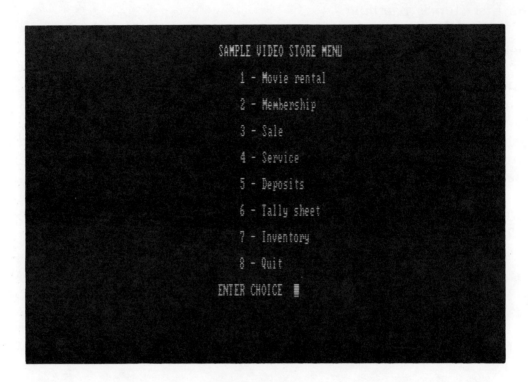

Screen 16 - 1

A diagram of how these selections fit together is shown in Figure 16-2.

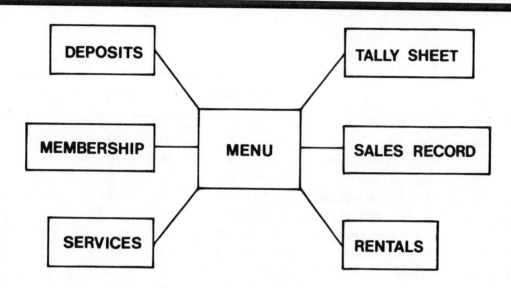

Figure 16-2

We first make the paper form into an electronic form. This requires a procedure and a database. The database plan— B:TALLY—is shown in Figure 16-3.

311

312

FIELD	DESCRIPTION	FIELDNAME	TYPE	SIZE	DECIMALS
1.	Date	DATE	D	8	
2.	Name of Employee	NAME	C	10	
3.	Starting Cash	STARTCASH	N	6	2
4.	Total Rental Income	RENTALS	N	7	2
5.	Lifetime Memberships	LIFEMEMB	N	2	
6.	Yearly Memberships	YEARMEMB	N	2	
7.	Other Memberships	SPECMEMB	N	2	
8.	Membership Income	MEMBERSHIP	N	7	2
9.	Services Income	SERVICES	N	7	2
10.	Non Taxable Sales	NONTAXSALE	N	8	2
11.	Taxable Sales	TAXSALE	N	8	2
12.	Deposits	DEPOSITS	N	7	2
13.	Cash Paid Out (total)	PAIDOUT	N	7	2
14.	End of Day Cash	ENDCASH	N	8	2
15.	No. of Checks	NOCHECKS	N	3	
16.	Value of Checks	TOTALCHECK	N	8	2
17.	VISA and MasterCard	CHARGES	N	8	2
18.	Next day starting cash	NEXTCASH	N	6	2
19.	Amount for deposit	BANKED	N	8	2

Figure 16-3. Plan For Cash Register Tally Sheet

One tally sheet equals one record in the tally sheet database. Several items on the paper tally sheet do not have corresponding fields in the electronic form because they result from calculations on items contained in the database (they appear on the report).

Figure 16-4 shows a simple procedure allowing the clerk to fill out field entries.

In this particular procedure, the clerk manually enters all of the information for each day's operations, just as he or she would using the paper tally sheet. The computer, however, performs all the required calculations. Potentially, the computer can do much more—for example, help count cash and enter checks and charges similar to the check register examples in Chapter Thirteen.

```
USE B:TALLY
SET TALK OFF
GO BOTTOM
IF .NOT.DATE=DATE()
APPEND BLANK
REPLACE DATE WITH DATE()
ENDIF
CLEAR
@ 1,10 SAY 'CASH REGISTER TALLY SHEET FOR:' GET DATE
@ 3,10 SAY 'NAME OF EMPLOYEE:' GET NAME
@ 4,10 SAY 'STARTING CASH:' GET STARTCASH
@ 5,10 SAY 'TOTAL RENT INCOME:' GET RENTALS
@ 6,10 SAY 'LIFETIME MEMBERSHIPS:' GET LIFEMEMB
@ 7,10 SAY 'YEARLY MEMBERSHIPS:' GET YEARMEMB
@ 8,10 SAY 'OTHER MEMBERSHIPS:' GET SPECMEMB
@ 9,10 SAY 'MEMBERSHIP INCOME:' GET MEMBERSHIP
@ 10,10 SAY 'SERVICES INCOME:' GET SERVICES
@ 11,10 SAY 'NON TAXABLE SALES:' GET NONTAXSALE
@ 12,10 SAY 'TAXABLE SALES:' GET TAXSALE
@ 13,10 SAY 'DEPOSITS:' GET DEPOSITS
@ 14,10 SAY 'CASH PAID OUT (TOTAL):' GET PAIDOUT
@ 15,10 SAY 'END OF DAY CASH:' GET ENDCASH
@ 16,10 SAY 'NUMBER OF CHECKS:' GET NOCHECKS
@ 17,10 SAY 'VALUE OF CHECKS:' GET TOTALCHECKS
@ 18,10 SAY 'VISA AND MASTERCARD TOTAL:' GET CHARGES
@ 19,10 SAY 'NEXT DAY STARTING CASH:' GET NEXT CASH
@ 20,10 SAY 'AMOUNT FOR DEPOSIT:' GET BANKED
READ
STORE RENTALS+MEMBERSHIP+SERVICES+NONTAXSALE+TAXSALE+DEPOSITS;
   TO TOTALSALES
STORE TOTALSALES-PAIDOUT+STARTCASH TO TOTAL
STORE ENDCASH+TOTALCHECK+CHARGES TO MONEY
```

```
CLEAR
@ 8,10 SAY 'STARTING CASH:' GET STARTCASH
@ 10,10 SAY 'TOTAL SALES:' GET TOTALSALES
@ 12,10 SAY 'AMOUNT CASH PAID OUT:' GET PAIDOUT
@ 14,10 SAY 'TOTAL MONEY IN REGISTER SHOULD BE:' GET TOTAL
@ 16,10 SAY 'TOTAL MONEY IN REGISTER IS:' GET MONEY
DO CASE
CASE MONEY> TOTAL
STORE MONEY-TOTAL TO DIFF
@ 18,10 SAY 'REGISTER IS OVER BY:' GET DIFF
CASE TOTAL>MONEY
STORE TOTAL-MONEY TO DIFF
@ 18,10 SAY 'REGISTER IS SHORT BY:' GET DIFF
ENDCASE
WAIT
SET TALK ON
RETURN
```

Figure 16-4

We spoke briefly before of video club memberships in this type of business. When such a membership is sold, the clerk fills out a form containing:

- Member's name
- Member's address
- Member's phone number
- Video club membership number
- Membership fee
- Kind of membership (life, yearly, monthly)
- Date of membership

This form becomes a single record in your membership database file, called B:MEMBERS in this example. The B:MEMBERS database plan is shown in Figure 16-5.

FIELD	DESCRIPTION	FIELDNAME	TYPE	SIZE	DECIMALS
1.	Date	DATE	D	8	
2.	Name of Member	MEMBNAME	C	30	
3.	Street Address	ADDRESS	C	20	
4.	City	CITY	C	20	
5.	Zip Code	ZIP	C	5	
6.	Telephone Number	PHONE	C	8	
7.	Kind of Membership	KINDMEMB	C	1	
8.	Membership Fee	FEE	N	6	2
9.	Membership Number	MEMBERNO	C	8	

Note: Database is to be indexed on Membership Number to MEMBID.

Figure 16-5. Plan for Video Club Membership

The database procedure allowing new member registration, B:MEMBERS, is extremely simple. It is shown in Figure 16-6.

```
USE B:MEMBERS INDEX B:MEMBID
SET TALK OFF
CLEAR
GO BOTTOM
STORE VAL(MEMBERNO)+1 TO M1
APPEND BLANK
IF RECNO()=1
REPLACE MEMBERNO WITH '10000000', DATE WITH DATE()
ELSE
REPLACE MEMBERNO WITH STR(M1,8), DATE WITH DATE()
ENDIF
@ 3,10 SAY 'SAMPLE COMPUTER MEMBERSHIP FORM'
@ 8,10 SAY 'MEMBERSHIP NUMBER' GET MEMBERNO
@ 8,40 SAY 'DATE' GET DATE
CLEAR GETS
@ 10,10 SAY 'NAME OF MEMBER' GET MEMBNAME
@ 12,10 SAY 'STREET ADDRESS' GET ADDRESS
@ 14,10 SAY 'CITY' GET CITY
@ 16,10 SAY 'ZIP CODE' GET ZIP
@ 18,10 SAY 'TELEPHONE NUMBER' GET PHONE
@ 20,10 SAY 'KIND OF MEMBERSHIP' GET KINDMEMB
@ 21,10 SAY '(L -Life Y - Year R - Renewel)'
READ
DO CASE
CASE KINDMEMB='L'
REPLACE FEE WITH 100.00
CASE KINDMEMB='Y'
REPLACE FEE WITH 50.00
CASE KINDMEMB='R'
REPLACE FEE WITH 25.00
ENDCASE

@ 22,10 SAY 'MEMBERSHIP FEE' GET FEE
READ
SET TALK ON
RETURN
```

Figure 16-6

317

FEATURING dBASE III

In establishing this procedure, we arrive at an important point. We can link the membership form (once we are sure it works correctly) back to the cash register tally sheet. Such linkage is particularly easy in this example, as both membership data and tally sheet data were entered manually. Now a membership sale can automatically update the tally sheet. This is accomplished by a simple addition to the procedure B:MEMBERS shown in Figure 16-6. The addition inserted between READ and SET TALK ON is shown in Figure 16-7.

```
READ (Same READ as bottom of Figure 16-6)
STORE KINDMEMB TO A1
STORE FEE TO A2
USE B:TALLY
GO BOTTOM
IF .NOT.DATE=DATE()
APPEND BLANK
REPLACE DATE WITH DATE()
ENDIF
DO CASE
CASE A1='L'
REPLACE LIFEMEMB WITH LIFEMEMB+1
REPLACE MEMBERSHIP WITH MEMBERSHIP+A2
CASE A1='Y'
REPLACE YEARMEMB WITH YEARMEMB+1
REPLACE MEMBERSHIP WITH MEMBERSHIP+A2
CASE A1='R'
REPLACE SPECMEMB WITH SPECMEMB+1
REPLACE MEMBERSHIP WITH MEMBERSHIP+A2
ENDCASE
SET TALK ON (this is also from the bottom of Figure 16-6)
RETURN
```

Figure 16-7

In this membership example we add all information to the membership database B:MEMBERS. At the same time, without any effort, we are able to update the cash register tally sheet.

VIDEO STORE RENTALS

A major part of this business is renting of videotaped movies. These movies may be either owned or leased by the store. When a movie is rented to a customer a form is filled out and signed by the customer. The form contains:

- Customer's name
- Customer's address
- Customer's phone number
- Driver's license number or
  Video club membership number
- Rental fee
- Amount of deposit (if any—club members avoid deposits)
- Number of movies rented
- Names of movies rented
- Date rented
- Date to be returned

When the movies are returned, the form is cancelled. The store uses this form to help keep track of:

- The cash transaction
- Where the movies are
- How many times each movie has been rented

At first glance, the straightforward way to handle the rental business on your computer would be to have one record for each transaction. The only problem with this approach is in keeping track of the *names* of movies rented. How do you decide about the amount of field space required to handle the names of the movies? If we do this with a paper form we can write small. You can't write small with a computer.

The way to handle this problem is to use more than one file for the rental database. The first file will contain all of the required information except for the movie titles. The title of each movie rented will become a record in a second database. The two databases will be linked with a transaction identifier. This transaction identifier must be unique for the transaction. It can require one or more fields. (For example, if name is used, two people might have the same name.) In this example, the unique transaction identification can be provided by the customer's driver's license number (or membership number) and the date.

The tie between the two database files is shown more graphically in Figure 16-8. The information that is to be contained in these two files is shown in two side-by-side columns.

320

	RENTAL DATABASE	MOVIE TITLE DATABASE
1.	Customer's Name	
2.	Customer's Address	
3.	Customer's Phone Number	
4.	Rental Fee	
5.	Amount of Deposit (if any) (club members avoid deposits)	
6.	Number of Movies Rented	
7.	Number of Days Rented	
8.	Club Member (y/n)	
9.	Driver's License Number or Video Club Membership Number	Driver's License Number or Video Club Membership Number
10.	Date Rented	Date Rented
11.		Movie Title
12.	.	VHS or BETA

Figure 16-8

At this point we believe that the combination of the date and the driver's license number is unique enough to identify each transaction. Each rental transaction results in a "Rental Database" record and a "Movie Title Database." This means that if a customer rents four movies, the Movie Title Database will have four movies added to it. Those titles are related to the rental record by the license number and the date.

We now have the core of the idea. However, in this example, a lot of typing is required on the part of the clerk. All of the customer information as well as the movie titles must be filled in. Fortunately, in many cases, we can minimize the typing by making use of information already stored in the computer.

If the rental customers are members of the store's video club, the membership database can be linked to the rental database by the membership number. The membership information can then be copied to the rental database—saving the clerk both time and effort (as well as minimizing the chance of error). This is also a terrific opportunity to add non-members to this database— thereby increasing its use as a mailing list.

321

When a field is used as a tie to link two database files together, the field should be the same size and type in both database files. "Alpha   " is not the same as "Alpha" to the computer. It considers the blank spaces also.

Movie titles are (or should be) a field in the Movie Rental Inventory Database. Basic inventory information includes:

Movie Title	Date Purchased or	Owned or Leased
VHS or BETA	Leased by Store	Supplier
Shelf Location	Purchase Price/Lease Rate	

The movie title is an awkward way for the store to deal with movie records. An identification number would enable the clerk to work more quickly and accurately with or without the computer. Therefore, in our example we will assume that a five-digit identification number has been assigned to each rental movie.

FEATURING dBASE III

CHAPTER SIXTEEN

If we add a few fields to the inventory database we can use it in place of the "Movie Title Database."

> Rental Fee
> Driver's License or Membership Number
> Rental Date
> Number of Times Rented
> Rented (Y/N)

There are a number of possible file combinations that one could use for this example. Each has advantages and disadvantages, depending upon the specific application. For the purposes of our example we will use the Inventory Database in the place of the Movie Database from now on.

A diagram of this rental procedure (so far) looks like that shown in Figure 16-9.

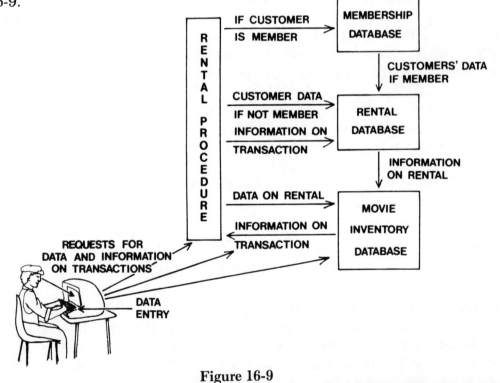

Figure 16-9

Let's take a look at where we are. When a customer rents a movie, the clerk fills out a form. This form becomes a single record in a rental database. The rental inventory database is used to identify the movies rented out. The driver's license number or club membership number and the rental date are common fields in the two database files. These two fields serve to tie the two files together. Each time a movie is rented, the "number of times rented" field gets increased by one. If the customer is a club member, much of the information is automatically retrieved from the membership database.

Taking the inevitable next step finds the computer calculating the total rental fee and adding this to the receipt. Just as in the last example, the value of the transaction can be automatically added to the Cash Register Tally Sheet.

Now let's put all of this together. A diagram of this database system is shown in Figure 16-10.

323

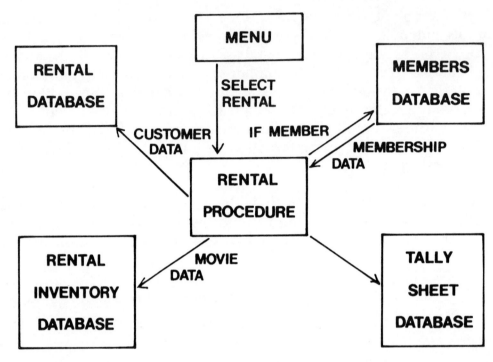

Figure 16-10

324

The process outlined above is a reasonable example of one way in which a computer system can be used to help with the operation of a small business. It is not the only way, and it is not necessarily the best way. However, it provides a useful demonstration of an approach to solving a business problem with a computer.

The next step is to write down the database plans for each of the database files used in this process. The plan for the membership file has already been described in Figure 16-5. The two new database files are shown in Figures 16-11 and 16-12. A procedure that will perform the rental process described above is shown in Figure 16-13. One word of caution: this procedure is intended to illustrate the process. It is necessarily somewhat simplified from one you might use for an actual business.

FIELD	DESCRIPTION	FIELDNAME	TYPE	SIZE	DECIMALS
1.	Customer's Name	NAME	C	30	
2.	Street Address	ADDRESS	C	20	
3.	City	CITY	C	20	
4.	Zip Code	ZIP	C	5	
5.	Telephone Number	PHONE	C	8	
6.	Identification	ID	C	8	
7.	Rental Fee	RFEE	N	5	2
8.	Amount of Deposit	DEPOSIT	N	6	2
9.	Number of Rentals	RENTAL	N	2	
10.	Number of Days Rented	TIME	N	2	
11.	Club Member (Y/N)	MEMBER	L	1	
12.	Date Rented	DATE	D	8	

Figure 16-11. Rental Database Plan

Though the procedure described in Figure 16-13 is the most elaborate in this book, it is not difficult. There is nothing tricky or complicated about it.

325

FIELD	DESCRIPTION	FIELDNAME	TYPE	SIZE	DECIMALS
1.	Movie Title	TITLE	C	30	
2.	VHS or BETA	VHS	L	1	
3.	Location	LOCATION	C	5	
4.	Date Acquired	IDATE	D	8	
5.	Price/Lease Rate	COST	N	5	2
6.	Owned or Leased	OWNED	L	1	
7.	Supplier	SUPPLIER	C	20	
8.	Identification	RID	C	8	
9.	Rental Charge	CHARGE	N	4	2
10.	Rental Date	RDATE	D	8	
11.	No. of Times Rented	RCOUNT	N	3	
12.	Rented (Y/N)	RENTED	L	1	
13.	Movie ID Number	MOVIEID	C	5	

Figure 16-12. Inventory Database

```
SET DEFAULT TO B
CLEAR ALL
SET TALK OFF
SELECT 1
USE TALLY
SELECT 2
USE INVENTRY
SELECT 3
USE MEMBERS INDEX MEMBID
SELECT 4
USE RENTAL
SET RELATION TO ID INTO MEMBERS
APPEND BLANK
REPLACE DATE WITH DATE()
CLEAR
@ 1,10 SAY 'SAMPLE VIDEO RENTAL FROM'
@ 2,10 SAY 'IS THE CUSTOMER A CLUB MEMBER? (Y/N)' GET MEMBER
READ
CLEAR GETS
IF MEMBER
   @ 8,10 SAY 'ENTER THE MEMBERSHIP NUMBER' GET ID
   READ
   GO RECNO()
ENDIF
IF ID = MEMBERS->MEMBERNO
   REPLACE  NAME WITH MEMBERS->MEMBNAME,   ;
            ADDRESS WITH MEMBERS->ADDRESS, CITY WITH MEMBERS->CITY, ;
            ZIP WITH MEMBERS->ZIP, PHONE WITH MEMBERS->PHONE
ENDIF
@ 3,10 SAY 'CUSTOMERS NAME' GET NAME
@ 4,10 SAY 'CUSTOMERS ADDRESS' GET ADDRESS
@ 5,10 SAY 'CITY' GET CITY
@ 6,10 SAY 'ZIP CODE' GET ZIP
@ 7,10 SAY 'TELEPHONE NUMBER' GET PHONE
```

```
IF ID = MEMBERS->MEMBERNO .AND. MEMBER
   CLEAR GETS
ELSE
   @ 8,10 SAY 'DRIVERS LICENSE NUMBER' GET ID
   @ 9,10 SAY 'ENTER AMOUNT OF DEPOSIT' GET DEPOSIT
READ
ENDIF
@ 10,10 SAY 'NUMBER OF DAYS RENTED' GET TIME
@ 10,45 SAY 'NUMBER OF MOVIES RENTED' GET RENTAL
READ
CLEAR GETS

STORE 0 TO MRENTAL
DO WHILE RENTAL->RENTAL > MRENTAL
   SELECT INVENTRY
   STORE '      ' TO MOVIENO
   @ 12,10 SAY 'MOVIE IDENTIFICATION NUMBER' GET MOVIENO
   READ
   LOCATE FOR MOVIEID=MOVIENO
   @ 13,0
   IF EOF()
      @ 13,10 SAY 'Movie number '+MOVIENO+' is not in the database'
      LOOP
   ENDIF
   IF RENTED
      @ 13,10 SAY 'Movie number '+TRIM(TITLE)+' is already rented'
      LOOP
   ENDIF
   @ 13,10 SAY TITLE
   REPLACE RDATE WITH DATE(),;
           RCOUNT WITH RCOUNT+RENTAL->TIME,;
           RENTED WITH .Y.,;
           RID WITH RENTAL->ID
   SELECT RENTAL
```

```
    REPLACE RFEE WITH RFEE + (INVENTRY->CHARGE * TIME)
    MRENTAL = MRENTAL+1
ENDDO

SELECT TALLY
GO BOTTOM
IF .NOT.DATE=DATE()
   APPEND BLANK
   REPLACE DATE WITH DATE()
ENDIF
REPLACE DEPOSITS WITH DEPOSITS+RENTALS->DEPOSIT,;
        RENTALS WITH RENTALS+RENTAL->RFEE

SELECT RENTAL
CLEAR
@ 5,10 SAY 'CUSTOMERS NAME' GET NAME
@ 7,10 SAY 'MOVIE RENTAL CHARGE' GET RFEE
IF DEPOSIT>0
@ 7,40 SAY 'REQUIRED DEPOSIT' GET DEPOSIT
ENDIF
STORE DEPOSIT+RFEE TO DUE
@ 9,10 SAY 'TOTAL AMOUNT DUE' GET DUE
CLEAR GETS

SELECT INVENTRY
DISPLAY OFF TITLE,CHARGE FOR RID=RENTAL->ID .AND. RDATE = DATE()
SELECT TALLY
SET TALK ON
RETURN
```

Figure 16-13

The first command SET DEFAULT TO B tells dBASE that all of the files used in the procedure are on the B drive unless otherwise indicated. CLEAR ALL closes any currently open database files, their associated index files, and format files. It initializes dBASE.

dBASE provides ten independent work areas to be used with up to ten different database files. The next step in this procedure is to open (USE) four database files in the first four work areas. To use a file in work area one, use SELECT 1—then open the database file with USE followed by the database name. This database name becomes the *ALIAS* for the database. From this point on we can switch back and forth between the work areas by using SELECT followed by the database name.

When we are using multiple files, they can be linked together by the SET RELATION command. In this case we want to link the database in work area four (RENTAL) to the MEMBERS database file. Specifically, we want to link these two files by the content of the ID field in RENTAL. To do this, the MEMBERS database file must be indexed on the corresponding field—which is MEMBERNO. The linkage is accomplished by:

SET RELATION TO ID INTO MEMBERS

From this point on, each time the RENTAL database is repositioned, the MEMBERS database will be repositioned to the record where the content of the MEMBERS field MEMBERNO is the same as the RENTAL field ID. If there is no matching record in MEMBERS, MEMBERS will be positioned to its end-of-file. It will appear to be positioned to a blank record.

Our next step is to add a blank record (APPEND BLANK) to the RENTAL file and set the content of the DATE field to the system date [REPLACE DATE WITH DATE()]. Next we clear the screen and ask you or whoever is entering data if the customer is a club member. The READ command allows you to answer the question. The result is stored in the RENTAL database as a logical yes or no.

In the RENTAL file, if MEMBER is true (yes), then you will be asked for the customer's club membership number. This number is entered into the field ID. The GO RECNO() command repositions the RENTAL database to same record. This was done to force the MEMBERS database to be repositioned to the record matching the membership number entered into ID.

Next we compare the field MEMBERNO in MEMBERS with the field ID in the current database file RENTAL. This is accomplished with

IF ID = MEMBERS->MEMBERNO
MEMBERNO will either match ID exactly, or it will appear to be all blanks. If we get a match we want to copy the contents of the fields MEMBNAME, ADDRESS, CITY, ZIP, PHONE from the file MEMBERS to the equivalent fields in the current work area of the RENTAL file. This is done with the REPLACE command. This command takes three lines. The semicolons indicate that the command is continued on the following line.

Next we display the customer's NAME, ADDRESS, CITY, ZIP, and PHONE using the @. . .SAY. . .GET. . . If the customer is a club member we use the CLEAR GETS command to prevent the cursor from being moved into these fields. If the customer is not a club member, the ELSE is activated and the customer's driver's license number and the amount of deposit are requested.

In either case the program will request the number of days of the rental, and the number of movies being rented. Once these items have been entered we issue a CLEAR GETS to prevent any changes to these items.

The next step stores a zero to a memory variable MRENTAL. The DO loop will process the commands between DO WHILE and ENDDO as long as the content of the variable MRENTAL is less than the content of the field RENTAL in the database file RENTAL.

330

Once inside the loop we SELECT the database file INVENTRY. Then we store five blank spaces to a memory variable MOVIENO. Once the movie number has been entered, we attempt to LOCATE a record where the contents of the field MOVIEID match the contents of MOVIENO. If the search is not successful [IF EOF()] we display an error message and LOOP back to the beginning of the DO WHILE. If the search is successful but the movie is already rented, we display an error message and again LOOP back to the beginning of the DO WHILE. If the search is successful and the movie is available for renting, we display the name of the movie. The command line @ 13,0 just prior to the line IF EOF() erases screen line 13 on each pass through the DO loop.

Note that you cannot get to the REPLACE command unless the search is successful and the movie is available for rental. The REPLACE command uses four lines, just for readability. (Again, the semicolons at the end of each line indicate that the command is to be continued.) Remember, the maximum length of a command line is 254 characters, and embedded blank spaces count. This REPLACE uses the system date [DATE()] as the rental date. The number of days for the rental (the content of the field TIME in the database file RENTAL) is added to the content of RCOUNT. We then set the rental flag RENTED to "yes," and enter the customer's ID code into RID, the rental ID field in the inventory database.

331

Next we switch back to the RENTAL database. When we switch, we maintain our place in the database we have just left. We must be selected to the database we are changing. We moved here so that we could add the rental fee (from the inventory database) times the number of days the movie is being rented to the content of the field RFEE.

Now we increment the variable MRENTAL by one and jump to the beginning of the DO WHILE. If the number stored in MRENTAL is larger than the content of the field RENTAL, we jump to the first command line following the ENDDO. Otherwise we go through the process until the MRENTAL is larger than RENTAL.

Next, we SELECT our tally sheet TALLY (See Figure 16-13). If the content of the DATE field in the last record is *not* the same as the system date DATE(), we add a record and enter the system date into the DATE field. Then we add the amount of the deposit from this customer (if any) to the content of the DEPOSITS field and the rental fees to the content of the RENTALS field.

Finally, we SELECT our RENTAL file, clear the screen, and display a summary of this customer's transaction. The bottom line is the amount of money the customer must pay. To cap off the program, we SELECT the INVENTRY file, and display the names and per day charge rates for each movie being rented.

As you can see, there is nothing complex about this example. The procedure is just a step-by-step list of instructions for the computer to execute. All the program does is describe the actions you would take if you were to undertake the same process using pencil and paper.

This example is particularly significant. There are four separate database files used. The procedure isolates you (and the clerk) from all of the database activity. As the information is filled in, the database management system moves from database to database adding and changing information as necessary.

The procedure B:RENTAL covers the basic elements in managing the movie rental aspects of this business. You should *not* consider it adequate for operating the movie rental business. The procedure has not considered all possible details that should be covered in a business procedure. Some elements were omitted in order to better illustrate the concepts of working with video screen forms and multiple database files.

332

A FEW
CLOSING REMARKS

Throughout this book we have demonstrated database management as an easy, effective, and natural way for you to get results from your computer. In illustrating various database concepts, we have used everyday examples to demonstrate the simple and versatile features of a database management system.

In retrospect, we realize that "database" is a concept we have long been familiar with. The specific terminology used in computer database systems may be a little unfamiliar, but it certainly isn't difficult. It doesn't take long to begin thinking of a column of data as a field. Nor does it take much effort to think of the title of the database as a filename. Once you have mastered the simple terminology, it is easy to master the system so that it works for you.

This, of course, is the whole idea behind microcomputer database management systems. They are supposed to do the work while you do the thinking. There is no need to become a computer specialist to make the computer work for you—you have seen in this book how really simple it is to make the computer work. Whether business or home oriented, a database management system provides the first-time user with an excellent opportunity to both increase work efficiency and get acquainted with computers. For the specialist, there is also increased efficiency as well as continuing satisfaction in the effective use of computing tools.

While you are still learning about your database management system, work with the applications that provide the most return for your effort. Remember our liquor store inventory—we actually did much less work when using the computer than if we had performed the inventory without it. By starting with simple applications, you will find it easier to progress to more complex ones—after all, you didn't run a marathon the first time you went to the track.

A common error is to purchase a computer and a database management system because you have a complicated problem to solve—and then, as your first task, to jump in and try to solve that complicated problem. This makes your problem (and your life) unnecessarily complex. You really need to become familiar with your computer and software first. It is too much to expect to relate your problem (especially if it is complicated) to the hardware and software all at the same time.

To familiarize yourself with your system, we suggest you practice by constructing "learning problems" that use small databases. The examples provided in this book should help direct you in constructing examples of your own. *The solutions to complicated problems are made up of many simple pieces.* It is much to your advantage to construct learning problems using small databases because they allow you to check your results fairly quickly to see whether or not you are getting the right answer. This is great background for dealing with larger databases. The examples in this book are varied enough to give you a good idea of an approach to a specific problem if you select the appropriate pieces from one or more examples and then assemble them into your solution. While it is valuable to work through the examples, you will learn more quickly by using them as a guide to work out a solution for a problem of your own.

Once you select the learning problem you'd like to construct, study your problem carefully and plan your solution methodically. If you understand your problem and are methodical in the planning and subsequent implementation of your system, you will always be successful. These three ingredients—understanding the problem, planning, and methodical step-by-step implementation—are essential to success in any computer system.

Success in the solution of an initial "easy" problem will give you the experience and confidence to begin attacking more and more complex problems. And as you do so, you will discover that these complex problems aren't difficult after all. Take a step-by-step approach, become familiar with the language, and you will have a winner.

We hope this book will be a useful guide to you as you learn to master a useful and versatile tool—the computer. Database management is probably the surest and most direct course towards attaining that goal. With it, we are sure you will find the computer a most helpful servant.

335

GLOSSARY

.AND.

A Boolean operator that is used to join two logic expressions so that the resulting expression applies to the shared characteristics of the expression. For example: GRADE='3'.AND.ROOM='122' restricts the expression to third graders who are assigned to room 122.

.NOT.

A Boolean operator which is used to invoke the opposite of the expression. For example: .NOT.GRADE='3' means all grades except the third.

.OR.

A Boolean operator which is used to join two groups within a logical expression. For example, the third and fourth grades can be joined within the logical expression GRADE='3'.OR.GRADE='4'.

?

A dBASE command for displaying selected items.

@

A dBASE operator that is used in conjunction with the SAY and GET commands to generate displays on either the CRT or the printer.

*

Normally used to indicate multiplication in computer systems. In *dBASE III* it is also used to indicate database records that have been marked for deletion. In program listings, works the same as NOTE (see NOTE).

#

338

The "pound sign" is used as a multipurpose function. It is normally used as a shorthand for "not equal to."

$

A dBASE operator that allows you to search for a sequence of characters contained in a field or memory variable. It is often called either a substring or string operator. It can be interpreted as "contained in." For example: 'Robert'$NAME would allow you to search the field NAME for the character string ROBERT.

ACCEPT TO [memory variable name]

A *dBASE III* command which allows the input of character strings into designated memory variables without the need for delimiters. Normally used within procedures (*dBASE III* command files).

ADL

Applications Development Language—the computer language used with *dBASE III*.

APPEND

The *dBASE III* command to add records to a database.

APPEND BLANK

A variation of APPEND which adds blank records to a database. Normally used within procedures.

339

APPEND FROM <FILENAME>

Used to append data from the named file to the file in use.

BACKUP

The process of copying a disk or disk file to another disk for protection against possible future loss. Also the backup copy of the file or disk.

BASIC

A computer language. An acronym standing for Beginners All Purpose Symbolic Instruction Code.

GLOSSARY

BOOLEAN

A method of computer logic based on the work of George Boole, who developed a certain type of algebra.

BOOTING

The process of starting up the computer.

BROWSE

A *dBASE III* command used for editing. Several records are displayed simultaneously for full screen editing.

BYTE

The amount of memory required to store a character such as an "A" or "#" or "9."

CANCEL

A command used to terminate a procedure and return control of the computer to the keyboard.

CASE

A variation of the IF statement. Case can only be used with DO CASE/ENDCASE.

CHANGE

A *dBASE III* command used for editing.

CHARACTER

Any keyboard symbol that can be printed, such as "A" or "$" or "1" or "a" (includes blank spaces).

CHARACTER FIELD

A database field that is intended to contain characters.

CHARACTER STRING

A continuous sequence of characters such as "John Doe."

CHR( )

A *dBASE III* command which allows you direct control of peripheral devices such as the printer and the CRT.

341

CLEAR

Erases the screen.

CLEAR ALL

This command resets *dBASE III*. All databases in USE are closed, all memory variables are released, and the system is just as it is when you initially enter *dBASE III*.

CLEAR GETS

A command which removes all pending GETS internally without altering the screen (as the ERASE command would). This will limit the domain of a READ to only those GETS issued after the CLEAR GETS command.

GLOSSARY

COBOL

A computer language used extensively in mainframe business application. The first English-like computer language. An acronym for Common Business Oriented Languages.

COMMAND

dBASE III terminology for a computer instruction.

COMMAND FILE

A set of computer instructions stored or saved on a disk for repetitive use. *dBASE III* terminology for a computer procedure.

CONDITION

A logical expression that can be used to more explicitly define a command such as DISPLAY. DISPLAY FOR NAME = 'JOHN DOE' modifies the command DISPLAY so that it applies only for records meeting the condition NAME='JOHN DOE'.

CONDITIONAL REPLACEMENT

A technique for changing the contents of a database where the replace command is modified by a condition. REPLACE TEACHER WITH 'ADAMS' FOR ROOM='171' will replace the contents of the field TEACHER with 'ADAMS' for only those records meeting the condition ROOM='171'.

CONFIG.DB

A special file used by a dBASE.ovl (overlay file) to determine the processing characteristics of dBASE.

CONFIG.SYS

A special file needed to configure the operating system. Consult you operating system manual.

CONTINUE

A command which positions the record pointer to the next record with conditions specified by the LOCATE command.

CONTROL KEY

A key which potentially gives a third value to all of the keys of the keyboard. Similar to the shift key, which gives a second meaning to each of the keys of the keyboard.

COPY TO <filename>

A *dBASE III* command which copies the database in use to the named database. Used to create a copy of the database for backup. Variations exist which will allow you to copy only selected parts of the database in use to the named database.

COUNT

A data displaying command which counts the number of records that meet some conditional expression.

CPU

Central Processing Unit—the central processor of the computer system. It contains the main storage, arithmetic unit, and special register groups.

343

CREATE

The *dBASE III* command to allow you to establish the structure of a new database file.

CRT

Cathode Ray Tube. Popularly used to denote the video display device used in conjunction with computers.

CTRL KEY

Control Key—used in combination with various keys to give them another meaning and function.

DASD

Direct Access Storage Device such as a disk.

344

DATA

A piece of information. Normally useless as an independent item. Can convey information when used with another item of data. For example, the phone number 555-3213 is relatively useless by itself. It conveys information when used in conjunction with another data item, Butch Johnson.

DATABASE

A repository of stored information organized in such a way that data is easily retrieved. Normally associated with an organized base of data stored within a computer that is usable by multiple applications. An everyday example of a non-computer database is the telephone directory.

DATE

A special data type designed to work with dates in the form mm/dd/yy. Date fields can be sorted or indexed chronologically.

DBMS

Database Management System.

DEFAULT

When the computer receives a command, it must take some action. Unless otherwise instructed, it will take a pre-programmed action. That pre-programmed action is called the default.

DELETE

A *dBASE III* command which marks records for deletion (see also PACK).

345

DELIMITERS

A way of identifying character strings to the computer. For example, allows the computer to distinguish between the field NAME and the word 'NAME'.

DIR <drive>

A *dBASE III* command which displays the filename, number of records, and date of last change of all database files on the named disk.

DISK DRIVE

A mechanical device used to read and write information onto a disk.

GLOSSARY

DISKS

A circular plate, coated with magnetic material, for storing data. The medium on which a computer may permanently or temporarily store information to be used or read at a later date.

DISPLAY

A *dBASE III* command to display the contents of a data record.

DISPLAY ALL

A variation of the DISPLAY command. This variation will display all records of the database in use—pausing every screenful.

DISPLAY FOR <condition>

A variation of the DISPLAY command. The FOR <condition> clause modifies the DISPLAY command so that all records meeting the condition will be displayed a screenful at a time.

DISPLAY MEMORY

A variation of the DISPLAY command which will display the name, type, size, and content of all memory variables.

DISPLAY OFF

A variation of DISPLAY which displays the database record without the record number.

DISPLAY STRUCTURE

A variation of the DISPLAY command which is used to display the structure of the database currently in use.

DO <filename>

A *dBASE III* command which instructs the computer to execute the named procedure (command file).

DO CASE

A *dBASE III* command which is used as an alternative to multiple nested IF, ENDIF statements. It must be accompanied by an ENDCASE command. Normally used in procedures.

DO WHILE <condition>

A *dBASE III* command which tells the computer to repeatedly execute the sequence of commands between the DO WHILE statement and its concluding ENDDO statement as long as the condition is satisfied. Used in *dBASE III* command files (procedures).

347

DOS

Disk Operating System—software.

EDIT <record number>

A command which allows changing a data field contents. In *dBASE III* it invokes a full screen operation which allows you to change the contents of desired fields by moving the cursor to the appropriate location and typing in the new data.

EJECT

A *dBASE III* command which ejects a page on the printer.

GLOSSARY

ELSE

A command file alternate path of command execution within IF.

ENDCASE

A command file command that terminates DO CASE.

ENDDO

A command file terminator for the DO WHILE command.

ENDIF

A command file terminator for the IF command.

EOF

End of File. A *dBASE III* function; also a special ASCII file character.

ESCAPE

A key (same as Ctrl-[) which allows you to interrupt a procedure or a command execution from the keyboard.

FIELD

In systems such as *dBASE III*, a field contains an item of information. It corresponds to a column of information on a paper database.

FIELD DESCRIPTION

A field description consists of three parts: the fieldname, field type, and the field width including decimal places (if any).

FIELDNAME

The field "title." Contains ten or fewer characters, must begin with a letter, and may not contain blank spaces.

FIELD SIZE

The number of character positions needed to contain the data to be placed in the field.

FIELDTYPE

The kind of data that may be stored in a field. The fieldtypes are character, numeric, logical, date, and memo.

FIELDWIDTH

The number of spaces needed in the field to contain the data.

349

FILE

A collection of information such as a database file or a command file stored as an identifiable unit on a disk.

FILENAME

Used to identify the file to the computer. Must contain eight or fewer characters, must begin with a letter, and may not contain any blank spaces.

FILETYPE

A three-character extension on the filename following the filename and a period. Used to distinguish among different file types with the same name and to identify to the computer certain kinds of files which it has been programmed to deal with in a specific way. As an example, a .dbf file is recognized by *dBASE III* as a database file.

FIND <key>

A *dBASE III* command to find the record with the key. May be used only with indexed files.

FLOPPIES

Floppy disks.

FLOPPY DISK

A storage medium commonly used on microcomputers. Information is stored on a thin, flexible mylar disk.

FLOPPY DISK SYSTEM

A computer system which uses floppy disks.

FORTRAN

A traditional computer language used mainly in scientific application. Acronym for Formula Translation.

GET

A dBASE command used in conjunction with the @ command to display the contents of a field or a memory variable. When used in conjunction with the READ command, the contents of the field or memory variable may be changed by simply typing in the new information.

350

GO BOTTOM

A command which makes *dBASE III* go to the last record in the database being used.

GO TOP

A command which makes *dBASE III* go to the first record in the database being used.

GOTO <record number>

This command is used to reposition the record pointer of the database to the named record number.

HARD DISK

A disk which is a rigid metal plate covered with magnetic film; capable of storing large amounts of data.

351

HARD DISK SYSTEM

A computer system which uses hard disks.

I/O

A mechanism by which the computer accepts and distributes the information among the peripheral devices. An acronym for Input/Output.

IF <condition>

A statement that tells the computer to execute a set of commands provided that a condition is satisfied.

INDEX ON <fieldlist> TO <filename>

A *dBASE III* command which creates an index file with the named filename. The index file causes the contents of the database file to appear to be arranged in the logical order of the contents of the listed fields.

INPUT TO <memory variable name>

A *dBASE III* command which allows keyboard input of numeric data to a memory variable. Only numeric data will be accepted. Normally used within procedures.

INSERT

A *dBASE III* command which inserts a new data record into the middle of a database file.

INT(n)

A function which will round off a number which has a decimal by throwing away everything to the right of the decimal point. Short for integer.

JOIN

A command which outputs the JOIN of two relational databases.

KEYBOARD

A device similar to a typewriter keyboard by which a user may "talk" to a computer.

LEN <memory variable name>

A *dBASE III* function that tells you how many characters are in the named string memory variable.

LIST

A dBASE command to display all data records in a database continuously.

LOCATE FOR <condition>

A dBASE command used to find a record that satisfies the condition.

LOGICAL FIELDS

Fields with only two possible contents. Used when there will only be two possible mutually exclusive entries such as .T. and .F. or .Y. and .N.

353

LOGICAL RECORDS

Records in an index file or another similar file which are images of part of the actual data. Normally used as an aid to using the actual data.

LOOP

A command which causes execution of a command file to skip back to the beginning of DO WHILE. It is used as an escape when some undesired condition is encountered.

MASS MEMORY

Peripheral storage devices such as disk drives and tape drives.

GLOSSARY

MEMO

A special kind of field used to store large blocks of variable length free-form text. Memo fields are stored in a special companion file to a database file. This companion file is called a database text (.dbt) file.

MEMORY VARIABLE

Allows you to store information in the computers main memory for your temporary use. Similar in concept to memory on an electronic calculator. All information is lost when machine is turned off.

MENU

A computer procedure that displays a set of choices for action.

MENU SYSTEM

A computer procedure that uses a menu selection to choose a course of action for the computer to follow.

MICROCOMPUTER

A small computer designed principally for use by a single person.

MILLISECOND

1/1000th of a second.

MINICOMPUTER

A small computer that is generally configured for simultaneous use by a small number of people. Slightly larger and more powerful than a microcomputer.

MODIFY COMMAND

A dBASE command that allows you to create and/or edit the contents of a procedure (command file).

MODIFY STRUCTURE

A dBASE command that allows you to change the structure of a database.

MS-DOS

A popular operating system for IBM PC compatible computers. It is a product of Microsoft, Inc.

NOTE <text material>

A dBASE command (normally used in procedures) which causes the computer to ignore the text that is written on the line. Used to describe the procedure for future reference.

355

NUMERIC FIELDS

Fields that contain numbers that are meant to be used in numeric calculation.

OPERATING SYSTEM

Software that coordinates the workings of your computer hardware system and software.

PACK

A command which physically DELETEs all records marked for deletion.

GLOSSARY

PASCAL

A computer language having some of the features of dBASE.

PC-DOS

The operating system used on the IBM PC and the IBM XT computers.

PERIPHERALS

Devices used with the computer such as a printer and disk drives.

PHYSICAL RECORDS

The actual data records.

PL/1

A computer language.

POINTER

A software mechanism that directs the computer to the database record of interest.

PRIMARY KEY

A unique way of identifying the record that is directly usable by the computer system. In *dBASE III*, the PRIMARY KEY is the record number.

PRINTER

A peripheral device which outputs data from the computer onto paper.

PROGRAM

A series of commands to be executed by the computer as a unit. A procedure is a program. In *dBASE III*, a command file is a program.

PROGRAMMER

Any person who writes programs.

PROMPT

An indication from the computer that it is ready to accept keyboard commands. Also a request for specific information to be input from the keyboard.

QUERY

A user request for information from the computer. Normally a keyboard request.

357

QUIT

A command that causes *dBASE III* to close all files currently being used and exit to the operating system.

RAM

An acronym for Random Access Memory. This is normally the computer's main memory. Random access memory is really computer memory that is directly addressable and can be written to as well as read from.

GLOSSARY

READ

A *dBASE III* command which is used in conjunction with the GET command to perform full screen (cursor) editing of the contents of memory variables and data fields.

RECALL

A *dBASE III* command which "undeletes" records previously marked for deletion.

RECNO

A *dBASE III* function used to identify the record number.

RECORD

An integral unit of data items. In *dBASE III*, it is that information which is contained on a row in a rectangular table of rows and columns.

RECORD LOCKOUT

An artifice to protect against possible simultaneous editing of a single data item in systems where there may be more than one user at a time.

RECORD NUMBER

An identifying number assigned to each data record by the database management system. The record number is unique for each record (no two records have the same record number).

RELATION

A technical term for a database file. SET RELATION is the dBASE III command to link two database files together.

RELATIONAL DATABASE SYSTEM

A type of database management system based on the use of rectangular tables of rows and columns. Different database files are linked (related) by the contents of a data field where the field contents may be common to both database files.

RELEASE <memory variable names>

A *dBASE III* command which "erases" the named memory variables.

RENAME <filename 1> TO <filename 2>

A dBASE command to rename a file. The file cannot be currently in use.

REPLACE <fieldname> WITH <new contents>

A dBASE command which replaces the contents of the named data field with the desired new contents. Most often used within procedures. May be effectively used from the keyboard in conjunction with FOR <condition>.

359

REPORT

A *dBASE III* command which prepares a report based on the contents of a database and your answers to a series of simple questions. The report is displayed on the CRT. The answers to the questions are entered from the keyboard for the first use of a specific report. The answers are saved in a .FRM file and the report will thereafter be generated automatically. There may be many reports available at any one time.

REPORT TO PRINT

A variation of REPORT that causes the report to be printed.

RETURN

A command which ends a command file and returns to the next higher procedure. Control returns to the keyboard if there is no higher procedure.

RETURN KEY

Similar to the carriage return key on a typewriter. Should probably be labeled as ENTER on a computer terminal.

ROM

An acronym for Read Only Memory.

RUB

A key which deletes the character to the left of the cursor.

SAVE

A command which copies the currently defined memory variables to mass storage.

SAY

A dBASE command used in conjunction with the @ operator to display information on the CRT or the printer.

SELECT 1

A command that selects the PRIMARY database.

SELECT 2

A command that selects the SECONDARY database.

SEQUENTIAL ACCESS

An access method for data records whereby the computer examines each record sequentially—beginning with the first record—until the desired record(s) are located.

SET ECHO ON/OFF

All commands which come from a command file are echoed on the screen as if they had been entered from the keyboard. ECHO is normally off and must be turned on if needed.

SET PRINT ON/OFF

361

Routes the computer output to the printer. Normally output is not directed to the printer.

SET TALK ON/OFF

The results from commands are normally displayed on the CRT. This is often undesirable when using command files.

SKIP [N]

A command which positions the database forwards or backwards a number of records.

SORT

A command which will cause the database to be physically rearranged into some desired order—normally by the numerical value of some field(s), or alphabetically according to the contents of a character field.

STORE

A command which stores data into memory variables.

STR(N,a,b)

A function to convert a number (N) to a character string. The argument (a) specifies the number of characters in the resulting character string. The optional argument (b) specifies the number of decimal places to be included. **SUBSTR(X,a,b)** is a function used to identify a substring within a larger character string. The argument (X) identifies the character string. The argument (a) is the starting character position of the substring withing the character string (X). The argument (b) specifies the length of the substring.

STRUCTURE

The predefined organization of your database. It is established by the fieldname, field type, and field width.

SUM <fieldname>

A command that adds the contents of the named fields.

TERMINAL

The means with which you communicate with your computer and it communicates with you. The most popular terminal devices with micro-computers are video display terminals.

362

TYPE

This function is the data type function and yields a C, N, L, D, M, (or U if unknown), depending on whether the one-character string is, respectively, Character, Numeric, Logical, Date, Memo, or undefined.

UPDATE

A command which merges records from two databases.

USE <filename>

A command which tells *dBASE III* which database you want to work with.

VAL(x)

Allows the contents of a character data field or memory variable to be used in arithmetic calculations.

363

VIDEO SCREEN

The video display device associated with your computer.

WAIT

A command file command that interrupts command file processing and waits for a single character input from the keyboard.

WAIT TO <memory variable name>

The same as WAIT except that the TO clause causes the keyboard character to be stored in the named memory variable.

WORK AREA

dBASE is divided into ten independent work areas. Each work area may contain one database file, its associated index files, a format file, a filter, and a specified linkage to another work area.

364

INDEX

365

366

367

369

370

SURVEY

Thank you for purchasing an Ashton-Tate book.

Our readers are important to us. Please take a few moments to provide us with some information, so we can better serve you.

Once we receive your reader card, your name will be kept on file for information regarding program disks to accompany the book.

Name: _____

Company Name: _____

Address: _____

City/State: _____ Zip: _____

Country: _____ Date: _____

1) How did you first learn about this publication?
21-1 ( ) Someone who saw or bought it
-2 ( ) Software dealer or salesperson
-3 ( ) Hardware dealer or salesperson
-4 ( ) Advertising
-5 ( ) Published review
-6 ( ) Computer store display
-7 ( ) Computer show
-8 ( ) Book store
-9 ( ) Directly from Ashton-Tate

2) Where did you purchase this publication?
22-1 ( ) Directly from Ashton-Tate™
-2 ( ) From my dBASE II® Dealer
-3 ( ) Computer show
-4 ( ) Book store

3) Have you purchased other Ashton-Tate books and publications?
23-1 ( ) Yes 23-2 ( ) No
If Yes, please check which ones:
23-3 ( ) *dBASE II for the First-Time User*
-4 ( ) *Data Management for Professionals*
-5 ( ) *System Design Guide*
-6 ( ) *dNEWS™*
-7 ( ) *Through the MicroMaze*
-8 ( ) *Everyman's Database Primer*
-9 ( ) *Reference Encyclopedia for the IBM® Personal Computer*
-10 ( ) *IBM PC Public Domain Software, Vol. I*

4) What type of software programs are you using now?
24-1 ( ) Accounting
-2 ( ) Spreadsheet
-3 ( ) Word Processing
-4 ( ) Other (Please specify) _____
_____

5) What type of software programs are you interested in?
25-1 ( ) Academic/Scientific
-2 ( ) Agriculture
-3 ( ) Building
-4 ( ) Business
-5 ( ) Financial
-6 ( ) Health Care
-7 ( ) Home/Hobby
-8 ( ) Insurance
-9 ( ) Membership/Registry
-10 ( ) Professional
-11 ( ) Real Property
-12 ( ) Software Utilities
-13 ( ) Spreadsheet
-14 ( ) Integrated

6) Whom are you purchasing the book for?
27-1 ( ) Business
-2 ( ) Self

7a) Who will be the actual reader?
28-1 ( ) I will be
-2 ( ) Someone else will be
Title: _____

7b) What make and model computer do you use?
28-3 _____

8) Do you expect to purchase other software programs during the next 12 months? If so, what type?
29-1 ( ) Accounting
-2 ( ) Sales
-3 ( ) Inventory
-4 ( ) Other (Please specify) _____
_____

9) What subjects would you like to see discussed?
30-1 _____
_____
_____

10) How can we improve this book?
31-1 _____
_____
_____

11) What is your primary business?
A. Computer Industry
32-1 ( ) Manufacturing
-2 ( ) Systems house
-3 ( ) DP supply house
-4 ( ) Software
-5 ( ) Retailing
-6 ( ) Other _____

B. Non-Computer Business
33-1 ( ) Manufacturing
-2 ( ) Retail trade
-3 ( ) Wholesale trade
-4 ( ) Financial, banking
-5 ( ) Real estate, insurance
-6 ( ) Engineering
-7 ( ) Government
-8 ( ) Education

34-1 ( ) Military
-2 ( ) Health services
-3 ( ) Legal services
-4 ( ) Transportation
-5 ( ) Utilities
-6 ( ) Communications
-7 ( ) Arts, music, film
-8 ( ) Other _____

12) What is your position and title? Please check one in each list
POSITION
35-1 ( ) Data processing
-2 ( ) Engineering
-3 ( ) Marketing/Advertising
-4 ( ) Sales
-5 ( ) Financial
-6 ( ) Legal
-7 ( ) Administration
-8 ( ) Research
-9 ( ) Operations/production
-10 ( ) Distribution
-11 ( ) Education
-12 ( ) Other _____
TITLE
35-13 ( ) Owner
-14 ( ) Chairperson
-15 ( ) President
-16 ( ) Vice President
-17 ( ) Director
-18 ( ) Manager
-19 ( ) Dept. head
-20 ( ) Independent contractor
-21 ( ) Scientist
-22 ( ) Programmer
-23 ( ) Assistant
-24 ( ) Other _____

13) How many employees are in your company?
36-1 ( ) Less than 10
-2 ( ) 10 to 25
-3 ( ) 26 to 100
-4 ( ) 101 to 300
-5 ( ) 301 to 1,000
-6 ( ) over 1,000

14) I would like to remain on your mailing list.
37-1 ( ) Yes 37-2 ( ) No

38-1 I'd like to purchase additional copies of the current edition of this book at $19.95 plus $1.50 handling.
☐ My check is enclosed
My MasterCard/Visa card number is:
_____

Expiration date _____

Signature _____

BUSINESS REPLY MAIL
FIRST CLASS   PERMIT NO. 959   CULVER CITY, CA

POSTAGE WILL BE PAID BY ADDRESSEE

ASHTON · TATE ■ ™
10150 WEST JEFFERSON BOULEVARD
CULVER CITY, CALIFORNIA 90230